poetics today

International Journal for Theory and Analysis of Literature and Communication

Volume 40, Number 3   September 2019

Introduction:
Cognitive Literary Studies and the Well-Lived Life

Nancy Easterlin
University of New Orleans

Abstract   In what ways does literary study contribute to human knowledge, understanding, and flourishing? This introductory essay emphasizes the importance of an
age-old question in the face of the devaluation of the humanities. Cognitive literary
studies are well situated to address the ethical and pedagogical functions of literature.
Broadly contextualizing the issue's contributions within literary and cognitive theory,
the essay describes their various explorations of reader processing and ethical involvement, including personal, social, and environmental improvement.

Keywords   aesthetics, cognition, ethics, literature, neuroscience

In the wake of the Enlightenment and Industrial Revolution, arguments in
defense of the humanities emerged as a response to the twin movements of the
ascendance of science and the reconceptualization of higher education in line
with new disciplines. But to this day, champions of the humanities are generally long on rhetoric rather than evidence.[1] Nonetheless, in literary studies
particularly, scholars are exhibiting increasing interest in the processes of
reading and imagining and the effects of both.[2] Cognitive literary studies

---

1. See, for instance, Helen Small's (2003) *The Value of the Humanities*, a primarily historical
account, and Joshua Landy's (2012) *How to Do Things with Fictions*, which posits the salutary
effect of engagement with aesthetic form.
2. In his recent book on reader processing, *The Gist of Reading*, literary scholar Andrew Elfenbein
(2018: 100) explains the complexity of reading processes and concept activation as well as the
difference between novice and skilled readers. Skilled or expert readers develop metacognitive

Poetics Today 40:3 (September 2019)   DOI 10.1215/03335372-7558038
© 2019 by Porter Institute for Poetics and Semiotics

occupy a special position in the debates over the purpose of higher education and the value of the humanities: through their varied interdisciplinary commitments, cognitive literary studies, including cognitive theater and film studies, seek to discover the processes, forms of knowledge, and ethical function of literary experience in its several modes — reading, viewing, contemplation, discussion, and analysis. If scholars wish to argue that the humanities are not a trivial pursuit, then they can best make their case by theorizing and, where possible, documenting the dynamic interactions of individuals, groups, texts, and environments that cumulatively produce the forms of knowledge specific to aesthetic engagement.

Whereas some research in this growing subdiscipline employs scientific methodology in efforts to determine, for example, the impact of reading on social awareness or critical thinking, other projects in the field are synthetic, bringing together cognitive science with literature and disparate disciplines as an interpretive and pedagogical tool. Through their application of psychology to literature and literary theory, the essays in this special issue explore the capacity of the literary humanities to enhance thought and action, whether through scholarship, teaching, mental flexibility, or human well-being.

This special issue was inspired not only by the general crisis in higher education, but, more specifically, by the conference *Why the Humanities: Answers from the Cognitive and Neurosciences*, which took place at Kent State University in July 2015. The conference was instrumental in bringing together psychologists and literary scholars with the shared goal of demonstrating the epistemic, ethical, and affective benefits of the humanities, and in so doing promoting the efficacy of cognitive perspectives for humanities scholarship, educational practice, and social awareness. Among the humanities, literary studies were especially well represented at the conference. Pursuing the same end, this issue presents ten essays by fourteen contributors, a few of whom attended the Kent State conference. Hailing from the fields of psychology, communications, and literary studies, these scholars represent diverse methodologies and a range of cognitive specializations, including empirical reading studies, empathy, neurophenomenology, and mindfulness psychology. They likewise explore varied literary areas, among them narratology, romantic drama, film, African American literature, ecocriticism, and meditative poetry. The essays are organized into three sections, though there is considerable overlap among them. Section 1 emphasizes reader processing and

---

awareness, which enables them to shift strategies during reading, a finding that has broad implications for literary pedagogy and the broad cognitive skills resulting therefrom. Like Donald's (2001) account of the evolutionary emergence and functioning human consciousness, Elfenbein's account of reading points to the rapidity of habituation in humans.

psychology; section 2 focuses on the empathy and ethics of human individuals and social groups; and section 3 addresses considerations of ethical well-being, including the nonhuman natural environment, other species, and the centered, integrated self.

For the better part of three decades, *Poetics Today* has been at the forefront of cognitive literary studies. Over those decades, the editors have regularly published not only a wealth of individual essays in the field but also numerous special issues devoted to its evolving perspectives. Other journals have rather more recently and cautiously opened up to scholarship crossing the science-humanities divide. Knowledge is a cumulative process, and one goal of this issue is to contribute new research and additional voices to this increasingly sophisticated conversation. Yet another is to embrace and strengthen the exchange between the social and hard sciences and literary scholars. This interaction presses us to consider the perspectives and concepts of our several disciplines, and therefore both furthers knowledge through cooperation and promotes a vital self-critical function. As Vittorio Gallese (in Wojciehowski 2011) notes, "Whenever people talk of multi- or interdisciplinarity, the first problem to be solved is the language, the linguistic barrier, and the jargons we employ. Often we use the same words but with totally different implications."

Last but not least, the collection foregrounds the means by which, through their particular manner of educating, aesthetic engagements may enhance human ethics. As Anthony Kwame Appiah (2008: 164) reminds us, "Ethics is, in that formulation of Aristotle's, about the ultimate aim or end of human life, the end he called *eudaimonia* [human flourishing]." It is not, on this account, simply subjective contentment but the life lived well that constitutes ethics, and like Appiah, the contributors here believe that literature has a role in this pursuit.

1. Reader Processing and Psychology

The essays in the first section draw on neuroscience and empirical studies to investigate reader processing and the consequent effects on cognition, understood as a combination of intellection and emotion. In the wake of second-generation cognitive science, cognitive literary studies has enjoyed a generalized shift away from a first-generation mind-as-machine approach to narrative and reader theory, largely embracing the mind's embodiment — that is, the inextricable links among ratiocination, emotion, memory, physical sensation, physiology, and the material and social surround.[3] To varying

3. As Jerome Bruner (1990: 1–11) explains, the cognitive revolution, which sought to place meaning and interpretation at the heart of psychology, was a proposed remedy to behavior-

degrees, those in the subdiscipline also acknowledge the evolved basis of such embedded cognition and its ubiquitously functional sociocultural dimension. Today, this viewpoint is dubbed "enactivist"; in fact, it has a long history beginning in nineteenth- and twentieth-century intellectual developments including evolutionary theory, pragmatic philosophy, and ecological psychology.[4] While at the theoretical level cognitive literary scholars and narratologists have shifted promptly away from a computer model of the mind to an enactivist perspective, frank assessment of existing literary theoretical models of reading and narrative influenced by the machine metaphor of the brain-mind is still ongoing. The essays in this group, then, underscore the need to reevaluate logically conceptualized paradigms that are often unidirectional and hierarchical; to define the terms applied to processes precisely and clearly; and to align the concepts of psychology and literary studies.

In the first paper, "Neuroscience, Narrative, and Narratology," Paul B. Armstrong addresses directly the mismatch between structuralist-influenced conceptualizations of reading on the one hand and the insights and findings of neuroscience, classical pragmatism, and select narrative theorists on the other. Laying out a neurobiological model of narrative that explains how stories arise from and set in motion fundamental neuronal and cortical processes, Armstrong then asks how the aims and methods of narratology might be aligned with what we know about language and the brain. Since, as Armstrong argues, the formalist goal of identifying orderly, universal structures of mind, language, and narrative conflicts with the probabilistic, reciprocal interactions in the brain through which cognitive patterns emerge from our embodied experiences of the world, cognitive narratology needs to break with the structuralist legacy still evident in the terminology of frames, scripts,

---

ism's simplifying, dichotomous view of human mental life. But this initial revolution — so-called "cognitivism" or first-generation cognitive science — quickly succumbed to the equally reductive mechanistic model of the mind emanating from the then-emergent computer sciences.

4. Pragmatistic philosophers William James and John Dewey critiqued the damaging reductionism of the subject-object dualism pervading nineteenth-century psychology, and their objections were repeated in the 1960s with the emergence of ecological psychology in the work of James J. Gibson (1966), followed by Roger Barker (1978), Edward Reed (1996), and others, which also took aim at simplistic models of stimulus-response. For extended discussion of the pragmatists in the context of embodiment psychology, see Johnson 2007; for an excellent historical account of the influence of post-Enlightenment science and sociohistorical elements on the development of American pragmatism, see Menand 2001; for brief glosses of these, see Easterlin (2012: 154–57, 103–14). For a crucial early discussion of extended mind, see Donald's (1991) *Origins of the Modern Mind*; for a more recent account, see Clark 2008. For an important recent theorization of narrative experientiality from an enactivist perspective, see Caracciolo 2014, and for an enactivist, "Bayesian" model of reader processing, see Kukkonen 2014. For an accessible introduction championing enactive, cognitive approaches to literature and addressed primarily to academics in English studies, see Cave 2016.

and preference rules and to embrace the paradigm shift proposed by various pragmatically oriented, phenomenological theories of narrative.

Whereas Armstrong is a literary scholar calling attention to the epistemic lag between current knowledge of brain processes and interdisciplinary models of literary reading, particularly those in cognitive narratology, the next two essays, coauthored by psychologists and communications theorists, highlight the complexity of empirical evidence on the topics, respectively, of personal relevance and social cognition. Currently, cognitive literary scholars are keen to assert that literary reading has demonstrable social and individual effects, and that emotional response triggered by empathy is the key to trans- formation in thought patterns and behavior. While the empirical evidence marshaled here suggests that, on the whole, this is almost certainly the case, it also illuminates the sheer range of cognitive processes operant in imagi- native reading and the attendant difficulty of assessing literature's impact. Those processes and that impact are highly influenced—and often, indeed, directed—by factors including the individual reader's self-concept and one or more of the various components of his or her background experience.

How does felt connection emerge from the interaction between individual experience and textual representation? Over the ages, many theories, from those insisting on an essential human nature to those asserting sociocultural identities to those claiming a panhuman cognitive substrate as the root of connection to literary arts, have either tacitly assumed or directly asserted a necessary or desired commonality between the contents of texts and the experiences of readers. But what is the cast and/or degree of this common- ality? Within the past fifty years, socially oriented movements, including feminist, Marxist, African American, and postcolonial approaches, have sensitized scholars to differences in aesthetic experience emerging from socio- cultural background, eschewing claims for a shared human nature. Con- joined with the long-perceived irrelevance of the humanities and the arts, this development has an ongoing influence on pedagogy, as faculty con- sciously ponder the relevance—or, to use our students' term, "relatability"— of the material they place at the center of their courses. But just as the phrase "relate to" most assuredly calls out for replacement with a more helpfully descriptive verb, *relevance* is not the simple concept we might be inclined to assume, nor is the function of its component aspects in reading and viewing processes by any means straightforward or predictable.

Personal relevance, although central to sustaining an audience's interest in any given narrative, has received little systematic attention thus far. In their comprehensive review article "Personal Relevance in Story Reading," Anežka Kuzmičová and Katalin Bálint document experimental and other empirical evidence on narrative processing in order to unravel which types of personal relevance are most likely to affect readers and what kinds of impact—for instance, aesthetic, therapeutic, persuasive—they appear to generate. Whereas research results suggest that narratives, irrespective of genre, appear to be read through the lens of the reader's self-schema, this finding does not imply that large-scale similarities between reader and character, such as gender, necessarily produce relevance effects. Instead, a variety of factors contribute to such effects and their perceived value. For example, certain groups of readers, especially in particular situations, may experience personal relevance and related effects more strongly than others. Likewise, although thematic saliency is undoubtedly important, emotional valence is a significant factor in perceptions of relevance.

In sum, as literary scholars consider relevance in critical, theoretical, and pedagogical engagements, the varieties, manifestations, and force of such effects must be weighed against a tendency to assume the efficacy of identification, especially since some research shows that the power of such effects can become excessive or outright detrimental to reader experience. This finding coheres with ongoing controversies about so-called trigger warnings at elite American universities, which precisely concern the unintended disturbance to students of some course content in the social sciences and humanities. Kuzmičová and Bálint's research review, then, suggests that literary scholars should engage in nuanced consideration of the meanings of relevance and its goals: for instance, Does perceived or wishful similarity occur prior to or as the product of reading? When do such identifications produce personal resonance or empathy and insight?[5] What is the impact of personality traits or crises at the time of reading?[6] However we might apply the results to theoretical formulations, the wealth of studies elucidated here limns a clear picture of the multifarious processes and circumstances through which relevance might emerge as awareness and insight.

Just as Kuzmičová and Bálint's essay asks us to consider the range of evidence on readers' connection to literature, Richard Gerrig and Micah Mumper explore the contribution of literature to social cognition, taking up

5. In a recent essay from the perspective of narratology, one that distinguishes sympathy from empathy (as does Caracciolo [2014: 130]), Faye Halpern (2018) focuses on unreliable narrators to highlight the complex ethical effects of "feeling with" and "feeling for" in three different works of film and literature. Her close analysis of the dynamics of feelings, ethics, and focalization counsels caution about claims for the emotional route to ethical insight or awareness.
6. David Michelson (2014a) has argued that the personality trait of "openness to experience" is a key factor in the enjoyment of literature. However, his classroom case study approach to personality and literary reading (Michelson 2014b) does not entirely converge with predictions related to personality assessments; in particular, for some students, negative experiences in high-school English classes rather than personality strongly colored attitudes toward literary reading.

the specific claim that mental simulation of narrative events constitutes the process of reader empathic engagement. Although research results indicate that engagement with works of fiction may benefit readers' social cognitive abilities of empathy and theory of mind, there is little direct evidence to support claims about the causal mechanisms underlying the positive impact of leisure reading. Summarizing simulation theory, which has emerged as the most common explanation, Gerrig and Mumper highlight the need for a more concrete theoretical instantiation, pointing to three other psychological accounts of the origins of the emotional content of readers' narrative experiences. Thus illuminating the diversity of processes that contribute to readers' affective responses, Gerrig and Mumper infer that ordinary processes of learning and memory, unaided by narrative simulation, might explain changes in readers' social cognition.

Adopting a definition of "simulation" as an offline functioning of the belief-desire system that enables readers to comprehend what characters are thinking and feeling—a definition generally accepted by a number of psychologists and cognitive literary scholars—Gerrig and Mumper point to the lack of specificity in the concept, which does not indicate whether simulations are strategic or spontaneous, as well as to more straightforward accounts of empathy.[7] Additionally, in all three of the accounts of emotional elicitation they discuss, reader feeling need not align with that of character. Like Kuzmičová and Bálint, then, Gerrig and Mumper underscore the complexity of response to literary reading; together, these two essays point to the variety of mechanisms and the multiple conditions that might affect emotional valence and potential changes in social awareness.

7. For a summary of the theoretical dimensions of simulation theory (ST) in philosophy of mind, see Barlassina and Gordon's (2017) encyclopedia entry, wherein the authors confess that ST is a family of theories rather than a single theory. At issue are the degrees of theory of mind and consciousness it entails and the exactitude of in-time affective repetition in simulative processes, ambiguities that render it akin to the outdated term "imagination." Kukkonen (2014) wisely avoids the concept *simulation*, in contrast to other literary scholars and reading psychologists, who use it flexibly; at times, theorists seem to assert the identity of actual and hypothetical experience. See, for instance, Hogan, following Oatley, in Aldama and Hogan (2014: 80–81, 13). Caracciolo (2014: 131–32) employs "simulation" to refer to consciousness-enactment in empathic engagement with others' mental states, a usage generally in line with what Wojciehowski and Gallese (2011) call "liberated embodied simulation." Weik von Mossner especially emphasizes the connection between bodily based affective response and narrative processing. However, Kuzmičová (2014: 279) notes the underdiscussed problem of consciousness in reading and cognitive literary theory, wherein "non-conscious sub-personal processes . . . and conscious experience (i.e., processes at least partly noticeable to the subject herself) . . . are treated as if they were the same thing," and further, she doubts the extensive repetition through time of another body's experience on the sound basis that it would overtax the reading mind. Kuzmičová herself only uses "simulation" to refer to the activation of the sensorimotor cortex to action-indicating language—thus, for subpersonal processes.

Given these complexities in relevance and emotional response, literary theorists should be cautious in hypothesizing the causal path leading to enhanced social cognition. Overall, the evidence and skeptical considerations of these social scientists harmonize with Armstrong's elucidation of neuroscience; as a group, the three essays together suggest that processes of narrative construction and ethical meaning-making are not only far from linear but also extremely context dependent.

2. Empathy and Literary Ethics

Do the arts make us better? In a book chapter with this title, John Carey (2006) voices skepticism about testing art's capacity to promote personal and social improvement. Citing Elliot W. Eisner's 2002 *The Arts and the Creation of Mind*, Carey largely concurs with Eisner that, while pedagogy in the arts certainly equips students to think with greater aesthetic sophistication, promising social and individual benefits beyond this seems unjustified based on the difficulty of gathering evidence. If

> the aim of education . . . is to help students lead personally satisfying and socially constructive lives outside school . . . setting up an experiment to find how far this is achieved by arts education would, [according to Eisner], be next-to-impossible. You would have to have two groups of students, one following an arts curriculum, the other not, and you would have to decide what kind of moral character you would like them to have, what could count as evidence of their having it, and how the extent to which they had it could be measured and evaluated. (Carey 2006: 102).

Here, in fact, Carey, following Eisner, gives a mere glimpse of the obstacles to controlled studies in this area, which also include individual differences in personality, development, and social class, not to mention other salient factors like family size and dynamics, interests, and preferences. Other complicating questions arise: Are the arts discussed inside and outside the home? If so, what is the nature of these discussions? How do existing relationships with other participants in these discussions color (or even determine) response? And so on.

But cognitive scholars who are, unsurprisingly, anxious to claim the epistemic and ethical value of literary pedagogy should not be demoralized by this vision of the impossibility of large-scale longitudinal studies and resultant thoroughgoing proofs for the efficacy of arts (including literary) education. The lesson here, it seems to me, is that while empirical studies produce critically significant evidence about parts of reading and viewing processes and their relation to self-development and social cognition, literary scholars need to embrace rather than reduce the dynamism, range, and idiosyncrasies of aesthetic engagements, self-consciously turning these features into solutions rather than trying to sweep them under the rug. As Gerrig and Mumper sensibly observe, if literature has an impact on social cognition, then this is clearly a double-edged sword: in plain terms, if the fuzziness of the line between everyday and fictional thinking can improve our sensitivity toward and treatment of others, then it can also do the opposite. Gerrig's extensive research in reader psychology, in fact, consistently demonstrates that fictional and factual information are not processed or stored in separate mental compartments.[8] "Simulation," as Joshua Landy (2012: 39) puts it, "by helping us plan, may assist us in implementing any altruistic schemes we happen to have, but simulation may also assist us in implementing a successful bank heist, a successful kidnapping, or a successful cull of spotted owls." Understanding that literature has effects on human thought and behavior, in short, compels us to ask how we can shape our scholarly and pedagogical projects in ways that promote the kinds of effects we seek, those that enhance our ethical disciplinary commitments.

Accordingly, whereas the essays in section 1 of this special issue address neuroscience and empirical findings that raise questions about the role, underlying processes, and function of imaginative literature, the contributions in section 2 focus directly on the empathic potential and ethical implications of literary experience and pedagogy. Of course, the Romantic-era author Joanna Baillie could not have known the results of empirical studies in reader psychology just emerging today, but her approach to writing two hundred years ago is a valuable reminder that there is a considerable history — dating, in fact, back to the classical origins of criticism — behind both the belief in literature's impact on behavior and the creation of psychologically informed art to produce desired effects. Collaborating across the disciplines of psychology and literary studies, M. Soledad Caballero and Aimee Knupsky, in "'Some Powerful Rankling Passion': An Interdisciplinary Exploration of Emotion Regulation Strategies in Joanna Baillie's Passion Plays," bring Baillie's work into alignment with contemporary psychological and neuroscientific discussions of emotion regulation. The authors elucidate

---

8. Gerrig (1993) critiques what he memorably calls "toggle" theories in *Experiencing Narrative Worlds*; taking up the tradition exemplified by Samuel Taylor Coleridge and others, he points out that empirical research does not support the view that readers and audiences switch back and forth between the fictional and the factual. Cognitive literary scholar Patrick Hogan, who defines fiction as "the simulation of emotionally consequential goal pursuit" and who has written at length about affect and narrative, also stresses the similarity between fictional characters, imaginative experience, and neurophysiological processes in actual situations and imaginative experience (Aldama and Hogan 2014: 13). For a brief discussion, see Aldama and Hogan 2014: 13–18.

Baillie's concept of "sympathetick curiosity," point to its correspondence with George A. Bonanno and Charles L. Burton's 2013 model of regulatory flexibility, and suggest that these theories, in conjunction with Baillie's "plays on the passions," demonstrate how art can improve self-regulation and self-knowledge. Focusing on two of Baillie's most popular "plays on the passions," Caballero and Knupsky argue that regulatory flexibility is a learned skill that can be enhanced by actively engaging sympathetic curiosity, thus concurring with Baillie, who insisted that her plays taught audiences how to avoid the destructive nature of the passions. They suggest that by watching protagonists' manifestations of and responses to an emotion, audiences learn to develop the regulatory flexibility essential to its expression and management. Since Baillie's plays dramatize not just differences in individual responses to emotion and in emotion regulation but also the role of the other in initiating, maintaining, or dampening emotion, they guide viewers to improve interpersonal regulatory skills.

Thus illuminating Baillie's self-conscious ethical intent and her didactic approach to playwriting, which was informed by eighteenth- and nineteenth-century Scottish psychology, Caballero and Knupsky endorse the immersive and pedagogical validity of this perspective based on present-day cognitive studies, explore potentially negative emotional motivations, and indicate empathic processes that facilitate conscious decision-making. Also addressing the problem of negative emotion and behavior but taking up post–Romantic era British and American examples, the next two essays span considerations of the wide-ranging impact and pedagogical value of texts including Richard Wright's *Native Son*, Harriet Beecher Stowe's *Uncle Tom's Cabin*, John Steinbeck's *Grapes of Wrath*, and Mary Shelley's *Frankenstein*.

In their essay on Wright's novel, beginning with a historical account of its impact on the Supreme Court's 1954 *Brown v. Board of Education* decision, Marshall Alcorn and Michael O'Neill develop the concept of *adaptive affective cognition*, highlighting emotion's decisive role in reason. In "Adaptive Affective Cognition in Literature and Its Impact," the authors employ research in neuroscience to argue that *Native Son*'s affective impact reorganized the cognitive practices that authorized segregation. Paradoxically, Wright's novel, triggering racist fears with the image of an angry, violent black man, also ultimately reduces those fears, according to Alcorn and O'Neill. Drawing on research on emotional bias in thought, the authors claim that emotional links in cognition, though they interfere with logical ratiocination, are nonetheless the only solution to the problem of bias, simply because emotion is deeply implicated in attention, memory, and reasoning. Openness to new information requires emotional priming; integration of new data within a reasoning system is facilitated by an aesthetic synthesis of bodily, affective, and cognitive data; and assignment of value, also dependent on emotion, consti-tutes a core feature of temporally durable emotionally informed reason. Along-side contemporaneous sociological research and the legal instrument of the Brandeis brief, Wright's *Native Son* contributed to legal and social change, exercising literature's distinctive capacity for affective involvement.

Just as Alcorn and O'Neill argue for the irreplaceable legal and social impact of emotionally powerful literary experiences on reasoned deci-sions, Mark Bracher insists that literary study strikingly and perhaps inevi-tably influences moral character and thereby contributes to social justice. In "Can—and Should—Literary Study Develop Moral Character and Advance Social Justice? Answers from Cognitive Science," Bracher reports on recent findings in the cognitive neurosciences indicating that morality, character, identity, and values are largely if not totally functions of social information processing. Commonsense views held by many literary scholars that see these as monolithic elements of personhood and thus unavailable to outside interventions are therefore most likely incorrect. Arguing against Stanley Fish's assumption that it is neither possible nor permissible for edu-cators to build character or advance social justice, Bracher presents compel-ling evidence that literature can alter the neurocognitive structures that produce and direct social information processing. According to Bracher, combining specific literary texts and pedagogical practices in the classroom alters the neurocognitive structures underlying social information processing, and the subsequently revised cognitive routines contribute not only to moral character and social justice but also to personal well-being. The nature and direction of this alteration, moreover, are profoundly ethical: far from indoc-trinating, they promote capabilities and habits of cognition that enable stu-dents to perceive and understand both others and themselves more clearly and comprehensively.

The first three essays in section 2, then, illuminate how emotion, intellec-tion, information processing, and pedagogy serve as interrelated elements of the ethical value of literature. But it is hardly beside the point that the primary works at the core of these arguments are self-consciously and indeed didac-tically constructed around notions of self- and social improvement. The difficulty and necessity of emotional self-control and the comprehensive destructiveness of racism are, respectively, at the heart of the decline and demise of Baillie's and Wright's characters, so literary scholars should be wary about universalizing claims for the direct moral effects of literature on emotion regulation, prejudice, and social change. Indeed, assertions of this kind would be false on their face, given the enormous diversity of the literary arts—so much literature simply does not work in this way. In her Tom Ripley novels, for instance, Patricia Highsmith, employing a spare, realistic style, focalizes the narrative through her sociopathic main character, thus both heightening suspense and eschewing moral commentary as Ripley repeatedly benefits from his crimes. In horror films such as John Carpenter's *The Thing* (1982) and Ari Aster's *Hereditary* (2018), all-powerful evil apparently wins out. Since literary art is so often about problems, it is not difficult to explain the epistemic and ethical value of immersion in a sociopathic personality or in the overwhelming make-believe threats of well-made horror films. However, because cognitive literary studies draw on theories about actual persons, they must guard against literalizing and moralizing biases that unintentionally elevate select realist modes and avoid transgressive or fantastical material. If such works forge swords that might cut in two directions, then scholars need to address the psychological and social functions they might serve and incorporate these considerations into research and course design.

In keeping with this perspective, the final essay in this section, "On Punishment and Why We Enjoy It in Fiction," addresses a perplexing problem for those highlighting the salutary impact of literature on social cognition: the fictional satisfaction of moral intuitions whose behavioral outcomes are no longer permissible in modern state society. Margrethe Bruun Vaage theorizes that spectators, even in Scandinavia where harsh punishment is roundly condemned, may enjoy excessive punishment when viewing fiction. Pointing out that humans have evolved as prosocial punishers whose emotions and intuitions facilitate collaboration and who desire punishment for wrongdoers even if no harm has been done to them personally, Vaage explains and adopts the dual-process model of morality, which posits both rational and intuitive routes to moral evaluation; however, she underscores the significance of intuition and emotions in this process. Vaage proposes a theory of *fictional reliefs*, noting that audiences embrace punishment more easily when the character who punishes is clearly fictional, and she hypothesizes that a mixture of filmic modes facilitates one of two paths to moral judgment. In films such as *The Girl with the Dragon Tattoo* (2009) and *Let the Right One In* (2008), the examples she employs here, excessive punishment is typically carried out by a vigilante avenger who is often a fantastic character with superhuman and/or supernatural attributes, thus relieving the spectator of the obligation to evaluate rationally. When fantastic elements permeate an otherwise realistic setting via such fictional reliefs, they permit the spectator to fully enjoy the main characters' vigilante revenge.

Vaage's essay is a reminder that the emergence of nation-states over the course of cultural evolution rests on the choice of large and diverse groups of persons to cooperate for the common good, a reconfiguration of human social organization that requires a revised morality and laws to enforce it. Vigilante and blood revenge served our human ancestors who lived in close-knit kinship groups, but today they create chaos. Following evolutionary psychologists who theorize that many of our adaptations are aligned with patterns of the distant past rather than our current lifeways, Vaage asks us to consider anachronistic moral response in our appreciation of art. Essays like Vaage's compel cognitive literary scholars to reflect on the role of forbidden thoughts and behaviors in literature. No less importantly, they ask us to raise these matters explicitly in the classroom. If emotion regulation, emotional response, and information processing can be altered through viewing, reading, and teaching, and if scholars choose to pursue these laudable ends, they need equally to confront and address pleasurable participation in the transgressive and sometimes frankly criminal elements of literary art. The idea of art as a pressure valve is not new, but understanding the why, when, and how of fictional relief as well as what works offer this outlet is just as ethical a goal of criticism as social justice.

3. Healing Planet, Species, and Self

A complete consideration of cognition, literature, and ethics takes into account processes of mentation and emotion in all dimensions of human experience: internal mental processes, interpersonal engagements, and transactions with the broader environment. Although this journal issue is generally organized from local to global topics, moving progressively outward toward larger scales, the aim is for the reader to think recursively—across and between the essays and issues offered here. In keeping with this purpose, the final section demonstrates the broader reach of cognitive approaches through literary engagements with the nonhuman natural world, then brings matters back to individual response and transformation in the conclusion, a reminder that the healthy individual is the point of origin for other kinds of ethical growth. Thus, engaging with the nature of ethics and healing across scales, this section explores both extra- and intrahuman dimensions.

Having asked how social cognition and justice might be improved through reading and pedagogy, the first essays in this section ponder how that ethos of concern might be extended to the nonhuman natural world. In "Why We Care about (Non)fictional Places: Empathy, Character, and Narrative Environment," Alexa Weik von Mossner extends the work of cognitive scholars to suggest how literary reading can lead us to care about natural environments, whether these environments are threatening for humans or threatened by human actions. Drawing on scholarship in philosophy, empirical psychology, cognitive science, and literary studies asserting that literary reading and pedagogy can develop emotional capabilities essential for responsible citizenship and social justice, Weik von Mossner conjoins these perspectives with the emerging subfield of cognitive ecocriticism. Cognitive ecocriticism maintains that species-typical cognition is a vital framework for studies in literature and the environment, explaining, among other things, emotional dispositions—loving, indifferent, and antipathetic—toward material environments. Weik von Mossner takes up Ann Pancake's novel *Strange as This Weather Has Been* (2007), exploring the ways in which it cues empathy for an actual environment, Appalachia, that is wounded and scarred. Pancake's choice not only of multiple focalization but also, in particular, of a preponderance of teenage narrators allows for highly emotional viewpoints. According to Weik von Mossner, through this use of *authorial strategic empathizing* (Keen 2010), Pancake facilitates readers' *liberated embodied simulation* (Wojciehowski and Gallese 2011) of characters' affective experience of their environment. Compelling readers to experience imaginatively what it is like to love an environment and then witness its destruction by mountaintop removal mining, Pancake engages readers in the social and moral issues around resource extraction.

Like Weik von Mossner, Erin James addresses bonds extending beyond persons and social groups. In "Nonhuman Fictional Characters and the Empathy-Altruism Hypothesis," she acknowledges the difficulty of presenting animal consciousness and employs cognitive approaches to literature to illuminate cross-species empathy. Highlighting a trend within current models of narrative empathy that suggests that readers' ability to feel for nonhuman characters is dependent wholly on anthropomorphism, James investigates how narrative point of view facilitates or inhibits knowledge and understanding between readers and chimp characters in two specific novels, Colin McAdam's *A Beautiful Truth* (2013) and Karen Joy Fowler's *We Are All Completely Beside Ourselves* (2013). First explaining the cognitive differences between humans and chimps to stress just how difficult it is to represent chimp cognition and emotion in narrative and to elaborate on the resulting challenges that this difficulty poses for models of narrative empathy, James then explores the mechanisms by which written narratives that refuse anthropomorphism, such as McAdam's and Fowler's novels, might inspire a real-world ethics of care for nonhuman subjects. Ultimately, James champions an expansion of current models of narrative empathy, surmising that human bridge characters serve as a vital affective link between human and nonhuman animals, thereby fostering real-world care for nonhuman subjects.

The development of literature and environment in the 1990s was bedeviled by the widespread assumption among Americanist ecocritics that representations of consciousness evinced a reprehensible bias toward the human and, presumably, against the nonhuman natural world.[9] Recognizing that our modes of knowing and the art objects we create are by their very nature inescapably human, Weik von Mossner and James can ask about the links between human understanding and feeling and a nurturing, productive relationship with nonhuman nature. Since persons, species, and nonhuman environments are inextricable from any human life, and because the far-reaching empathic and ethical engagements that scholars aspire to through literature can only be achieved from the vantage point of personal well-being, a meditation on the healthy self sounds this collection's final note. In "The Poetry and Practice of Meditation," Elizabeth Bradburn specifically asks, Is reading poetry therapeutic? And further, could the great religious lyricists of the seventeenth century have understood it that way? Citing neurophysiological evidence that reading poetry involves some of the same brain structures as those upon which human psychological well-being depends, Bradburn argues that George Herbert's devotional lyrics, long understood as Christian meditations, are structurally consistent with the modern practice of mindfulness meditation. Neurally, meditation entails the reduction of activity in the brain's default mode network; phenomenally, it requires repeatedly bringing the wandering attention back to a chosen meditation object. Seventeenth-century devotional poetry likewise centers on a recurring image, indicating significant overlap between that century's Christian meditative tradition and modern secular and therapeutic theory and practice.

Attending to several examples, Bradburn demonstrates that Herbert's poetry is isomorphic to meditative practice because the image of meditation has a distinctive pattern of movement—spontaneous wandering and controlled return—that can be created in several sensory modalities. This image, complex enough to define Herbert's poetry as meditative, also potentially typifies a meditative literary mode with a distinctive relationship to the imagination. Bradburn maintains, therefore, that meditative poems create, by design, aesthetic experiences that provide some of the same emotional benefits as meditation, such as greater compassion, increased ability to regulate emotions, moderation of anxiety, and better focus and attention. As with meditation, however, the skill of reading poetry takes time, practice, and humanist teaching to master; therefore, she concludes that the therapeutic potential of meditative poetry speaks to the value not just of poetry but of humanist education in general.

Bradburn's insights harmonize with the recent essay "Literature and Happiness," wherein D. J. Moores (2018: 260) declaims at the outset, "It's not

9. For a critique of this realist bias and of the reification of the nature-culture dichotomy in ecocriticism, see Easterlin 2012: 93–105.

literary unless it's depressing." Pointing out along the way that a bias toward narrative settles conflict-based genres at the heart of literary studies, Moores sensibly observes that literature is not just about problems. Indeed, citing the work of social psychologist Jonathan Haidt, he reports that the psychological processes of elevation may be more complex than those of negative emotions. At a time when anxiety and depression are at record levels among young people, literary scholars would do well to heed the insights of Moores and Bradburn: this hard work of feeling good and of exploring varied moods and psychological states through literature may be worthwhile after all. Literature has a special capacity to raise awareness and the means to do it by its elicitation of experiential engagement, but the changes to self and in social cognition are not always easily arrived at or readily accepted.[10] In this light, combining the hard lessons of Baillie, Wright, Larson, Pancake, and others with a positive, intellectually and literarily grounded sense of the route to flourishing may well give humanity the personal security and peace of mind to be better caretakers of ourselves and our environment.

Because aesthetic behaviors are both evolutionarily expensive — that is, requiring a lot of time and energy — and complex, they are a puzzle not to be neglected by students of natural selection. Faced with these and other costly behaviors and adaptations, evolutionists seek to explain their utility, since an effortful activity unconnected with survival or reproduction is not, in today's jargon, favorable to a species' long-term enactive embedment in the environment. But knowing the cause of art's emergence is a complex quest, not very amenable to the tools of science.[11] On the other hand, studying how

10. Carey (2006: 172, 177) maintains that "disagreement is ... a necessary condition for the existence of ethics as an area of discourse" and, following this logic, claims the superiority of literature over the other arts, because it "is not just the only art that can criticize itself, it is the only art ... that can criticize anything, because it is the only art capable of reasoning." While these claims are too unqualified for blanket acceptance — ethics as Appiah has defined it does not always entail disagreement or conflict, and movements in music and painting, for instance, most certainly criticize the art of earlier eras without the intervention of language and reason — Carey still has a point about literature's special capacity for criticism (broadly defined). Written literature has a unique relationship to higher levels of consciousness, given two things, the nature of language processing and the capacity for symbolic text to supersede the biological limitations of short-term memory, enabling extended or hybrid mind. See Donald 1991.

11. How to define the concept *art* is a matter that must be settled at the outset of any such theorization. Carey (2006: 3–31) glosses the major theories, and concludes that anything ever considered an artwork by a single person constitutes art. Carey's approach privileges the plastic arts, as does most theory treating the arts as a category, and the theories he surveys are for the most part traditional in that they seek to define the essence of art. By contrast, Ellen Dissanayake (1992) considers the arts from an evolutionary anthropological perspective, therefore foregrounding function over essence. Dissanayake (42) proposes that art is "making special," which functioned for our human ancestors as a means of exerting control in the face of environmental uncertainties. Since, in this perspective, many ancient art activities are communal (ritual, dance, music, body adornment, and so forth), art activities also served to consolidate

the arts function in the here and now, and exploring how literary scholars might extend the value and impact of a specific art form such as literature, is fully within our reach. The multifarious affective, personal, and social engagements with literary art documented and considered in this issue illuminate the power of the humanities as a vital, shaping context, compelling scholars to self-consciously foreground ethical ends in the design of curricula and in research programs. Joining the insights of the contemporary sciences and humanities, literary studies can actively enhance the lives of socially committed and personally satisfied individuals, thus serving as a part of no less than a contribution to the life well lived.

References

Aldama, Frederick Luis, and Patrick Colm Hogan. 2014. *Conversations on Cognitive Cultural Studies.* Columbus: Ohio University Press.

Appiah, Kwame Anthony. 2008. *Experiments in Ethics.* Cambridge, MA: Harvard University Press.

Barker, Roger. 1978. *Habitats, Environments, and Human Behavior: Studies in Ecological Psychology and Eco-Behavioral Science from the Midwest Psychological Field Station, 1947 – 1972.* San Francisco, CA: Jossey-Bass.

Barlassina, Luca, and Robert M. Gordon. 2017. "Folk Psychology as Mental Simulation." In *The Stanford Encyclopedia of Philosophy*, edited by Edward N. Zalta. plato.stanford.edu /archives/sum2017/entries/folkpsych-simulation/.

Bruner, Jerome. 1990. *Acts of Meaning.* Cambridge, MA: Harvard University Press.

Caracciolo, Marco. 2014. *The Experientiality of Narrative: An Enactivist Approach.* Berlin: DeGruyter.

Carey, John. 2006. *What Good Are the Arts?* Oxford: Oxford University Press.

Cave, Terrance. 2016. *Thinking with Literature: Towards a Cognitive Criticism.* Oxford: Oxford University Press.

Clark, Andy. 2008. *Supersizing the Mind: Embodiment, Action, and Cognitive Extension.* Oxford: Oxford University Press.

Dissanayake, Ellen. 1992. *Homo Aestheticus: Where Art Comes From and Why.* New York: Free Press.

Donald, Merlin. 1991. *The Origins of the Modern Mind: Three Stages in the Evolution of Culture and Cognition.* Cambridge, MA: Harvard University Press.

Donald, Merlin. 2001. *A Mind So Rare: The Evolution of Human Consciousness.* New York: W. W. Norton and Company.

Easterlin, Nancy. 2012. *A Biocultural Approach to Literary Theory and Interpretation.* Baltimore: Johns Hopkins University Press.

Elfenbein, Andrew. 2018. *The Gist of Reading.* Stanford, CA: Stanford University Press.

Gerrig, Richard J. 1993. *Experiencing Narrative Worlds: On the Psychological Activities of Reading.* New Haven: Yale University Press.

Gibson, James J. 1966. *The Senses Considered as Perceptual Systems.* Boston: Houghton Mifflin.

Halpern, Faye. 2018. "Closeness through Unreliability: Sympathy, Empathy, and Ethics in Narrative Communication." *Narrative* 26, no. 2: 125 – 45.

Johnson, Mark. 2007. *The Meaning of the Body: Aesthetics of Human Understanding.* Chicago: University of Chicago Press.

human bonds, thus enhancing the sociality of the group as well as the psychological perception of control.

Keen, Suzanne. 2010. "Narrative Empathy." In *Toward a Cognitive Theory of Narrative Acts*, edited by Frederick Louis Aldama, 61 – 94. Austin: University of Texas Press.

Kukkonen, Karin. 2014. "Presence and Prediction: The Embodied Reader's Cascades of Cognition." In Kukkonen and Caracciolo 2014: 367 – 84.

Kukkonen, Karin, and Marco Caracciolo, eds. 2014a. "Cognitive Literary Study: Second Generation Approaches." Special issue, *Style* 48, no. 3.

Kukkonen, Karin, and Marco Caracciolo. 2014b. "Introduction: What Is the 'Second Generation'?" In Kukkonen and Caracciolo 2014: 261 – 74.

Kuzmičová, Anežka. 2014. "Literary Narrative and Mental Imagery: A View from Embodied Cognition." In Kukkonen and Caracciolo 2014: 275 – 93.

Landy, Joshua. 2012. *How to Do Things with Fictions*. Oxford: Oxford University Press.

Menand, Louis. 2001. *The Metaphysical Club*. New York: Farrar, Straus and Giroux.

Michelson, David. 2014a. "Personality and the Varieties of Fictional Experience." *Journal of Aesthetic Education* 48, no. 2: 64 – 85.

Michelson, David. 2014b. "Where Readers Meet the Road: On a Class Project Integrating Personality with the Evolutionary Study of Literature." In "Cognition in the Classroom," edited by Nancy Easterlin. Special issue, *Interdisciplinary Literary Studies* 16, no. 1: 180 – 202.

Moores, D. J. 2018. "Literature and Happiness." *Philosophy and Literature* 42, no. 1: 260 – 78.

Reed, Edward S. 1996. *Encountering the World: Toward an Ecological Psychology*. New York: Oxford University Press.

Small, Helen. 2013. *The Value of the Humanities*. Oxford: Oxford University Press.

Weik von Mossner, Alexa. 2017. *Affective Ecologies: Empathy, Emotion, and Environmental Narrative*. Columbus: Ohio State University Press.

"Why the Humanities? Answers from the Cognitive and Neurosciences." 2015. Academic conference, Kent State University Hotel and Conference Center, Kent, OH, July 9 – 12.

Wojciehowski, Hannah Chapelle. 2011. "An Interview with Vittorio Gallese." *California Italian Studies* 2, no. 1. escholarship.org/uc/item/56f8v9bv.

Wojciehowski, Hannah Chapelle, and Vittorio Gallese. 2011. "How Stories Make Us Feel: Toward an Embodied Narratology." *California Italian Studies* 2, no. 1. escholarship.org/uc/item/3jg726c2.

I. READER PROCESSING AND PSYCHOLOGY

Neuroscience, Narrative, and Narratology

Paul B. Armstrong
Brown University

Abstract Cognitive narratology needs a neuroscientifically sound understanding of language. This essay lays out a neurobiological model of narrative that explains how stories arise from and set in motion fundamental neuronal and cortical processes, and it then asks how the aims and methods of narratology should be aligned with what we know about language and the brain. The formalist goal of identifying orderly, universal structures of mind, language, and narrative does not match up well with the probabilistic, reciprocal interactions in the brain through which cognitive patterns emerge from our embodied experiences of the world. Cognitive narratology needs to break with the structuralist legacy still evident in the terminology of frames, scripts, and preference rules and to embrace the paradigm shift proposed by various pragmatically oriented, phenomenological theories of narrative that have contested the formalist program.

Keywords cognitive narratology, embodied cognition, neuroscience, phenomenology, language, reading, temporality, action, empathy

The ability to tell and follow a story requires cognitive capacities that are basic to the neurobiology of mental functioning. Neuroscience cannot of course reveal everything we might want to know about stories, but it is also true that our species would probably not produce narratives so prolifically if they weren't somehow good for our brains and our embodied interactions with the world. What kind of brains do we have that enable us to tell each

Poetics Today 40:3 (September 2019) DOI 10.1215/03335372-7558052
© 2019 by Porter Institute for Poetics and Semiotics

other stories? And how do stories configure our brains? How plots order events in time, how stories imitate actions, and how narratives relate us to other lives, whether in pity or in fear — these central concerns of narratological theorists from Aristotle to Paul Ricoeur are perhaps surprisingly aligned with a variety of hot topics in contemporary neuroscience: temporal synchrony and the binding problem, the action-perception circuit in cognition, and the mirroring processes of embodied intersubjectivity. The processes through which stories coordinate time, represent embodied action, and promote social collaboration are fundamental to the brain-body interactions through which our species has evolved and has constructed the cultures we inhabit.

Triangulating our phenomenological experience as tellers and followers of stories with neuroscientific findings about embodied cognition and with narrative theories about plots, fiction, and reading is an attempt to understand the relation between language, cognition, and narrative — a goal that many thoughtful investigators across a variety of disciplines have pursued. One of the reasons why philosophers, literary theorists, and everyday readers have wondered about why and how we tell stories is that narrative has seemed to hold the key to how language and the mind work. Narratology is now at a turning point in its understanding of the relation between language, cognition, and narrative, poised between formalist models of schemes, scripts, and preference rules inherited from structuralism and pragmatically oriented theories of narrative as embodied, intersubjective interaction. Whether and how these models can be reconciled is an important, unsettled question. Understanding the neurobiological bases of narrative may help solve this problem by showing how the ability to tell and follow stories aligns with how the brain processes language. The first section of this essay lays out a neurobiological model of narrative that explains how stories arise from and set in motion fundamental neuronal and cortical processes, and the second section then asks how the aims and methods of narratology should be aligned with what we know about language and the brain.

1. The Neuroscience of Narrative

Stories help the brain negotiate the never-ending conflict between its need for pattern, synthesis, and constancy on the one hand and for flexibility, adaptability, and openness to change on the other. The brain's remarkable, paradoxical ability to play in a to-and-fro manner between these competing imperatives is a consequence of its decentered organization as a network of reciprocal top-down, bottom-up connections among its interacting parts. Narrative theorist Seymour Chatman (1978: 47, 45) attributes plot formation to "the disposition of our minds to hook things together"; as he notes, "our minds inveterately seek structure." This is, indeed, a basic axiom of contemporary neuroscience. Against the cognitive need for consistency, however, the psychologist William James ([1890] 1950: 1:139) describes the brain as "an organ whose natural state is one of unstable equilibrium," constantly fluctuating in ways that enable its "possessor to adapt his conduct to the minutest alterations in the environing circumstances." The brain knows the world by forming and dissolving assemblies of neurons, establishing the patterns that through repeated firing become our habitual ways of interacting with the environment, even as ongoing fluctuations in these syntheses combat their tendency to rigidify and promote the possibility of new cortical connections. The brain's ceaseless balancing act between the formation and dissolution of patterns makes possible the exploratory play between past equilibria and the indeterminacies of the future that is essential for successful mental functioning and the survival of our species.

Stories contribute to this balancing act by playing with consonance and dissonance. Borrowing Frank Kermode's (1967) well-known terms, Ricoeur (1984: 65–66) describes emplotment as "concordant discordance" — "a synthesis of the heterogeneous" that configures parts into a whole by transforming the "diversity of events or incidents" into a coherent story. According to Ricoeur, the act of "composing plots" converts "the existential burden of discordance" into narrative syntheses that give meaning to life's imbalances by constructing patterns of action (33, 31). Even in the simplest narratives that approach what Gérard Genette (1980: 35–36) calls the hypothetical "zero degree" of difference between the order of events in the telling and their order in the told, the conjunctions that join together the elements of the plot are invariably disrupted by twists and turns on the way to resolution. What Genette calls temporal "anachronies" (flash-forwards and flashbacks, for example, that disrupt the temporal correspondence between the telling and the told) further play with the competing impulses toward consonance and dissonance that are basic to narrative. The imbalances between pattern-formation and dissolution in the brain make possible this narrative interaction between concord and discord, even as the construction and disruption of patterns in the stories we tell each other help the brain negotiate the conflicting imperatives of order and flexibility. The neuroscience of these interactions is part of the explanation of how stories give shape to our lives even as our lives give rise to stories.

Stories can draw on experience, transform it into plots, and then reshape the lives of listeners and readers because different processes of figuration traverse the circuit of interactions and exchanges that constitute narrative activity. First, the neural underpinnings of narration start with the peculiarly decentered temporality of cognitive processes across the brain and the body—disjunctions in the timing of intracortical and brain-body interactions that not only make possible but also actually require the kind of retrospective and prospective pattern-formation entailed in the narrative ordering of beginnings, middles, and ends. Next, the strangely pervasive involvement of processes of motor cognition not only in the understanding of action and gesture but also in other modalities of perception suggests why the work of creating plots that simulate structures of action can have such a profound effect on our patterns of configuring the world. Finally, if stories can promote empathy and otherwise facilitate the cointentionality required for the collaborative activity unique to our species, the power and the limits of their capacity to transform social life ultimately depend on embodied processes of doubling self and Other through mirroring, simulation, and identification, processes whose limitations are reflected in the strengths and weaknesses of narratives as ethical and political instruments. In each of these areas, narratives configure lived experience by invoking brain-based processes of pattern-formation that are fundamental to the neurobiology of mental functioning.

1.1. *Narrative Time and the Temporality of the Brain*

The concordant discordance of emplotment is based on the decentered, asynchronous temporality of the brain. One of the many ways in which the brain differs from a computer is that its temporal processes are not instantaneous and perfectly synchronized (see Armstrong 2013: 91–130). Unlike electrical signals that discharge simultaneously at nearly the speed of light, action potentials at the neuronal level take more than a millisecond to fire, and different regions of the cortex respond at varying rates. For example, as neuroscientist Semir Zeki (2003: 215) observes, in the visual cortex "colour is perceived before motion by [approximately] 80 ms [milliseconds]," and "locations are perceived before colours, which are perceived before orientations." The integration of neuronal processes through which conscious awareness emerges may require up to half a second. As Zeki points out, however, this "binding" (as it is called) is itself not perfectly homogeneous: "The binding of colour to motion occurs after the binding of colour to colour or motion to motion" because "binding between attributes takes longer than binding within attributes" (216, 217). More time is needed to integrate inputs from vision and hearing, for example, than to synthesize visual signals alone. Although we typically don't notice these disjunctions, the nonsimultaneity of the brain's cognitive processes means that consciousness is inherently out of balance and always catching up with itself.

This imbalance is not a bad thing, however, because it allows the brain to play in the ever-changing horizontal space between past patterns and the indeterminacies of the future, the space that plots organize into beginnings, middles, and ends. Concord with no trace of discord would be disabling. In waking life, as neuroscientists Gerald Edelman and Guilio Tononi (2000: 72) observe, "groups of neurons dynamically assemble and reassemble into continuously changing patterns of firing." The synchronization of brain waves across the cortex makes possible the formation of neuronal assemblies and coordinates the workings of different regions of the brain (see Buzsáki 2006). As cognitive scientists Bernard Baars and Nicole Gage (2010: 246) explain, "normal cognition requires selective, local synchrony among brain regions," "highly patterned and differentiated" oscillatory patterns in which "synchrony, desynchrony, and aperiodic 'one-shot' waveforms constantly appear and disappear." But as Edelman and Tononi (2000: 36) explain, "If a large number of neurons in the brain start firing in the same way, reducing the diversity of the brain's neuronal repertoires, as is the case in deep sleep and epilepsy, consciousness disappears." In those conditions, "the slow, oscillatory firing of . . . distributed populations of neurons is highly synchronized globally" (72), and global hypersynchrony paralyzes normal functioning by disrupting the to-and-fro of synchronization and desynchronization. In contrast to sleep and epilepsy, "consciousness requires not just neural activity," Edelman and Tononi point out, "but neural activity that changes continually and is thus spatially and temporally differentiated" — "distributed, integrated, but continuously changing patterns of neural activity . . . whose rich functioning actually *requires* variability" (73, 74–75). The ability of a plot to join concord and discord through temporal structures that order events while holding them open to surprise, variation, and refiguration is one instance of this necessary tension between pattern and change, synchrony and fluctuation, coordination and differentiation.

Stories set in motion reciprocal processes of pattern-formation that are always already occurring beneath our awareness and that are fundamental to the brain's operation as a to-and-fro ensemble of neuronal assemblies that are constantly coming and going, waxing and waning. The concordant discordances of narrative play off of the brain's necessary, never-ending alternation between synchronization and desynchronization. By manipulating the time lags built into cognition, narratives can reinforce established patterns through the pleasures of recognition, providing support for the structures that build coherence across our temporal experience, or they can disrupt the expectations through which we build consistency and thereby make possible new patterns of synchronization. The conjunctions that smooth over temporal discordances can facilitate configurative activity, but the disjunctions inherent in these time-lags can also be productive by combating habitualization and promoting flexibility.

One narrative correlative of these temporal discrepancies is the relation between discourse and story—the sometimes concordant, sometimes discordant interplay between the order of events in the telling and their sequence in the told. When the telling and the told reinforce each other, the formation of cognitive syntheses is facilitated; when they veer off and diverge, the possibility emerges of interruptions and disjunctions through which the ordinarily invisible temporal operations of cognitive pattern-formation can come into view. As narratologist Christian Metz (1974: 18) observes, "Narrative is a . . . doubly temporal sequence," and "one of the functions of narrative is to invent one time scheme in terms of another time scheme." Even the classic formula "Once upon a time . . . " has the basic temporal structure of doubling one time over against another. The capacity to play with temporal differences is a defining characteristic of narrative, and this is possible only because of the asynchronous temporality of the embodied brain. Were cognitive processes temporally homogeneous and globally hypersynchronized, they would not give rise to the doublings entailed by the interaction of discourse and story.

1.2. Narrative Action and the Action-Perception Circuit

The temporality of the decentered brain makes mimesis possible because imitation is not a static correspondence of sign to thing but a dynamic configuration of an action. Narration is a kind of action (a linguistic making) that produces an organization of events (an emplotment of actions) that the reader or listener follows and reconstructs (the activity of comprehension). According to Ricoeur (1984: 54), "The composition of the plot is grounded in a preunderstanding of the world of action, its meaningful structures, its symbolic resources, and its temporal character." The lived experience of action is characterized by "temporal structures that evoke narration," and so Ricoeur (1987: 434) describes life "as an activity and a desire in search of a narrative." The configuration of existential patterns of action into plots and stories is, however, not an end in itself: "Structuration is an oriented activity that is only completed in the spectator or the reader" (Ricouer 1984: 48) through the potentially transfigurative action of comprehending the narrative. And so the circuit is completed, only to stand ready to begin again, as culturally shared and shaped patterns of action are taken up and refashioned by poets, writers, and storytellers of all kinds who offer refigured narratives to ever-new audiences that in turn may play with and transform the configurations through which they experience the world. It may be, as Ricoeur (1987: 425) observes, that "stories are told and not lived" whereas "life is lived and not told," but there is a circuit between living and telling that is mutually formative and potentially transformative, and that is because the work of figuration crosses and joins these modes of narrative activity.

Contemporary neuroscience suggests that the biological basis of these connections is an action-perception circuit that makes action fundamental to many cognitive processes that might seem unrelated to the control of various body parts by the motor cortex. Plots can play a central role in structuring our understanding of the world because action is thoroughly implicated in perception and cognition. Seeing, hearing, and touching are all active processes, for example, that are especially attuned to difference and change. According to neurophilosopher Alva Noë (2004: 8), "The basis of perception . . . is implicit practical knowledge of the ways movement gives rise to changes in stimulation."[1] As he points out, "the world makes itself available to the perceiver through physical movement and interaction" (1). For all modes of perception, exploratory activity of the environment provides ever-changing information about regularities and irregularities, and it is these differences to which the organism responds. Noë consequently claims that "all perception is touch-like," even vision (1): "As in touch, the content of visual experience is not given all at once. We gain content by looking around just as we gain tactile content by moving our hands" (73). As he notes, for example, "in normal perceivers, the eyes are in nearly constant motion, engaging in saccades (sharp, ballistic movements) and microsaccades several times a second. If the eyes were to cease moving, they'd lose their receptive power" because "optic flow contains information that is not available in single retinal images" (13, 20).

One reason for this is that the workings of "opponency" make the retina more sensitive to changes in light than to a uniform, constant illumination (see Livingstone 2002: 54–55). Similarly, as neuroscientists Mark Bear, Barry Connors, and Michael Paradiso (2007: 420) observe, the responsiveness "of warm and cold receptors" on the skin is "greatest during, and shortly after, temperature changes"; "with thermoreception, as with most other sensory systems, it is the sudden change in the quality of a stimulus that generates the most intense neural and perceptual responses." Perception is an exploratory

1. Noë is affiliated with various intellectual traditions that also inform my analysis of cognition and narrative. His theories about action and perception have much in common with the neurophenomenology of Varela (Varela, Thompson, and Rosch 1991; Varela 1999), Thompson (2007), and Gallagher (2012) that in turn derives from the work of Husserl, Heidegger, and Merleau-Ponty. The phenomenological tradition and its recent neurocognitive offshoots also inform my theoretical framework for neuroaesthetics and reading (Armstrong 2013, 2015). Noë also belongs to the tradition of American pragmatism descending from Charles Sanders Peirce and William James through Dewey and Bruner. The convergences between phenomenology and pragmatism have been much discussed (see Wilshire 1968; Rosenthal and Bourg 1980; Corrington, Hausman, and Seebohm 1987) and were an inspiration for my early book on Henry James, William James, and phenomenology (Armstrong 1983; see also 2018). On the history of these intellectual traditions, also see my entry on phenomenology in *Contemporary Literary and Cultural Theory: The Johns Hopkins Guide* (Armstrong 2012).

activity that can bring all of the modalities of sensation into interaction with each other as the organism's changing relation to its world produces differences to which our sensory equipment responds, even as changes in how we direct that equipment toward the world — moving our eyes or hands or the direction of our ears — can produce differences that are rich in information.

Recent experimental evidence on the responsiveness of the brain to imagined action and even to action words suggests that the brain is primed to respond to linguistically staged configurations of action, and these can have a profound effect on our cognitive processes because perception in many different modalities depends on embodied action (see Pulvermüller 2013). As neuroscientist Marc Jeannerod (2006: 28, 39) points out, many different experiments have shown that "imagining a movement relies on the same mechanisms as actually performing it," and that is because "imagined actions are indeed actions in their own right: they involve a kinematic content, they activate motor areas almost to the same extent as executed actions, they involve the autonomic system as if a real action was under way." If the motor cortex and even muscle tissue can be excited by mental rehearsal of an action, that should also be true of linguistic simulations of actions, and there is experimental evidence that this is so. Cognitive scientist Lawrence Barsalou (2008: 628) reports, for example, that, "when reading about a sport, such as hockey, experts produce motor simulations absent in novices." This is consistent with a 2009 fMRI study by Speer et al. that showed correlations between six different kinds of changes represented in stories and the brain regions activated by "analogous activities in the real world" (changes in the location, cause, goal, character, timing, or the object involved in an action) (Speer et al. 2009: 990). These and many other similar studies point to some of the neurobiological processes set in motion by the feigned figuration of action and sensation in narrative, brain-body interactions in response to imitation that could have the power to reinforce or reshape the recipient's pattern-forming habits across many cognitive domains.

Action seems to perform a fundamental role in coordinating different modalities of cognition, and this organizing role is crucial not only for language but also for narrative and our ability to construct and follow plots. The anatomical region of the brain central to these interactions is Broca's area, a section of the inferior frontal cortex adjacent to the parts of the motor cortex that control the mouth and the lips: "Studies have shown this area to be active in human action observation, action imagery and language understanding" (Pulvermüller and Fadiga 2010: 351). Impairments in Broca's area have long been known to result in difficulties producing and comprehending grammatical sentences. Patients with lesions in this part of the brain can understand and pronounce single words, "but they have great difficulty in aligning scrambled words into a sentence or in understanding complex sentences," and these deficiencies are "paralleled in non-linguistic modalities" (357). Similarly, a number of brain-imaging studies have shown that musical syntax is processed in Broca's area and that listening to musical rhythms activates the motor cortex (Maess et al. 2001; Chen, Penhune, and Zatorre 2008).

This region of the brain is also apparently crucial for narrative. A recent experiment by Patrik Fazio et al. (2009: 1987, 1980) revealed that "a lesion affecting Broca's area impairs the ability to sequence actions in a task with no explicit linguistic requirements." His group showed patients with Broca's aphasia "short movies of human actions or of physical events," and they were then asked to order, "in a temporal sequence, four pictures taken from each movie and randomly presented on the computer screen." Curiously, although these patients could still recognize before-after relations between physical events, they had a harder time using the pictures to reconstruct the order of human actions. Their ability to remember and compose a sequence of represented actions was impaired. This result suggests that the patients in Fazio's study suffered a deficiency in the capacity for emplotment, the ability to produce and follow configurations of action. Such an inference is consistent with Fazio's claim that "the complex pattern of abilities associated with Broca's area might have evolved from its premotor function of assembling individual motor acts into goal-directed actions" (1987). This capacity for organizing action into meaningful sequences makes the brain ready for language, but it also prepares the brain for narrative. Broca's area is vital for language as well as narrative because both entail the structuration of symbolic action.

1.3. Following a Story, Empathy, and the Social Brain

Our intuitive, bodily based ability to understand the actions of other people is fundamental to social relations of many kinds, including the relation between storyteller, story, and audience. This ability undergirds the circuit between the representation of a configured action emplotted in a narrative and the reader's or listener's activity of following the story as he or she assimilates its patterns into the figures that shape our worlds. In an illuminating analysis of the "kinematics" of narrative, cognitive literary theorist Guillemette Bolens (2012: 1–3) distinguishes between "kinesic intelligence" and "kinesthetic sensations" — "our human capacity to discern and interpret body movements" of other people as opposed to the "motor sensations" we may have of our own actions, whether voluntary or involuntary:

> Kinesthetic sensations cannot be directly shared, whereas kinesic information may be communicated. I cannot feel the kinesthetic sensations in another person's arm.

Yet I may infer his kinesthetic sensations on the basis of the kinesic signals I perceive in his movements. In an act of kinesthetic empathy, I may internally simulate what these inferred sensations possibly feel like via my own kinesthetic memory and knowledge.

The ability to understand the actions represented in a story (what is told) as well as to follow the movements of the narration (the telling) requires both kinds of cognitive competence—the hermeneutic capacity to configure signals into meaningful patterns (kinesic intelligence) and the intuitive sense of how the structures emplotting the actions and the forms deployed in the narration resonate with my own unreflective, habitual modes of figuring the world (embodied in my kinesthetic sensations).

The kinesic intelligence and kinesthetic empathy that we use to understand stories entail a kind of doubling between self and Other that, according to Maurice Merleau-Ponty, makes the alter ego fundamentally paradoxical. As Merleau-Ponty ([1945] 1962: 362, 358) explains, "the social is already there when we come to know or judge it" because the intersubjectivity of experience is primordially given with our perception of a common world—and yet, he continues, "there is ... a solipsism rooted in living experience and quite insurmountable" because I am destined never to experience the presence of another person to him- or herself. The kinesthetic empathy Bolens describes is paradoxically both intersubjective and solipsistic, for example, inasmuch as I "internally simulate" what the other must be feeling as if her sensations were mine, which, of course, they are not (otherwise I wouldn't need to infer them on the basis of my own). Following a story is a similarly paradoxical process, with both intersubjective and solipsistic dimensions, whereby my own resources for configuring the world are put to work to make sense of another, fictive, narrated world that may seem both familiar and strange and that may either reinforce or disrupt my sense of the world's patterns, since its figurations both are and are not analogous to mine. Reading is an "as-relation" whereby I think the thoughts of someone else, but think them as if they were my own—a doubling of the "real me" I bring to the text and the "alien me" I produce by lending it my powers of consciousness (see Iser 1978).

The doubling of self and Other in the exchange of stories can have a variety of beneficial or potentially noxious social consequences. Following a story is a fundamentally collaborative transaction that can promote the "shared intentionality" that Michael Tomasello and other neurobiologically oriented cultural anthropologists identify as a unique human ability that other primates seem to lack (Tomasello et al. 2005; Tomasello 2014). What Tomasello et al. (2005: 676) call "'we' intentionality" is the capacity for "participating in collaborative activities involving shared goals and socially coordinated action plans (joint intentions)" (see Armstrong 2013: 131–74). The fundamental "skills of cultural cognition" made possible by shared intentionality begin with parent-infant "proto-conversations" that involve "turn-taking" and "exchange of emotions"—activities also entailed, of course, in telling and following stories—and such collaborative interactions culminate in what is known as the "ratchet effect" of cumulative cultural evolution (Tomasello et al. 2005: 681, 675; see Easterlin 2012, Boyd 2009). This ability to engage in coordinated activity is analogous to what neuroscientists of music observe in the predisposition of infants "to attend to the melodic contour and rhythmic patterning of sound sequences" and in their attunement "to consonant patterns, melodic as well as harmonic, and to metric rhythms" (Trehub 2003: 13–14). The back-and-forth interaction of telling and following the configured patterns of action in a narrative is similar to how, according to cognitive scientist Ian Cross (2003: 48, 50), music "enables the sharing of patterned time with others and facilitates harmonicity of affective state and interaction"—a "communal experience of affect elicited by moving together rhythmically in music and dance [that] could have enhanced cooperative survival strategies for early humans, for example, in hunting or in inter-group conflict." The coordination of action across subjectivities in the exchange of stories—emplotted patterns of actions reconfigured in the listener's patterns of reception—would similarly enhance the "'we'-intentionality" that makes culturally productive collaboration possible.

The comparison to music is instructive because rhythmically coordinated action beneath conscious awareness can be both enabling and disabling. The sensation of boundaries dissolving in experiences of rhythmic interaction and harmonic unification—what Nietzsche ([1872] 1994) famously attributed to the Dionysian powers of music to overwhelm Apollonian line and form—may miraculously, even sublimely, transport us outside of ourselves, but it can also result in well-documented contagion effects (the shared thrills of an audience response at a concert, for example, or the collective enthusiasm of a crowd at a sports event or a political rally) that disable cognitive capacities for criticism and evaluation (see Garrels 2011; Lawtoo 2013). Although perhaps less sweepingly powerful, the experience of being carried away by a narrative may similarly transport the listener and seem to erase boundaries between worlds. If not as intoxicating as the Dionysian abandon that Nietzsche describes, such an erasure of self-Other differences may facilitate the inculcation of patterns of feeling and perceiving and have a more powerful impact on habitual pattern-formation than cooler, less absorbing, less transportive exchanges of signs and information. For better or worse (and it can be both), the power of stories to reshape or reinforce the listener's unreflective patterns of configuring the world may increase to the extent that the difference between self and Other in the "as" of empathic identification is reduced or erased. The ideological workings of narrative—its ability to inculcate, perpetuate, and naturalize embodied habits of cognition and emotion— are optimized as the "not" in the doubling of "me" and "alien-me" disappears. If stories ask us to suspend disbelief to immerse ourselves in the illusion they offer, this invitation may be a temptation to the dissolution of boundaries that the demystifying suspicions of ideology-critique rightly resist in order to shake the hold on us of habits of thinking and feeling whose power we may not recognize because they are so deeply ingrained, familiarized, and naturalized.

The capacities of stories to facilitate beneficial social collaboration and to habitualize ideological mystification are two sides of the same coin. This doubleness complicates in important ways the oft-heard claim that a culture's narratives constitute a valuable source of collective knowledge and social cohesion. This argument has recently been reformulated in the terminology of "distributed cognition" based on Andy Clark's (2011) influential notion of the "extended mind." Surveying the various tools and "affordances" (see Gibson 1979) provided by the environment that extend our cognitive capacities, Clark (2011: 226) observes that a "linguistic surround envelops us from birth"—a "sea of words ... and external symbols [that] are thus paramount among the cognitive vortices which help constitute human thought." These include, of course, the stories we find circulating around us. Stories are equipment for navigating the world and solving problems, but they are not entirely defined by their instrumental dimension. The "as if" of aesthetic experience has a noninstrumental quality that is potentially more playful and open-ended than the use of tools for particular ends. If the to-and-fro play between telling and following stories sets in motion the brain's habitual sense-making patterns, then the "as if" of the aesthetic dimension opens up more room for experimentation, flexibility, and play than may be available in the instrumental use of patterns for problem-solving (although here too, of course, the brain needs to be open to adjustments and realignments when anomalies don't fit the patterns it typically deploys). Paradoxically, perhaps, the pragmatic usefulness of stories for keeping our cognitive processes from congealing into rigid patterns—for holding open their capacity to be reshaped and re-formed–may be enhanced by the noninstrumental play of the aesthetic (see Iser 1978; Jauss 1982; Easterlin 2012: 39–89). An important cognitive, moral, and political value of exchanging stories, then, may be to loosen the habitual, ideological hold of any particular set of narrative patterns on our individual and social minds.

2. Neuroscience and Narratology

The goal of classical narratology was to construct the ideal taxonomy—the classificatory scheme that would identify the fundamental elements of narrative and their rules of combination, based on the model of how grammar and syntax determine meaning by establishing the structural relations between the constituent parts of a logical, ordered system (see Phelan 2006: 286–91; Todorov 1969; Barthes 1975; Lotman 1990). Whether inspired by Ferdinand de Saussure's prioritization of *langue* over *parole* (the presumably stable, orderly structures of language as opposed to the contingencies of speech) or Noam Chomsky's claims about universal grammar (the inborn cognitive structures that constitute what Steven Pinker memorably calls the "language instinct"), the assumption was that the structures of mind, language, and narrative are homologous, innate, and universal. Classical narratologist Ann Banfield (1982: 234) expressed a view shared by many narrative theorists, for example, when she asserted that "the ingredients for represented speech and thought" in a story "are . . . given in universal grammar" and that the ease with which we create and understand stories is explained by fundamental homologies between the structures of narrative and "the speaker's internalized grammar."

Some versions of cognitive narratology still operate within the structuralist paradigm, either tacitly or explicitly. For example, the editors of the recent anthology *Stories and Minds: Cognitive Approaches to Literary Narrative* assert that "rather than turning away from structuralist narratology, cognitive narratologists . . . build on the insights of structuralism and combine them with cognitive studies" (Bernaerts et al. 2013: 13). As James Phelan (2006: 286) explains, "cognitive narratology . . . shares with [structural narratology] the same goal of developing a comprehensive formal account of the nature of narrative" and "conceives of its formal system as the components of the mental models that narratives depend on in their production and consumption." These "mental models" are the frames, scripts, and preference rules that Manfred Jahn (2005: 67–71) defines and explains in his authoritative account of cognitive narratology in the *Routledge Encyclopedia of Narrative Theory*. Spelling out the aims of "postclassical narratology," Jan Alber and Monika Fludernik (2010: 11) endorse this project: "Cognitive narratologists . . . show that the recipient uses his or her world knowledge to project fictional worlds, and this knowledge is stored in cognitive schemata called frames and scripts."

Whether these mental constructs can do justice to the cognitive processes they purport to describe is highly questionable, however. The formalist goal of identifying orderly, universal structures of mind, language, and narrative does not match up well with the unstable equilibrium of the temporally decentered brain or the probabilistic processes through which cognitive connections develop and dissolve. There is a growing scientific consensus that the formalist model of innate, orderly, rule-governed structures for language should be cast aside because it does not fit with what we know about how the brain works. As the science of cognition and language has shifted, so too must narratology adjust its methods and aims.

New versions of cognitive narratology have arisen to challenge the structuralist paradigm. Advocates of an "embodied, enactive" view of cognition argue that, rather than "conceiv[ing] of the mind" as a structure of "abstract, propositional representations" like "frames" and "scripts," narrative theory should understand "the human mind as shaped by our evolutionary history, bodily make-up, and sensorimotor possibilities, and as arising out of close dialogue with other minds, in intersubjective interactions and cultural practices" (Kukkonen and Caracciolo 2014: 261–62). Whereas first-generation cognitive science was "firmly grounded in a computational view of the mind," with "frames, scripts, and schemata" functioning as "mental representations that enable us to make sense of the world by serving as models of specific situations or activities," second-generation cognitive science shares with phenomenology and the pragmatism of John Dewey and William James an emphasis on the interactions between embodied consciousness and the world in "feedback loops" through which "experience shapes cultural practices" even as "cultural practices help the mind make sense of bodily experience" (Caracciolo 2014: 45; Kukkonen and Caracciolo 2014: 267). Rather than prioritizing the construction of taxonomies, schemata, and systems of rules to explain how the mind works and to account for narrative by disclosing its underlying cognitive structures, second-generation narratology "insist[s] on the situated, embodied quality of readers' engagement with stories and on how meaning emerges from the experiential interaction between texts and readers" (Caracciolo 2014: 4). A quest for structures and rules has been displaced by an emphasis on the interactions between embodied minds, stories, and the world.

Instead of viewing this change as a paradigm shift, some prominent narrative theorists with roots in the first generation have sought ways of reconciling embodied, enactivist narratology with schema theory and formalist, grammatically based models. For example, rejecting the idea that second-generation cognitive science has replaced earlier theories, Monika Fludernik (2014: 406) proposes that they should be regarded as approaches that can coexist and inform one another: "A history of cognitive studies might perhaps better start out from an inherent duality in cognitive work–research that is static and abstract flanking research that looks at the body and human experience." Reminiscent of how structural linguistics juxtaposed synchronic and diachronic approaches to language, this proposal would view frames and scripts as "static, abstract" structures that are actuated in experience, much as the structuralists thought the rules of *langue* are manifested in the speech-acts of *parole*. David Herman (2002: 1–24) seems to have cast aside his earlier project of constructing a "story logic" that reflects transcendental, universal "mental models" in favor of what he calls "discursive psychology" (Herman 2010: 156), which regards meaning not as a product of "mental processes 'behind' what people say and do" but, rather, holds that "the mind does not preexist discourse, but is ongoingly accomplished in and through its production and interpretation." Still, hoping like Fludernik to rescue formalism and schema theory, he nevertheless asks "how we might work toward a rapprochement between (1) discourse-oriented approaches to the mind as a situated interactional achievement and (2) the work in cognitive grammar and cognitive semantics that likewise promises to throw light on the mind relevance of narrative structures but that focuses on discourse productions by individual speakers?" (175). Again echoing structuralism's opposition between *langue* and *parole*, Herman proposes that we think of language as having social and individual sides that could be separately but compatibly studied—but with the switch that pragmatic, interactive theories rather than formal structures would explain the social side and grammatically based schema theory would provide models for individual mental structures. (As I show below, formalist models and modes of analysis still pervade Herman's 2013 book *Storytelling and the Sciences of Mind*, even though he claims to have embraced enactivism and to have abandoned the structuralist assumptions of his earlier narratological work.)

The problem with both of these proposals, however, is that the epistemological assumptions of first- and second-generation cognitive science are irreconcilably opposed, viewing meaning either as a manifestation of underlying frames, scripts, and rules or as a product of mutually formative, historically evolving interactions between brain, body, and world. The narratological programs based on these opposing epistemologies are also fundamentally at odds—focusing on the figurative, interactive processes through which stories are constructed and experienced as opposed to the schemes, structures, and rules presumably underlying them. This opposition is a reprise of the debates between structuralism and its phenomenological and pragmatic opponents (see Ricoeur 1968; Merleau-Ponty [1945] 1962: 174–99). The problem is not whether to emphasize what happens in interactions between the body and the world or, alternatively, what goes on in the head. What is at issue is how to correlate neuronally based, embodied cognitive processes with our experience of the social world and with our capacities to tell and follow stories. Two questions are at stake here: How are we to understand the pattern-forming capacities of our cognitive equipment that first-generation cognitive narratologies would formalize into frames, scripts, and preference rules? And how should we understand the regularities of language that formalists would systematize into orderly classificatory schemes and rule-governed structures? Cognitive narratology needs a neuroscientifically sound understanding of language that explains how neuronal and cortical processes interact with our lived experience of the social world.

One obstacle to seeking such correlations is the bogeyman of Cartesian dualism that haunts literary studies. To inquire about the cognitive workings of the brain, it is sometimes feared, is to commit the fallacy of assuming that reality is constituted in the mind of an ego that thinks, thereby overlooking the fact that the cogito is always situated in a body and a social, historical setting and that cognition entails interactions across the boundaries joining brain, body, and social world. Advocates of enactive embodied cognition sometimes similarly worry that asking about processes in the brain may wrongly neglect its situation in a body and a world of natural and socially constructed affordances (for example, see Cook 2018). Enactivism risks becoming a distorting dogma, however, if it refuses to investigate cortical and neuronal processes inside the skull on the grounds that cognition is not only a matter of what happens in the head. By no means mutually exclusive, these perspectives are interdependent and inextricably linked. Usefully reminding us that "the brain is one element in a complex network involving the brain, the body, and the environment," Noë (2004: 214, 222) advises that we need both "to look inward, to the neural plumbing" that gives rise to experience, and "to look outward, too, to the way that plumbing is hooked up to the world."

2.1. "Seeing as" in Language and Cognition

Not everything, to be sure, in first-generation cognitive narratology need be abandoned. Jahn (2005: 67) describes "'seeing X as Y' as a foundational axiom" of cognitive narratology, and this idea is indeed scientifically sound. Configurative processes of categorization and pattern-formation—what existential phenomenologist Martin Heidegger ([1927] 1962) similarly calls the "as-structure " (*Als-Struktur*) of understanding—are crucial to embodied cognition and narrative, but they need to be understood in nonschematized, interactive form. One reason why gestalt theory has been a resource from which neuroscientists like Semir Zeki (2004), cognitive psychologists like James J. Gibson (1979), and phenomenologists like Merleau-Ponty ([1945] 1962) have all repeatedly drawn is its appreciation of the role that figuration or "seeing as" plays in cognition. This is, for example, the epistemological moral of the famously ambiguous rabbit-duck gestalt (the beak of the duck shifting if we see the shape as a rabbit, a new part-whole configuration that transforms it into a pair of ears). This gestalt is a model of cognition because the circular, recursive work of configurative pattern-building ("seeing as") animates not only vision but cognitive processes of all kinds. Making a case for what he calls "carnal hermeneutics," phenomenologist Richard Kearney (2015: 20) similarly observes that the "'as-structure' is already operative in our most basic sensations." This is because, as Merleau-Ponty ([1945] 1962: 159) points out, "the smallest sense-datum is never presented in any other way than integrated into a configuration and already 'patterned.'" It is consequently a basic principle of contemporary neuroscience that "categorization (or conceptualization) is a fundamental process in the human brain. . . . There are ongoing debates about how categorization works, but the fact that it works is not in question" (Lindquist et al. 2012: 124).

The "as-structure" of categorization—how seeing always entails "seeing as"—is also evident in the circularity of literary interpretation (see Armstrong 2013: 54–90). Literary theorists have long recognized that interpretation is inherently circular because one can understand a text or any state of affairs only by grasping in advance the configurative relation between part and whole. Any act of interpretation sets in motion a reciprocal interaction between part and whole because a detail makes sense only if it can be seen as somehow relating to the entire text, even as the whole can only be understood by working through its parts. This epistemological theory about the need for pattern—the reciprocal construction of part and whole that are together construed as a configurative relation of some kind—is common ground between the humanities and the cognitive sciences.

It is a mistake, however, to reify these configurative processes into mental modules that bear no relation to the anatomy of the embodied brain or to posit linear logical models of cognitive decision-making that do not correspond to the reciprocal, to-and-fro movements of figuration in experience, in the cortex, or in the interactions between brain, body, and world. These are some of the problems with the terminology of frames, scripts, and preference rules employed by cognitive narratology. As Jahn (2005: 69; see also 1997) acknowledges, these notions were developed by "artificial intelligence" theorists "to replace the concept of context by more explicit and detailed constructs" that "aim at reproducing a human cogniser's knowledge and expectations about standard events and situations"—with "frames" referring to "situations such as seeing a room or making a promise," and "scripts" encompassing "standard action sequences such as . . . going to a birthday party, or eating in a restaurant." The brain is not a computer, however. As hermeneutic phenomenologist Hubert Dreyfus (1992) points out, computers lack context, background, and prior experience that we as embodied conscious beings typically employ in testing hypotheses about how to configure a situation we encounter, whether in a text or in the world, and replacing this deficiency by positing preset mental constructs that do the work only displaces the problem that needs to be solved. Rather than explaining the processes whereby the embodied brain configures experiential contexts, these constructs instead call attention to what computers can't do.

"Seeing as" sets in motion interactions between brain, body, and world that are fluid, reciprocal, and open-ended, and preset schemata like frames and scripts are too rigid and linear to do justice to these sorts of dynamic, recursive processes. This is why psychologist Richard Gerrig (2010: 22), whose work on reading is widely (and rightly) respected among cognitive narratologists, has recently parted company from what Jahn describes as the mainstream view, in the process rejecting the term *schema* as too rigid and formulaic. Gerrig prefers instead to speak of "memory-based processing," a concept that recognizes that "readers' use of general knowledge" is "more fluid and more idiosyncratic" than the terminology of frames and scripts can capture.

The linear, overly tidy notion that cognition is governed by preference rules also needs to be abandoned. According to Jahn (2005: 69), "a preference rule is usually cast in the form *Prefer to see A as B given a set of conditions C.*" In its favor, the notion of *preference* is not absolute and leaves a little wiggle room for probabilistic variation, but the problem with structuring preferences into "rules" is that these posit a linear chain of decision-making, following the form of a logical proposition: if C, then A implies B. This linear, mechanical, logical structure is not an adequate representation of how cognitive decision-making happens either in neurobiology or experience. Neurobiologically, it bears little relation to the interactive, top-down, bottom-up processes of the dynamical systems of synchronization and desynchronization in the brain. Neuronal assemblies form and dissolve according to patterns of habituation that result from the reciprocal reinforcement of connections that can be displaced by other syntheses, and these interactions are not like linear, mechanical algorithms. Experientially, the unidirectional logic of preference rules is unable to capture the to-and-fro circularity of "seeing as" in the phenomenological process of configuring part-whole relations in a text or in life. Reading is not linear logical processing, and embodied cognition cannot be adequately modeled either by ordered hierarchies of modules or mechanical, linear algorithms.

2.2. Brain-Body-World Interactions and the Patterns of Language and Cognition

The work of "seeing as" is not localizable in any particular region of the cortex but extends across the brain, the body, and the world. It is not governed by rules but develops habitual patterns through repeated experiences and is consequently always open to disruption, variation, and change. The formalist goal of identifying orderly, universal structures of mind, language, and narrative doesn't match up well with the messiness of the brain or with how cognitive patterns emerge from our embodied experiences of the world. The consensus among neuroscientists is that the brain is a bushy ensemble of anatomical features whose functions are only partly fixed by genetic inheritance and are to a considerable extent plastic and variable depending on how they connect in networks with other, often far-flung cortical areas. These connections develop and change through experience according to Hebb's law (Hebb [1949] 2002), a fundamental axiom of neuroscience: "Neurons that fire together, wire together." As neuroscientist Stephen E. Nadeau (2012: 1) points out, "Brain order is chaotic rather than deterministic; rules are not defined but instead emerge from network behavior, constrained by network topography" and connectivity (not all parts of the cortex can do everything, and they cannot interact if they are not linked by the axons through which neurons exchange electro-chemical charges). Whatever order can be found in language and cognition results, he explains, from patterns of reciprocal relationship "acquired through experience," and these patterns are attributable less to innate, genetically determined anatomical structures than to "statistical regularities of experience."[2]

The brain, in short, is not an orderly structure consisting of rule-governed relations between fixed elements like a computer with hardwired connections

2. Nadeau's fascinating book provides a thorough and rigorous (although technically difficult) explanation of the neuroscientific case against universal grammar. See Changeaux (2012: 206–8) for a more concise and accessible explanation of why contemporary neuroscience has rejected the Chomksyan model that "mental organs" are "innate," "determined genetically," and "suited to a given species." For comprehensive reviews of the neuroscientific findings that cast doubt on the claim that language is based on inborn, universal cognitive structures, see Evans and Levinson (2009) and Christiansen and Chater (2008). Berwick and Chomsky (2016) have recently attempted to reconcile the assumption of an innate "language faculty" with contemporary neurobiology and evolutionary theory. The scientific community generally remains skeptical, however, for reasons outlined in reviews by cognitive linguist Vyvyan Evans (2016: 46), who politely notes that their "position seems less reasonable today than it once did," and by neuroscientist Elliot Murphy (2016: 8), who more pointedly criticizes their reliance "on outdated assumptions" about "how the brain actually operates (via oscillations and their various coupling operations)" and shows in detail that their assertions about the localization of linguistic operations do not fit the experimental evidence. Also see the highly critical review by the language columnist for the *Economist* (Greene 2016).

between components that operate according to logical algorithms. Much messier, more fluid, and more open to unpredictable (if not unlimited) developments than this linear, mechanical model assumes, the brain is an ever-changing ensemble of reciprocally interacting parts whose functions may vary according to how they combine with other elements. Modular models of the brain (see Fodor 1983), once popular during the heyday of "artificial intelligence" models in cognitive science, have fallen out of favor because cortical regions are not autonomous and orderly. As neurophenomenologist Shaun Gallagher (2012: 36) observes, the brain is "a dynamical system [which] cannot be explained on the basis of the behavior of its separate components or in terms of an analysis that focuses on the synchronic, or static, or purely mechanical interactions of its parts"; "the parts of a dynamical system do not interact in a linear fashion" but, rather, "in a non-linear way, reciprocally determining each other's behavior." Patterns of relationship can become established over time as particular interactions recur and reinforce existing connections or propagate and strengthen new ones, but how repeated experiences lead to the formation of habits through Hebbian "firing and wiring" is a better model for understanding these patterns than the genetically fixed, orderly structures assumed by the epistemological formalists. Preprogrammed modules and linear algorithms are not a good model for understanding the workings of the brain.

The structures of neural anatomy are limiting but not ultimately defining. Different cortical locations have particular functions that can be disabled if they are damaged, but no region works alone, and its role can vary according to how it reciprocally interacts with other areas. Function and connectivity can change with experience. The visual cortex of a blind person, for example, can adapt and become responsive to touch when reading Braille (see Changeux 2012: 208), and some sight-deprived people as well as animals have been shown to have superior sound localization because the unused parts of their visual cortex are recruited for auditory functions (see Rauscheker 2003). These instances of plasticity may seem exceptional, but they are examples of the general rule that, as Kristen A. Lindquist et al. (2012: 123) explain, the "function of individual brain regions is determined, in part, by the network of brain regions it is firing with." According to Lindquist et al., this is why there is "little evidence that discrete emotion categories can be consistently and specifically localized to distinct brain regions" (121). Her review of the experimental evidence shows, for example, that the amygdala is not uniquely and exclusively associated with fear but is also active "in orienting responses to motivationally relevant stimuli" that are "novel," "uncertain," and "unusual" (130). Various studies have similarly shown, she points out, that the anterior cingulate cortex, typically connected with disgust, "is observed in a number of tasks that involve awareness of body states," including "awareness of body movement," "gastric distention," and even orgasm (133–34).

This research calls into question Patrick Colm Hogan's claim (2010: 255; see also 2011) that "emotion is . . . the response of dedicated neurobiological systems to concrete experiences, not a function of the evaluation of changing situations relative to goals." Lindquist is a member of Lisa Feldman Barrett's group that has led the challenge to the theory of "basic emotions" promulgated by Paul Ekman and Silvan Tomkins. As Barrett (2017: 22, 23, 33) explains, a large and growing body of neuroscientific and psychological research has called into question the view that emotions are universal classes with objective biological markers:

> Overall, we found that no brain region contained the fingerprint for any single emotion. . . . Emotions arise from firing neurons, but no neurons are exclusively dedicated to emotion. . . . An emotion word, like "anger," does not refer to a specific response with a unique physical fingerprint but to a group of highly variable instances that are tied to specific situations. . . . The emotions you experience and perceive are not an inevitable consequence of your genes. . . . Your familiar emotion concepts are built-in only because you grew up in a particular social context where those emotion concepts are meaningful and useful, and your brain applies them outside your awareness to construct your experiences.

Emotions are mixed products of biology and culture that are better thought of as variable, internally heterogenous populations than logical categories or universal classes with fixed neurobiological foundations.

Anatomical location and cortical structure alone cannot explain embodied cognition. Brain-body-world interactions can affect not only internal connectivity but also the functions of particular cortical regions. To understand a complex cognitive phenomenon like vision, emotion, or language, it is not enough to identify structure and modularity (as the formalist models assume); it is necessary, rather, to trace the configurative, nonlinear, to-and-fro processes through which various components of our dynamic cognitive systems interact and reciprocally constitute each other.

A good example of the brain's combination of anatomical specialization and openness to change through experience is the manner in which the visual cortex adapts inherited functionalities in order to support the unnatural, culturally acquired capacity to read written texts (see Armstrong 2013: 26–53). As neuroscientist Stanislas Dehaene (2009: 4) points out, we learn to read Shakespeare by adapting cortical capacities that our species acquired on the African savannah. This is an instance of what cognitive scientist M. L. Anderson (2010) calls "neural re-use" — the capacity of cortical regions to acquire functions for which they did not first evolve. New, unpredictable experiences with the world may set in motion variable interactions between different areas of the brain and the body as well as with other members of our species that can produce fundamental changes in cortical structure and functionality. As the visual and auditory cortices interact during the often arduous processes through which beginning readers learn to associate word-shapes with phonetic sounds (also activating parts of the motor cortex associated with the mouth and the lips that fire not only in the articulation but also during the recognition of speech), connections get established and reinforced between different regions of the brain that have the effect of converting a specific area of the visual cortex to a culturally specific use (the recognition of visual word forms) for which it was not innately, genetically predetermined. The acquisition of the ability to read may be an extraordinary cultural and neurobiological accomplishment, but as an example of neural reuse, it is simply an illustration of what Anderson (2010: 245) calls "a fundamental organizational principle of the brain."

Our species' development of the capacity to read illustrates the dual historicity of cognitive functions (see Armstrong 2015). Some of our epistemological equipment is based on long-term, evolutionarily stable capacities like the responsiveness of the visual system to edges, orientation, lines, and shapes, but these capacities are open to change depending on learning and experience—they can be recruited, in this case, to identify alphabetic signs—because the function of a cortical region depends on how it interacts with other components of the dynamical system in which it is engaged. The brain can be molded by cultural institutions (like literacy) that adapt particular areas and capacities for their purposes, but as with reading, these capabilities need to be relearned with each generation until or unless the neural reuse through which they are repurposed becomes evolutionarily adapted into the biological makeup of the species. The structures and functions of the brain are historical, not universal, because they are the products of evolution, but some capacities are more enduring than others and are shared by members of our species across time and around the globe, even as they get reshaped and repurposed through particular, historical, culturally situated experiences of learning.

2.3. Language and Narrative as Biocultural Hybrids

Language is what neuroscientists call "a bio-cultural hybrid" (Evans and Levinson 2009: 446) that develops through the interaction of inherited functions and anatomical structures in the brain with culturally variable experiences of communication and education. Although some parts of the brain are known to be linked to language (lesions in Broca's and Wernicke's areas, for example, can disrupt syntactical or semantic processes), Nadeau (2012: 83) points out that "linguistic function taps the entire cerebrum," and recent fMRI-based research has confirmed that language entails far-flung syntheses of cortical areas and connections between the brain and the body (see Huth et al. 2016). There is no single module that governs language and no discrete, anatomically identifiable set of regions that would constitute the grammar unit predicted by structural linguistics. As Nadeau (2012: 164–65) explains, "The grammar anyone of us uses is not intrinsically universal. . . . Instead it is based on the statistical regularities of our own linguistic experience (instantiated in neural connectivity), which have been determined by the modest community of people we have conversed with or read." Cases of aphasia in different languages reveal not an anatomically based, universal grammar system that gets knocked out with the loss of language function but rather what Nadeau calls "graceful degradation" (17). Everything doesn't simply collapse and disappear, but some functions are more or less strongly preserved, in different patterns of vulnerability that depend on cross-cerebral connections and redundancies and that vary between linguistic communities. This evidence is better accounted for by the stochastic, probabilistic regularities established through Hebbian connections and developed through experience than by a logically ordered, innate grammar.

   Such a probabilistic model also helps to explain the duality of language as a set of regularities open to innovation, variation, and change. As neuroscientist Jean-Pierre Changeux argues, the Hebbian explanation of stochastic regularities offers a better account of the creative capacities of language than prefixed formal systems can provide (see Changeux 2012: 206–7, 316–17). On the one hand, language is a set of shared codes, evident in its recurring patterns that support intersubjective communication and well-formed sentences. On the other hand, the irregularities of language are also vitally important because they make possible unpredictable if constrained possibilities for linguistic innovation through rule-governed or rule-breaking creativity. In accord with a probabilistic model, structures do not completely decide in advance all the ways they can be used (innovation within the rules is possible), and sometimes new configurations can emerge as previous connections are replaced by new ones (transgressing existing rules is not always wrong, as with a novel metaphor that at first may seem like a category mistake but then becomes accepted and gets adopted into the lexicon).

   If language and narrative are biocultural hybrids, any transcultural, transhistorical regularities in their functions and forms are a product of variable but constrained interactions between brain, body, and world and not universals that are homologous to logical structures of the mind. The sources of these regularities are typically both biology and culture; it's not simply that nature is fixed and culture variable. Similarly, any recurring patterns in the stories we typically tell each other are the mixed products of interactions between our species' neurobiological equipment and repeated experiences we are likely to undergo. If stories across the world have recurrent forms, this is not a result of narrative structures that reflect universal cognitive schemata. Rather, as biocultural hybrids, the patterns identified by various narrative theories have probably developed because evolved cognitive proclivities shared by members of our species have interacted with recurrent, typical experiences to produce configurative relations between brain, body, and world that demonstrate statistical regularities. These patterns are not logical structures but habitual configurations that are variable but constrained within limits that are attributable to the regularities of both biology and experience.

Consider, for example, cognitive narratologist Patrick Colm Hogan's (2003: 230–38) claim that certain "narrative universals" characterize "the mind and its stories" — "story structures" that he identifies as the romantic, the heroic, and the sacrificial. The question of how to understand cross-cultural "universals" is notoriously difficult. For example, arguing that the claims of relativism overstate the differences between cultures, Donald E. Brown (1991: 9–38) carefully distinguishes between different kinds and degrees of universality — universals of "essence," attributable to the biological characteristics of our species, as opposed to universals of "accident," produced by widely shared experiences, some of which may be "near universals," probably all-encompassing but at least broadly evident, and "statistical universals" that may not be omnipresent but are more common than would be predicted by chance. Hogan (2010: 48–49) admits different kinds and degrees of universality, but he thinks and talks like a structuralist: "Hierarchies of universals are defined not only by the schematization of techniques and by a receding series of explanatory abstractions but by a series of conditional relations. . . . Much as unconditional universals may be subsumed into hierarchies of abstraction, implicational universals may be organized into typologies." This kind of logical formalism is not a good way of thinking about the messy, probabilistic development of regularities that characterize biocultural hybrids like language and narrative.

If narrative patterns like those identified by Hogan recur across cultures, that is not because they reflect universal cognitive structures. They are better understood as biocultural hybrids — recurrent configurations that develop because certain repeated characteristics of our species' shared experiences of birth and death, collaboration and competition, propagation and violence interact with biologically based cognitive proclivities to produce statistically discoverable regularities in cultural institutions, including the stories we circulate in our communities. Given the commonalities in the basic experiences members of our species typically undergo in their journeys from birth to death, it would be surprising if the cognitive configurations established through Hebbian connectivity between our brains, bodies, and worlds did not demonstrate various regularities that would show up in our narratives. Members of our species fall in love and have sexual relations, engage in conflicts that produce winners and losers, and form communities that join some members and exclude others, and the configurative powers of pattern-formation based on the connective capacities of our embodied brains build narratives about these experiences that may evince various regularities (Hogan's stories of romance, heroism, and sacrifice).

It is misleading to call these "narrative universals" or to attribute them to a structural logic of "the mind and its stories," because these terms are too static, orderly, and ahistorical to do justice to the messy, dynamic processes through which biocultural hybrids get produced in the interactions of brain, body, and world. These interactions may produce patterns that demonstrate regularities because habitual connections are established through Hebbian processing and neural reuse and are then passed on by cultural sharing of the kind through which, for example, literacy is developed and handed down. But formalist terminology and structuralist models are not good tools for describing these processes because such concepts misrepresent the way habitual patterns of connection and configuration get made and transformed in experience and in the brain. Formal taxonomies are not sufficient to explain these interactions.

2.4. Describing (without Reifying) Narrative Worlds

The term *world* is often employed in narrative theory to describe these interactions. For theorists in the traditions of phenomenology and pragmatism, the term refers to the configurations of meaning-making activity that characterize experience—what Merleau-Ponty ([1945] 1962: vii–xxi) calls the unreflective, "operative intentionality" that we find already at work when we reflect on our lives and discover various patterns of relationship that give shape to our typical, habitual interactions with people, places, and things. Narratives bring worlds into relationship as patterns of configurative activity cross back and forth in the circuit joining lived experience, the construction of stories, and their reception by listeners and readers. This circuit entails an interaction between worlds—between what Edmund Husserl ([1954] 1970) calls the *Lebenswelt* or lived world, the fictional worlds constructed by storytellers, and their re-creation in the imaginative worlds built by their recipients. As Ricoeur (1987: 430–31) explains, "The intersection of the world of [the] text and the world of the reader ... opens up a horizon of possible experience, a world in which it would be possible to dwell." The process of telling and following stories sets in motion interactions between the patterns of configuration that characterize these different worlds. Pragmatically oriented psychologist Jerome Bruner (1986: 66) similarly invokes this term to characterize stories not as logical, formal structures but as aspects of our lived experience—projections of "possible worlds in which action, thought, and self-definition are possible (or desirable)." What matters for theorists like Ricoeur and Bruner in the phenomenological and pragmatic traditions is how the pattern-making powers of stories contribute to what Nelson Goodman (1978) memorably calls our "ways of worldmaking," a concept also adopted by phenomenological reading-theorist Wolfgang Iser (1993: 152–70) in his "literary anthropology."

It is once again a mistake, however, to reify worldmaking by reducing it to formal, schematic models of the sort sometimes proposed to map the structures of "storyworlds." The interactions between worlds as we tell and follow stories cannot be reduced to grids and schemes. For example, the good thing about David Herman's (2013: x–xi) somewhat awkward, confusing description of "narrative worldmaking" as "worlding the story" and "storying the world" is its recognition that the configurative work of narrative is a dynamic process. It is not necessary to turn nouns into verbs to describe this activity, however. More problematic is the taxonomic drive to construct classificatory schemes to account for these processes. Herman's much-discussed book *Storytelling and the Sciences of the Mind* (2013) offers one classificatory scheme, diagram, and taxonomy after the other and proliferates terms, categories, and distinctions in an almost manic attempt to reduce the dynamism of worldmaking to an orderly system. Rather than clarifying the configurative activity through which worlds are projected and interact in narratives and lived experience, this elaborate edifice of maps, grids, and definitions necessarily fails to capture the processes it attempts to reduce to static schemes.

The fundamental problem with this approach is evident in two of Herman's (2013: 56) central claims about narrative worldmaking—namely, that "interpreters map textual patterns onto WHO, WHAT, WHERE, WHEN, HOW, and WHY dimensions of storyworlds," and that "the patterns in question emanate from reasons for (text-producing) actions" that can be systematically categorized. A static map of positions on a grid charting the answers to these questions cannot do justice to the configurative processes of meaning-making through which worlds are experienced and exchanged. Herman's interrogatory map is reminiscent of the stock questions that newspaper reporters are instructed to ask as they gather material for their stories, but any journalist knows that the answers they jot down in their notebooks are *not* the story but only the bits and pieces out of which it must still be put together when they return to the newsroom. What is missing are the configurative processes of pattern-formation that connect the dots and fill in the blanks. Resistant to reduction to a classificatory scheme, the patterns of intentionality that animate a world cannot be explained by positions on a map. The spatial, formal logic of Herman's maps of storyworlds cannot account for the dynamic, to-and-fro processes by which fictional worlds arise and through which they interact with the worlds of readers.

A similar problem afflicts Mark Turner's (1996) diagrams of what he calls "conceptual blending," none of which can do justice to the interaction between a word and a context through which metaphorical innovation occurs. This interaction is characterized by what Nietzsche ([1873] 2015) calls *"das Gleich-setzen des Nicht-gleichen,"* the "setting equal" of what is "not the same." As Ricoeur explains, a novel metaphor is a category mistake — a term that is surprising because it doesn't fit its context in the expected manner. This incongruity is not simply dismissed as an error, however, but instead produces new meaning because of the interpreter's adjustments through which its initial incoherences are made coherent and, thereby reconfigured, come to seem "right" in unanticipated and new ways. A novel metaphor can then become dead when its incongruities are so assimilated and conventionalized that they are no longer noticed. Turner's schemata necessarily miss this interaction — the category mistake and the readjustments it provokes — and his term *blending* does not do justice to the necessity of incongruity and discordance to the production of new congruence (see Easterlin 2012: 163–79; Armstrong 1990: 67–88; 2013: 87–88). The maps, grids, and schemes that Herman and other structurally oriented narratologists use to characterize the concordant discordance of narrative are similarly destined to miss the processes of figuration, configuration, and refiguration that they reduce to static taxonomies.

This schematic approach is a legacy of the first-generation prioritization of frames and structures. By contrast, various forms of second-generation narratology focus on precisely these interactions. For example, Terence Cave (2016: 4, 5) describes "thinking with literature" as a collaborative process of inquiry, improvisation, and conversation that "conscript[s] our capacity for cognitive inference" and may "alter the cognitive environment of the reader in ways that are powerful, potentially disturbing, and not at all self-evident." Cave's model of reading, based on relevance theory, emphasizes the "bold and highly precise modes of underspecification" of literature that may "act like a prompt or a trampoline, creating unlimited possibilities for imaginative leaps into the blue – or into the minds of others" (27) through improvisatory responses to the world of the text that go beyond mapping dimensions of a story world onto a spatial grid. For Cave, "thinking with literature" is a cocreative response to a literary work "not as [a] neutral text but as an animated affordance" (9) that encourages and makes possible but does not fully determine our interpretations. According to Cave, "what happens when we redescribe literary conventions as affordances" is that "what was static and merely constraining" turns out to open up "all kinds of unexpected possibilities, ways of breaking out into new territory" (55–56). Mapping a world as points on a grid misses this dynamism and "the human ability to think beyond the immediate demands of their environment" that a text invokes through its "implicatures," "intended meanings that can be derived inferentially from a given utterance" (77, 33).

Other contemporary narratologists have made important attempts to theorize these interactions. Describing narrative as "a purposeful communicative exchange between authors and readers," James Phelan (2015: 121; see 2017) offers a "rhetorical theory" that "defines narrative as somebody telling somebody else on some occasion and for some purposes that something happened." Carrying on the tradition of his teachers at the University of Chicago from before the days of cognitive literary criticism, Phelan's theory of rhetoric as a purposeful communicative exchange deserves "second generation" status because it foregrounds the configurative, mutually formative processes of the text-reader interaction. Drawing on phenomenological and pragmatic theories of text-reader interaction, Marco Caracciolo's (2014: 4) "enactivist approach" similarly insists on "how meaning emerges from the experiential interaction between texts and readers"—"stories offer themselves as imaginative experiences because of the way they draw on and restructure readers' familiarity with experience itself"—a to-and-fro, temporally unfolding, dynamic relationship between the world of the reader and the world of the text in a mutually formative experiential transaction.

Nor can narrative actions be reduced to a logic of "reasons" from which they "emanate." According to Herman (2010: 169–70), "Readers are able to understand the characters' *behaviors* as *actions* in part because of the models of emotions on which they rely to interpret the text"—what he calls an "emotionology," defined as "the collective emotional standards of a culture as opposed to the experience of emotion itself": "An emotionology specifies that when an event X inducing an emotion Y occurs, an agent is likely to engage in Z sorts of actions." Once again adopting a model based on scripts, frames, and preference rules, Herman contends that "the characters' activities can be construed as more than just a series of individual, unrelated doings because of the assumption, licensed by a model of emotions, that those behaviors constitute a coherent *class*" (170). There are several problems with this taxonomic, rule-based approach to character, action, and emotion. To begin with, as explained above, the best contemporary neuroscience of emotions (Barrett 2017) suggests that "anger" or "embarrassment" should be viewed not as a coherent, homologous "class," but rather as a "population" of related, overlapping, but diverse subjective states. Further, the research on the relation between real and imagined action suggests that our response to the action staged in a text is less like the linear, logical application of a rule from a class than the sort of bodily based resonances that Guillemette Bolens (2012) describes in her kinematic theory of narrative. These intuitive, embodied resonances unfold over our engagement with a text at the level of primary intersubjectivity through unreflective, operative intentionality, and they cannot be adequately described by a logic of models and rules. These interactions are "as-relations" that have the power to reconfigure our sense of the world because they are not simply applications of schemata we already know. They are, rather, dynamic and unpredictable enactments of the paradox of the alter ego, the doubling of the "real me" of my kinematic sensations that I experience while reading and the "alien me" of the world I set in motion as I empathize and identify with the actions of the text.

A scheme outlining an underlying logic of actions cannot do justice to the processes through which these configurations of embodied intentionality emerge, develop, and change across the horizons joining past, present, and future in to-and-fro, reciprocal interactions. What matters is not only where actions come from, but where they are headed to — not just their sources but their goals and directions — and it is the variable, often unpredictable interaction between these that makes actions dynamic. For example, as Elaine Auyoung (2013: 60) observes, narrated actions can seem lifelike because their gaps and indeterminacies draw on "our readiness to contend with partial representational cues in everyday, nonliterary experience." With the actions represented in stories as in those we encounter in everyday life, she notes, we fill out what lies beyond our limited perspective by our expectations about their future course and direction (see Auyoung 2015). Similarly, as Karin Kukkonen (2016) points out, the various kinds of action set in motion by a text — not only the characters' behaviors (the action of the plot) but also our responses to stylistic cues (the action of the narration) — are less like the unilinear application of preference rules than "affordances" that make possible but do not fully prescribe our responses, guiding our actions but leaving open room for improvisation, innovation, and surprise. Drawing on a Bayesian, predictive-processing model of embodied cognition, Kukkonen explains that the narrative environment makes certain actions probable and others less so, thereby motivating not only the development of the plot but also our expectations about the course of the narration in a dynamic, interactive process of "feedback loops" that "cascade" into each other, reinforcing or disrupting the pattern-making work set in motion by different kinds of narrative figuration. The eventfulness of worldmaking and the unpredictability of the interaction of worlds in the experience of narrative that these second-generation theorists are attempting to describe are essential to how "storyworlds" work, and these are necessarily lost in spatial maps and classificatory schemes.

3. Conclusion

Cognitive narratology needs to break with its structuralist legacy and embrace the paradigm shift proposed by the various pragmatically oriented, phenomenological theories of narrative that have contested the formalist program. If we want to understand stories, logical structures and taxonomies won't do the job. What we need to know, rather, is how elements combine into patterns through their interactions in lived experience and embodied cognition. "How do narratives participate in the formation and dissolution of patterns in the embodied brain's interactions with the world?" is the right question to ask if what we have is not a logically ordered, formally structured mind but a bushy brain that is an ensemble of relationships that get fixed over time but are open to a future of variation. Those interactions are the means by which stories help the brain negotiate the tension between pattern and flexibility thanks to the play of their concordant discordances. Charting the to-and-fro processes of figuration and refiguration through which we tell and follow stories is the dynamic, ever-shifting ground on which neuroscience, narrative, and narratology meet.

References

Alber, Jan, and Monika Fludernik, eds. 2010. *Postclassical Narratology: Approaches and Analyses.* Columbus: Ohio State University Press.

Anderson, M. L. 2010. "Neural Reuse: A Fundamental Organizational Principle of the Brain." *Behavioral and Brain Sciences* 33, no. 4: 245–66.

Armstrong, Paul B. 1983. *The Phenomenology of Henry James.* Chapel Hill: University of North Carolina Press.

Armstrong, Paul B. 1990. *Conflicting Readings: Variety and Validity in Interpretation.* Chapel Hill: University of North Carolina Press.

Armstrong, Paul B. 2012. "Phenomenology." In *Contemporary Literary and Cultural Theory: The Johns Hopkins Guide,* edited by Michael Groden, Martin Kreiswirth, and Imre Szeman, 378–82. Baltimore: Johns Hopkins University Press.

Armstrong, Paul B. 2013. *How Literature Plays with the Brain: The Neuroscience of Reading and Art.* Baltimore: Johns Hopkins University Press.

Armstrong, Paul B. 2015. "How Historical Is Reading? What Literary Studies Can Learn from Neuroscience (and Vice Versa)." *REAL: Yearbook of Research in English and American Literature,* no. 31: 201–18.

Armstrong, Paul B. 2018. "Henry James and Neuroscience: Cognitive Universals and Cultural Differences." *Henry James Review* 39, no. 2: 133–51.

Auyoung, Elaine. 2013. "Partial Cues and Narrative Understanding in *Anna Karenina.*" In Bernaerts et al. 2013: 59–78.

Auyoung, Elaine. 2015. "Rethinking the Reality Effect: Detail and the Novel." In Zunshine 2015: 581–92.

Baars, Bernard J., and Nicole M. Gage. 2010. *Cognition, Brain, and Consciousness: Introduction to Cognitive Neuroscience*. Amsterdam: Elsevier.

Banfield, Ann. 1982. *Unspeakable Sentences: Narration and Representation in the Language of Fiction*. Boston: Routledge and Kegan Paul.

Barrett, Lisa Feldman. 2017. *How Emotions Are Made: The Secret Life of the Brain*. New York: Houghton Mifflin Harcourt.

Barsalou, Lawrence W. 2008. "Grounded Cognition." *Annual Review of Psychology* 59: 617–45.

Barthes, Roland. 1975. "An Introduction to the Structural Analysis of Narrative." *New Literary History* 6, no. 2: 237–72.

Bear, Mark, Barry W. Connors, and Michael A. Paradiso. 2007. *Neuroscience: Exploring the Brain*, 3rd ed. Baltimore: Lippincott Williams and Wilkins.

Bernaerts, Lars, Dirk de Geest, Luc Herman, and Bart Vervaeck, eds. 2013. *Stories and Minds: Cognitive Approaches to Literary Narrative*. Lincoln: University of Nebraska Press.

Berwick, Robert C., and Noam Chomsky. 2016. *Why Only Us: Language and Evolution*. Cambridge, MA: MIT Press.

Bolens, Guillemette. 2012. *The Style of Gestures: Embodiment and Cognition in Literary Narrative*. Baltimore: Johns Hopkins University Press.

Boyd, Brian. 2009. *On the Origin of Stories: Evolution, Cognition, and Fiction*. Cambridge, MA: Harvard University Press.

Brown, Donald E. 1991. *Human Universals*. Philadelphia: Temple University Press.

Bruner, Jerome S. 1986. *Actual Minds, Possible Worlds*. Cambridge, MA: Harvard University Press.

Buzsáki, György. 2006. *Rhythms of the Brain*. Oxford: Oxford University Press.

Caracciolo, Marco. 2014. *The Experientiality of Narrative: An Enactivist Approach*. Berlin: De Gruyter.

Cave, Terence. 2016. *Thinking with Literature: Towards a Cognitive Criticism*. Oxford: Oxford University Press.

Changeux, Jean-Pierre. 2012. *The Good, the True, and the Beautiful: A Neuronal Approach*. Translated by Laurence Garey. New Haven: Yale University Press.

Chatman, Seymour. 1978. *Story and Discourse: Narrative Structure in Fiction and Film*. Ithaca, NY: Cornell University Press.

Chen, Joyce L., Virginia B. Penhune, and Robert J. Zatorre. 2008. "Listening to Musical Rhythms Recruits Motor Regions of the Brain." *Cerebral Cortex* 18, no. 12: 2844–54.

Christiansen, Morten H., and Nick Chater. 2008. "Language as Shaped by the Brain." *Behavioral and Brain Sciences* 31, no. 5: 489–509.

Clark, Andy. 2011. *Supersizing the Mind: Embodiment, Action, and Cognitive Extension*. Oxford: Oxford University Press.

Cook, Amy. 2018. "4E Cognition and the Humanities." In *The Oxford Handbook of 4E Cognition*, edited by Albert Newen, Leon De Bruin, and Shaun Gallagher, 875–90. Oxford: Oxford University Press.

Corrington, Robert S., Carl Hausman, and Thomas M. Seebohm, eds. 1987. *Pragmatism Considers Phenomenology*. Lanham, MD: University Press of America.

Cross, Ian. 2003. "Music, Cognition, Culture, and Evolution." In Peretz and Zatorre 2003: 42–56.

Dehaene, Stanislas. 2009. *Reading in the Brain: The New Science of How We Read*. New York: Penguin.

Dreyfus, Hubert L. 1992. *What Computers Still Can't Do: A Critique of Artificial Reason*. Cambridge, MA: MIT Press.

Easterlin, Nancy. 2012. *A Biocultural Approach to Literary Theory and Interpretation*. Baltimore: Johns Hopkins University Press.

Easterlin, Nancy. 2015. "Thick Context: Novelty in Cognition and Literature." In Zunshine 2015, 613–32.

Edelman, Gerald M., and Giulio Tononi. 2000. *A Universe of Consciousness: How Matter Becomes Imagination.* New York: Basic Books.

Evans, Nicholas, and Stephen C. Levinson. 2009. "The Myth of Language Universals: Language Diversity and Its Importance for Cognitive Science." *Behavioral and Brain Sciences* 32, no. 5: 429–92.

Evans, Vyvyan. 2016. "Let's Talk About It." *New Scientist* 229, no. 3062: 46–47.

Fazio, Patrik, Anna Cantagallo, Laila Craighero, Alessandro D'Ausilio, Alice C. Roy, Thierry Pozzo, Ferdinando Calzolari, Enrico Granieri, and Luciano Fadiga. 2009. "Encoding of Human Action in Broca's Area." *Brain* 132, no. 7: 1980–88.

Fludernik, Monika. 2014. "Afterword." In "Cognitive Literary Study: Second Generation Approaches." edited by Karin Kukkonen and Marco Caracciolo. Special issue, *Style* 48, no. 3: 404–8.

Fodor, Jerry A. 1983. *The Modularity of Mind.* Cambridge, MA: MIT Press.

Gallagher, Shaun. 2012. *Phenomenology.* New York: Palgrave Macmillan.

Garrels, Scott R., ed. 2011. *Mimesis and Science: Empirical Research on Imitation and the Mimetic Theory of Culture and Religion.* East Lansing: Michigan State University Press.

Genette, Gérard. 1980. *Narrative Discourse: An Essay in Method.* Ithaca, NY: Cornell University Press.

Gerrig, Richard J. 2010. "Readers' Experiences of Narrative Gaps." *StoryWorlds* 2, no. 1: 19–37.

Gibson, James J. 1979. *The Ecological Approach to Visual Perception.* Boston: Houghton Mifflin.

Goodman, Nelson. 1978. *Ways of Worldmaking.* Indianapolis, IN: Hackett.

Greene, Robert Lane. 2016. "The Theories of the World's Best-Known Linguist Have Become Rather Weird." *Economist* 418, no. 8982: 96.

Hebb, Donald O. (1949) 2002. *The Organization of Behavior: A Neurophysiological Theory.* Mahwah, NJ: Erlbaum.

Heidegger, Martin. (1927) 1962. *Being and Time*, translated by John Macquarrie and Edward Robinson. New York: Harper and Row.

Herman, David. 2002. *Story Logic: Problems and Possibilities of Narrative.* Lincoln: University of Nebraska Press.

Herman, David. 2010. "Narrative Theory after the Second Cognitive Revolution." In Zunshine 2010: 155–75.

Herman, David. 2013. *Storytelling and the Sciences of Mind.* Cambridge, MA: MIT Press.

Hogan, Patrick Colm. 2003. *The Mind and Its Stories: Narrative Universals and Human Emotion.* Cambridge: Cambridge University Press.

Hogan, Patrick Colm. 2010. "Literary Universals." In Zunshine 2010: 37–60.

Hogan, Patrick Colm. 2011. *What Literature Teaches Us about Emotion.* Cambridge: Cambridge University Press.

Husserl, Edmund. (1954) 1970. *The Crisis of European Sciences and Transcendental Phenomenology*, translated by David Carr. Evanston, IL: Northwestern University Press.

Huth, Alexander G., Wendy A. de Heer, Thomas L. Griffiths, Frédéric E. Theunissen, and Jack L. Gallant. 2016. "Natural Speech Reveals the Semantic Maps That Tile Human Cerebral Cortex." *Nature* 532, no. 7600: 453–58.

Iser, Wolfgang. 1978. *The Act of Reading: A Theory of Aesthetic Response.* Baltimore: Johns Hopkins University Press.

Iser, Wolfgang. 1993. *The Fictive and the Imaginary: Charting Literary Anthropology.* Baltimore: Johns Hopkins University Press.

Jahn, Manfred. 1997. "Frames, Preferences, and the Reading of Third-Person Narratives: Towards a Cognitive Narratology." *Poetics Today* 18, no. 4: 441–68.

Jahn, Manfred. 2005. "Cognitive Narratology." In *Routledge Encyclopedia of Narrative Theory*, edited by David Herman, Manfred Jahn, and Marie-Laure Ryan, 67–71. London: Routledge.

James, William. (1890) 1950. *Principles of Psychology.* 2 vols. New York: Dover.

Jauss, Hans Robert. 1982. *Toward an Aesthetic of Reception*, translated by Timothy Bahti. Minneapolis: University of Minnesota Press.

Jeannerod, Marc. 2006. *Motor Cognition: What Actions Tell the Self.* Oxford: Oxford University Press.

Kearney, Richard. 2015. "The Wager of Carnal Hermeneutics." In *Carnal Hermeneutics*, edited by Richard Kearney and Brian Treanor, 15–56. New York: Fordham University Press.

Kermode, Frank. 1967. *The Sense of an Ending.* New York: Oxford University Press.

Kukkonen, Karin. 2016. "Bayesian Bodies: The Predictive Dimension of Embodied Cognition and Culture." In *The Cognitive Humanities: Embodied Mind in Literature and Culture*, edited by Peter Garratt, 153–67. London: Palgrave Macmillan.

Kukkonen, Karin, and Marco Caracciolo, eds. 2014. "Introduction: What Is the 'Second Generation'?" In "Cognitive Literary Study: Second Generation Approaches." Special issue, *Style* 48, no. 3: 261–74.

Lawtoo, Nidesh. 2013. *The Phantom of the Ego: Modernism and the Mimetic Unconscious.* East Lansing: Michigan State University Press.

Lindquist, Kristen A., Tor D. Wager, Hedy Kober, Eliza Bliss-Moreau, and Lisa Feldman Barrett. 2012. "The Brain Basis of Emotion: A Meta-Analytic Review." *Behavioral and Brain Sciences* 35, no. 3: 121–43.

Livingstone, Margaret. 2002. *Vision and Art.* New York: Abrams.

Lotman, Yuri M. 1990. *Universe of the Mind: A Semiotic Theory of Culture*, translated by Ann Shukman. Bloomington: Indiana University Press.

Maess, Burkhard, Stefan Koelsch, Thomas C. Gunter, and Angela D. Friederici. 2001. "Musical Syntax Is Processed in Broca's Area: An MEG Study." *Nature Neuroscience* 4, no. 5: 540–5.

Merleau-Ponty, Maurice. (1945) 1962. *Phenomenology of Perception*, translated by Colin Smith. London: Routledge and Kegan Paul.

Metz, Christian. 1974. *Film Language: A Semiotics of the Cinema*, translated by Michael Taylor. Chicago: University of Chicago Press.

Murphy, Elliot. 2016. "The Human Oscillome and Its Explanatory Potential." *Biolinguistics*, no. 10: 6–20.

Nadeau, Stephen E. 2012. *The Neural Architecture of Grammar.* Cambridge, MA: MIT Press.

Nietzsche, Friedrich. (1872) 1994. *The Birth of Tragedy Out of the Spirit of Music*, translated by Shaun Whiteside. New York: Penguin.

Nietzsche, Friedrich. (1873) 2015. *Über Wahrheit und Lüge im außermoralischen Sinne (On Truth and Lie in an Extra-Moral Sense).* Stuttgart, DE: Reclam.

Noë, Alva. 2004. *Action in Perception.* Cambridge, MA: MIT Press.

Peretz, Isabelle, and Robert Zatorre, eds. 2003. *The Cognitive Neuroscience of Music.* Oxford: Oxford University Press.

Phelan, James. 2006. "Narrative Theory, 1966–2006: A Narrative." In Robert Scholes and Robert Kellogg, *The Nature of Narrative*, 283–336. Oxford: Oxford University Press.

Phelan, James. 2015. "Rhetorical Theory, Cognitive Theory, and Morrison's 'Recitatif': From Parallel Play to Productive Collaboration." In Zunshine 2015: 120–35.

Phelan, James. 2017. *Somebody Telling Somebody Else: A Rhetorical Poetics of Narrative.* Columbus: Ohio State University Press.

Pulvermüller, Friedemann. 2013. "How Neurons Make Meaning: Brain Mechanisms for Embodied and Abstract-Symbolic Semantics." *Trends in Cognitive Sciences* 17, no. 9: 458–70.

Pulvermüller, Friedemann, and Luciano Fadiga. 2010. "Active Perception: Sensorimotor Circuits as a Cortical Basis for Language." *Nature Reviews Neuroscience* 11, no. 5: 351–60.

Rauscheker, Josef P. 2003. "Functional Organization and Plasticity of the Auditory Cortex." In Peretz and Zatorre 2003: 357–65.

Ricoeur, Paul. 1968. "Structure, Word, Event." In *The Philosophy of Paul Ricoeur*, edited by Charles E. Regan and David Stewart, 109–19. Boston: Beacon.

Ricoeur, Paul. 1984. *Time and Narrative*, translated by Kathleen McLaughlin and David Pellauer. Vol. 1. Chicago: University of Chicago Press.

Ricoeur, Paul. 1987. "Life: A Story in Search of a Narrator." In *A Ricoeur Reader: Reflection and Imagination*, edited by Mario J. Valdés, 425–37. Toronto: University of Toronto Press.

Rosenthal, Sandra B., and Patrick L. Bourg. 1980. *Pragmatism and Phenomenology: A Philosophic Encounter*. Amsterdam: Grüner.

Speer, Nicole K., Jeremy R. Reynolds, Khena M. Swallow, and Jeffrey M. Zacks. 2009. "Reading Stories Activates Neural Representations of Visual and Motor Experiences." *Psychological Science* 20, no. 8: 989–99.

Thompson, Evan. 2007. *Mind in Life: Biology, Phenomenology, and the Sciences of Mind*. Cambridge, MA: Harvard University Press.

Todorov, Tzvetan. 1969. "Structural Analysis of Narrative." translated by Arnold Weinstein. *Novel: A Forum on Fiction* 3, no. 1: 70–76.

Tomasello, Michael. 2014. *A Natural History of Human Thinking*. Cambridge, MA: Harvard University Press.

Tomasello, Michael, Malinda Carpenter, Josep Call, Tanya Behne, and Henrike Moll. 2005. "Understanding and Sharing Intentions: The Origins of Cultural Cognition." *Behavioral and Brain Sciences* 28, no. 5: 675–91.

Trehub, Sandra E. 2003. "Musical Predisposition in Infancy: An Update." In Peretz and Zatorre 2003: 3–20.

Turner, Mark. 1996. *The Literary Mind: The Origins of Thought and Language*. Oxford: Oxford University Press.

Varela, Francisco J. 1999. "The Specious Present: A Neurophenomenology of Time Consciousness." In *Naturalizing Phenomenology: Issues in Contemporary Phenomenology and Cognitive Science*, edited by Jean Petitot et al., 266–314. Stanford, CA: Stanford University Press.

Varela, Francisco J., Evan Thompson, and Eleanor Rosch. 1991. *The Embodied Mind: Cognitive Science and Human Experience*. Cambridge, MA: MIT Press.

Wilshire, Bruce. 1968. *William James and Phenomenology*. Bloomington: Indiana University Press.

Zeki, Semir. 2003. "The Disunity of Consciousness." *Trends in Cognitive Sciences* 7, no. 5: 214–18.

Zeki, Semir. 2004. "The Neurology of Ambiguity." *Consciousness and Cognition*, no. 13: 173–96.

Zunshine, Lisa, ed. 2010. *Introduction to Cognitive Cultural Studies*. Baltimore: Johns Hopkins University Press.

Zunshine, Lisa, ed. 2015. *The Oxford Handbook of Cognitive Literary Studies*. Oxford: Oxford University Press.

Personal Relevance in Story Reading: A Research Review

Anežka Kuzmičová
Department of Culture and Aesthetics, Stockholm University
Institute of Literature, Czech Academy of Sciences

Katalin Bálint
Department of Communication Sciences, VU University Amsterdam

Abstract　Although personal relevance is key to sustaining an audience's interest in any given narrative, it has received little systematic attention in scholarship to date. Across centuries and media, adaptations have been used extensively to bring temporally or geographically distant narratives "closer" to the recipient under the assumption that their impact will increase. In this article, we review experimental and other empirical evidence on narrative processing in order to unravel which types of personal relevance are more likely to be impactful than others, which types of impact (e.g., aesthetic, therapeutic, persuasive) they have been found to generate, and where their power becomes excessive or outright detrimental to reader experience. Together, the evidence suggests that narratives are read through the lens of the reader's self-schema independently of genre, although certain groups of readers, especially in certain situations, may experience personal relevance and related effects more strongly than others. The literature further suggests that large-scale similarities between reader and character (e.g., gender) may not per se be enough for relevance effects to arise and that emotional valence has a role to play in the process alongside thematic saliency.

Keywords　reader response, literature, narrative processing, personal relevance

Part of this work was completed within READ-IT, a Joint Programming Initiative project funded by the Ministry of Education, Youth and Sports of the Czech Republic, reg. nr. 8F18003.

Poetics Today 40:3 (September 2019)　DOI 10.1215/03335372-7558066

In the past century, emotional responses to literary narratives were regarded as unsystematic, personal, and unphilosophical, and therefore largely excluded from scholarly discourse. With the recent cognitive turn in the humanities (Kuzmičová 2014; Caracciolo 2016), however, scholars are increasingly willing to consider the question of actual readers' responses to literary texts. Theories of emotions in reading have become more sophisticated (Miall 2011; Mar et al. 2011), acknowledging that responding emotionally can help readers better understand and appreciate literature (Robinson 2007). Importantly, these theories also acknowledge the role of individual differences in the personal histories and belief systems of readers as part of their explanations of how emotions emerge. This review article focuses on an undertheorized facilitator of emergent emotions in response to narrative, namely, *personal relevance*. Thus, it deals with the general mechanics of narrative processing, but with a particular focus on the individual reader, forging connections between humanities and science perspectives on reading.

A narrative is defined as personally relevant if the information presented carries special importance with respect to the individual reader's self, knowledge, or past experiences. Personal relevance is a key factor at many stages and levels of literary reading. It is empirically proven that literary texts, besides evoking fresh and new emotions, also activate existing memory structures, which then feed into the narrative experience (Cupchik, Oatley, and Vorderer 1998). Studies show that the presence or absence of self-related, personally salient, and familiar issues in a fictional narrative influence, for instance, what people select to read and how they evaluate a text (Fuller and Rehberg Sedo 2012), what level of engagement they achieve (Sikora, Kuiken, and Miall 2011), and how much insight they gain from reading it (Miall and Kuiken 1995; Koopman 2011). Bálint and Tan (2019) analyzed twenty-five in-depth interviews with readers of fiction and found that self-character comparison is an important component in highly absorbed narrative experiences. Participants frequently referred to similarities, dissimilarities, and wished-for similarities with the protagonist when describing their subjective experiences of absorption in fiction.

Analyses of reading group discourse (Peplow et al. 2015) also attest to the salience of relating fictional stories, characters, and situations to one's past and present personal life. For instance, when discussing books, reading group members draw extensively on their direct experiences of the time periods and places rendered in the story (Swann and Allington 2009), bouncing back and forth between "on-book" and "off-book" talk. They even deliberately divide the conversational floor between themselves on the basis of story-relevant real-life expertise (Peplow et al. 2015). Readers sometimes report employing these widespread "mimetic" (Peplow et al. 2015) or "autobiographical"

(Collinson 2009) reading strategies with the express objective of deepening their knowledge of themselves and their life circumstances (Todd 2008).

In literary studies as well as literary education research (Fialho, Zyngier, and Miall 2011), personal relevance has been neglected, despite its obvious implications for reader experience and interpretation. The concept may seem an epitome of the so-called *affective fallacy* (Wimsatt and Beardsley 1949), an approach to literature traditionally derided for diverting the literary expert's focus from authoritative meaning production to personal idiosyncrasy. With the current interest in emotions, especially empathy (Keen 2010; Koopman and Hakemulder 2015; Burke et al. 2016), we feel the moment is ripe for a systematic exploration of personal relevance and related concepts. Indeed, experiments prove that empathy is facilitated by readers' own personality characteristics (Komeda et al. 2013) or personal life experiences (Koopman 2015a; 2015b; 2016), when similar to those rendered in a story.

The weight of individual readers' prior experiences may seem commonplace to the advocates of cultural theory, who make the case for underrepresented subjectivities in the discourse of and on culture (Booker 2010). Our purpose is distinct from that of cultural theory. Rather than postulating that the language used in particular works of literature necessarily has distinct meanings for the underrepresented and theorizing how these meanings are formulated, we review experimental and other empirical evidence on narrative processing in order to unravel which types of personal relevance are more likely to be powerful than others, which types of impact (e.g., aesthetic, therapeutic, persuasive) they generate, and where their power might become excessive or outright detrimental to reader experience. In other words, this review focuses on the workings of personal relevance as a psychological process. Psychological approaches to literary reading are sometimes met with skepticism in the humanities, because they seem to reduce away subjective differences between individuals (van Peer, Hakemulder, and Zyngier 2012). This review attempts to show that the issue of personal relevance is precisely where subjectivist humanities perspectives intersect with the generalist ethos of psychology.

The review draws primarily on empirical literary studies, a broadly defined interdisciplinary field applying empirical-experimental methods of the cognitive and social sciences in the study of aesthetic responses to fiction (van Peer, Hakemulder, and Zyngier 2012). We also supplement the review with insights from the fields of psychology and communication, which use experimental stimuli in a wider variety of media that are not always fictional or not ostensibly presented as such. Focusing on the psychological processes of persuasion and belief change, psychology and communication often have the individual reader's characteristics and their malleability at the very core of inquiry. In addition, literary theory will be cited as appropriate.

1. Concepts of and around Personal Relevance

In this section, we list the basic theoretical concepts applied to phenomena and processes linked to personal relevance. The section is structured following the nomenclature of psychology and communication, which is more unified and systematic in comparison to that of empirical literary studies. Where applicable, the concept presented is first accompanied by a review of the basic psychology and communication literature. It is then followed by a review of work in empirical literary studies that explores the phenomenon in question, albeit labeling it differently.

1.1. Personal Relevance

In psychology and communication, *personal relevance* is defined as the steady tendency in readers to ascribe relative saliency to a certain issue presented in a text (Petty and Cacioppo 1979). Terms synonymous with personal relevance are issue involvement (Kiesler, Collins, and Miller 1969), ego-involvement (Rhine and Severance 1970), and personal involvement (Apsler and Sears 1968). Readers perceive an issue presented in a narrative as personally relevant when it is intrinsically important, carries an emotionally loaded personal meaning, or has significant effects on the reader's own life (Petty and Cacioppo 1979). Experiments show that high levels of personal relevance enhance the processing of text, which means that people process personally relevant texts with more care and attention (for a review, see Petty and Cacioppo 1979). Personal relevance occurs together with increased levels of involvement with the issue dealt with in the text. This involvement has to be distinguished from readers' general susceptibility for engagement with narratives, also known as transportability (Bilandzic and Busselle 2011). Personal relevance is closely related but not necessarily identical to prior knowledge about (Green 2004) or familiarity with an issue (Hoffner and Cohen 2012). Under these latter labels, the amount of prior information or personal contact is mostly measured without considering the personal importance attached to the topic.

Empirical literary studies use varied terms for familiarity and personal relevance as defined above, including the following: recognition of aspects of one's own life (Miall and Kuiken 1995), personal truth (Oatley 1999b), familiarity with situation (Braun and Cupchik 2001), knowing from lived experience (Therman 2008), or personal experience with subject matter (Koopman 2015a). These terms serve different purposes. For instance, in

Miall and Kuiken's (1995) Literary Response Questionnaire, which is widely used for the assessment of literary reading styles, the Insight section comprises items closely related to personal relevance, such as "When I begin to understand a literary text, it's because I've been able to relate it to my own concerns about life." *Insight* is defined as the recognition of previously unrecognized qualities in the self and surrounding world. Braun and Cupchik (2001) and Therman (2008), on the other hand, primarily link personal relevance and familiarity to mental imagery. That is, they found that familiarity with the story situation increases the amount and quality of readers' mental images. In yet other studies, Koopman (2015a; 2015b; 2016) found that personal experience with story topic predicts empathy with the protagonist as well as insight and postreading reflection.

The above literature treats personal relevance as one of many factors contributing to a more complex outcome, for example, insight or empathy. It does not answer the question of what it may be like for a reader, in the moment, to experience personal relevance as such. In this sense, personal relevance was more closely explored by Larsen and László (1990) under the term *personal resonance*. Personal resonance (see also Seilman and Larsen 1989; Halász 1991) stands for the experience proper that a text relates to one's personal history or life circumstances. In this account, personal resonance becomes manifest as a tangle of conscious associations from personal memory, so-called *remindings*. While all text elicits some remindings and all readers have some remindings when prompted by an experimenter, the degree of personal resonance is inferred from the quality of each individual reader's reported remindings. The more the remindings refer to the phenomenal detail of firsthand lived experience rather than, for example, recounting events or secondhand knowledge schematically, the more the text is understood to resonate with the reader. Personal resonance is reportedly higher for literary compared to expository text (Seilman and Larsen 1989) as well as for culturally proximate compared to culturally distant text (Larsen and László 1990).

1.2. Perceived Similarity

Personal relevance has to be distinguished from *perceived similarity* (also known as homophily), a concept used in psychology and communication for readers' recognition that in one way or another they share some features with a character in a narrative (de Graaf 2014). Readers can feel similar to characters in objective, demographic characteristics (e.g., age, gender, nationality, religion, health status) or more subjective features, such as actual life situation, past life experiences, attitudes, or opinions (de Graaf 2014; Hoffner and Buchanan 2005). People tend to share the perspective and motivation of those mediated others whom they perceive as more similar to themselves (Eyal and Rubin 2003; Hoeken, Kolthoff, and Sanders 2016).

Perceived similarity can be an antecedent but also an outcome of reading, meaning that prior similarity can have an effect on the reading experience but also that the reading experience itself can shape one's perceptions of similarity. Similarity in objective characteristics between readers and characters can prompt readers to exhibit more similar attitudes or opinions to the characters after reading (Andsager et al. 2006; Hoffner and Buchanan 2005). In one experiment (de Graaf 2014), participants read a story of a young woman fighting cancer. In one version of the story, the protagonist lived at home, whereas in the other version, she lived in student housing. Readers who read a version matching their own living arrangements felt more similar to the character in general and also more at risk of cancer compared to readers who read the story with a protagonist that had dissimilar living arrangements. This indicates that similarity can enhance the incorporation of a fictional protagonist's characteristics into the self. In a recent study (Cohen, Weimann-Saks, and Mazor-Tregerman 2018), however, effects of similarity on identification could not be replicated.

Hoffner and Buchanan (2005) found that perceived attitude similarity is associated with *wishful identification*, defined as the wish to be like a character. Bálint and Tan's (2019) interview analysis showed wishful identification with psychological features of characters to be an important component of absorbed reading experiences. People tend to report higher wishful identification with those characters who have the same gender and whom they perceive as more similar in attitudes to themselves (Hoffner and Buchanan 2005). However, story characters have been found to elicit wishful identification on the basis of different features depending on whether they are male or female (Hoffner 1996). Another study (Tsay and Krakowiak 2011) found that participants tend to morally disengage (i.e., accept immoral actions) to a greater extent when a character is felt to be more similar to them.

As aesthetic experiences, *wishful identification* and *similarity identification* have been teased apart in empirical literary studies (Andringa 2004). The former term refers to the reader's recognition of personal characteristics that the reader desires to possess, occasionally resulting in behavioral imitation. The latter term refers to the recognition of similarity proper, mediating outcomes such as consolation, support, or distraction in relation to the reader's life situation (Andringa 2004; Charlton, Pette, and Burbaum 2004; Koopman 2014) and also deepening their involvement in the text (Charlton, Pette, and Burbaum 2004).

Another distinction concerning similarity and identification has been suggested by Kuiken, Miall, and Sikora (2004). These authors understand perceived similarity, which they term *simile-like identification*, as only one possible but not sufficient stage on a reader's way to self-modification through literature. Simile-like identification ("A is like B") is then distinguished from *metaphor-like identification* ("A is B"), wherein readers' selves are felt to instantaneously merge with the text not only at the level of human characters but at a more abstract level of affective themes and inanimate forces. Readers come to recognize a character as a member of a class to which they also belong, thus realizing something new about life, a possibly lingering effect.

Empirical literary studies have shown that readers relate to both positive and negative features of characters (Andringa 2004), presumably with specific outcomes for varied aspects of the reading experience such as empathy, participatory responses, and transportation (Gerrig and Mumper 2017) or aesthetically productive mixed emotions (Hoorn and Konijn 2003). Exploring the potentially edifying power of literature, Miall and Kuiken's (1995) Literary Response Questionnaire also features items specifically targeting the recognition of one's own shortcomings in story characters as well as feelings of wanting to change one's life on the basis of a reading experience.

1.3. Self-Referencing

Personal relevance, perceived similarity, and wishful identification are subjective experiences in a reader's consciousness, fueled by the underlying cognitive process of *self-referencing* (Burnkrant and Unnava 1995). To understand the importance of self-referencing, we need to briefly clarify the psychological concept of self-schema. *Self-schema* is defined as a mental representation of our own self, stored and constantly updated in our mind (Conway 2005). It is a highly organized and complex mental structure containing memory traces of factual knowledge about the self (e.g., gender, age, nationality) and autobiographical events (e.g., important time points in life, significant places, associated emotions, etc.) gathered over the course of life (Conway 2005). Krishnamurthy and Sujan (1999) distinguish between anticipatory (future-oriented) and retrospective (past-oriented) self-referencing. When exposed to a narrative text, readers—either consciously or wholly subconsciously—often engage in self-referencing, or searching for similarities and dissimilarities between the content of self-schema and story-schema (Escalas 2007). Through this process, story content is connected to the reader's own past experiences, which can then become manifest to consciousness in above-mentioned remindings (Seilman and Larsen 1989).

Self-referencing is closely associated with other key processes of reading. Psychological studies suggest that self-referencing during reading improves readers' attention and recall of the text (Bower and Gilligan 1979; Klein and Loftus 1988). Rogers, Kuiper, and Kirker (1977) asked participants to pay attention either to the structural, phonemic, semantic, or self-relevant aspects of adjectives and found that words rated for self-relevance were recalled best. Other findings in psychology and communication showed that activated self-referencing increases the persuasive impact of a message (Burnkrant and Unnava 1989), and readers' identification with characters (Chen, Bell, and Taylor 2016). These findings are most probably due to the fact that when readers actively relate their own self and life story to the narrative, they allocate more attention to the details and elaborate more on the topic (Cacioppo, Petty, and Sidera 1982; Burnkrant and Unnava 1995).

As a subconscious mechanism, self-referencing per se has not been explored in empirical literary studies, where the reader's subjective experience, such as conscious remindings, is the main focus of inquiry. Finally, it is important to mention here that too much self-referencing can overtax the reader's attention and divert it from features of the text, especially in cases of autobiographical retrievals (Sujan, Bettman, and Baumgartner 1993). We return to this scenario further on in our review.

2. Individual Differences and Situational Factors

The likelihood of being affected by personal relevance and related phenomena varies greatly due to differences in individual readers' psychological traits, their cultural and situational dispositions, and characteristics of the text being read. In most cases, the variation probably cannot be ascribed to one single factor but rather emerges as a result of interaction. In this section, we review the reader-related factors most frequently proposed in the research literature.

2.1. Reading Habits

Like many other aspects of reader response, personal relevance seems to be more or less prominent depending on one's reading habits, reading style, and general attitude to literature (Miall and Kuiken 1995). Different reader profiles have been proposed, with different degrees of empirical corroboration, to associate most closely with self-implicating reading styles. In literary theory, the classical twentieth-century approach was to deride self-referencing as an epitome of the affective fallacy (Wimsatt and Beardsley 1949), reserved for the inexperienced, less "competent" reader (Culler 1980). Caracciolo and van Duuren (2015) offer a different theory. These authors concur that, of all readers, those who frequently read innovative literary narratives may be especially prone to self-referencing during reading. Caracciolo and van Duuren's argument is based on the idea that, in comparison to more formulaic texts, innovative literature poses higher demands on cognitive-affective flexibility and increases awareness of one's own self as narratively structured.

Within empirical literary studies, Caracciolo and van Duuren's hypothesis is indirectly supported by Cupchik, Oatley, and Vorderer (1998), who found narrative passages of higher stylistic complexity to elicit a higher degree of first-person emotional memories, compared to more stylistically straightforward passages. But direct empirical evidence confirms neither the assumption that self-referential reading is typical of less experienced readers, nor the hypothesis that it is a hallmark of niche expertise. For instance, a representative large-scale survey of German readers conducted by Charlton, Pette, and Burbaum (2004) revealed that the most "committed style of reception," in terms of self-referencing and the cultivation of personal meanings, was typical of the sociocultural "group that consumes high cultural as well as trivial offerings" (Charlton, Pette, and Burbaum 2004: 206) rather than of the sociocultural groups that favor either very demanding or very undemanding reads. Based on complex interactive effects found in a reader response experiment, Koopman (2015b) makes the following similar observation: In order to achieve the state of being "shaken up" by reading, "it may be helpful if people are already empathic persons, find something that connects to their personal experience in the work, and, perhaps, have *not read too much yet*, since that seems to spoil the surprising effects of literature" (Koopman 2015b: 439, emphasis added). We may conclude that self-referencing is not specific to a type of audience with particular expertise or taste in reading. Rather, it is to some degree inherent in story-reading. However, the overall aesthetic impact associated with personal relevance may be relatively higher in nonexpert readers.

2.2. Gender and Age

A common notion regarding gender differences is that female readers are more prone than males to empathizing (Charlton, Pette, and Burbaum 2004; Mar et al. 2011; Koopman 2016), which is a type of response to real and fictional others reportedly mediated by similarity and/or personal relevance (e.g., Preston and de Waal 2002; Decety, Echols, and Correll 2010; Igartua and Barrios 2012; Komeda et al. 2013; McKeever 2015; Koopman 2015a; 2015b; 2016). Oatley (1999a, 1999b) reports a reader-response experiment in which young adult female readers scored significantly higher than their male counterparts on the quantity of self-relevant memories as well as emotions elicited by stories, across both protagonist gender conditions. The author sees a connection between this finding and the fact that "more women than men read fiction ... that concerns relationships" (Oatley 1999a). Charlton, Pette, and Burbaum's (2004) findings likewise suggest that, compared to men, women tend to identify more frequently with story characters and situations, seeking "critical self-confrontation." Based on a study of readers' autobiographies, Andringa (2004) also reports gender differences in reading styles from childhood to adulthood, with female readers reporting more self-referencing and identification. However, gender differences are far from universally validated in experimental research (see, e.g., Bortolussi, Dixon, and Sopčák 2010).

Andringa (2004) found that adult respondents recalled identification experiences more frequently in connection with children's books and with their earlier life stages than with their current life stage and reading materials. An analysis of the earlier reading episodes suggested a gradual evolution from wishful identification in early childhood (see also Hynds 1989) to similarity identification in subsequent years. This effect occurred in male and female respondents alike. A plausible interpretation concerning age may be found in a study by Halász (1991), who explains a surprising lack of story-elicited self-relevant remindings (as opposed to remindings of mediated knowledge) in a teenage sample by the fact that teenagers simply have relatively limited firsthand life experience to draw on when reading *adult* literature. In sum, there is evidence that gender and age modulate the saliency of personal relevance in reading.

2.3. Specific Life Situations

In addition, reading motivated by or focused on personal relevance has been connected with difficult life situations, such as personal crises, periods of grief, or illness. Experiencing such situations at the time of reading (Charlton, Pette, and Burbaum 2004; Koopman 2014) or having done so in the past (Goldstein 2009; Sikora, Kuiken, and Miall 2010; Koopman 2015a; Koopman 2015b) reportedly increases the probability of picking up relevance cues from fiction, especially if the story deals with serious existential themes.

A survey of cultural consumption patterns during periods of distress conducted by Koopman (2014) revealed that those who generally turn to literary reading for coping with difficult life situations tend to be older than those who either turn to music or engage with neither of the two media. This finding was independent of any possibly confounding effect of age as a factor in overall life experience, as Koopman exclusively analyzed responses from individuals who had had distressing life episodes. While Charlton, Pette, and Burbaum (2004) identify literary reading for self-confrontation as a distinctly female strategy, a finding likewise linked to difficult life situations in particular, in Koopman's (2014) study, gender differences were only marginally significant. Not only the imminent experience of a distressing situation but also the sheer memory of it can affect how readers process literature with respect to personal relevance (Goldstein 2009; Sikora, Kuiken, and Miall 2010; Koopman 2015a; 2015b). These effects are further reviewed below.

3. Relevance Domains and Emotional Valence

The previous section reviewed the effects of dispositions for personal relevance on the part of the individual reader. Let us now proceed to the elusive nexus of reader and text. Which types of cues in the content of a text can potentially prompt personal relevance? Across centuries and even across artistic media, adaptations have been used extensively to bring temporally or geographically distant narratives "closer" to the recipient under the assumption that affective impact will increase. Early modern religious paintings depict Jesus' apostles consuming roasts or eel at the Last Supper, and Romeo and Juliet frequently wear bomber jackets on stage. Generally speaking, these adaptations attempt to exploit what Keen (2010), in a literary-theoretical treatise on empathy and the novel, has termed *bounded empathy*. They suggest an easily recognizable link to one's time, place, or other identity marker. There is of course no guarantee of the success of such relatively superficial manipulations. In our focus research disciplines, readers have been subject to experimental designs measuring the effect of various potential links.

3.1. Personality Trait, Demographic, and Locative Relevance

Personality traits are difficult to match between reader and story character. Komeda et al. (2013) made one such attempt in an experimental study that had participants read artificially designed micronarratives rendering protagonists who were highly extroverted, highly neurotic, or neither, while also measuring participants' personalities along these dimensions. Personality matches between participants and protagonists predicted self-reported empathy over and above measures of general empathy dispositions. Analogous reader-character match effects were found in the domain of gender role orientation as well (not to be confused with biological gender; Jose 1989). Because of the complexity entailed in modeling personality traits in natural-length stories and in comparing them to those of live readers, however, most of the research literature reports on more easily operationalized, demographic characteristics such as biological gender, sexual orientation, socio-cultural background, and so forth.

Results obtained on the basis of literary stimuli are mixed. For instance, a cross-national experiment by Bortolussi, Dixon, and Sopčák (2010) manipulated the biological gender of literary characters but found no effect of reader-character gender match on readers' evaluative ratings with regard to character appreciation, clarity of style, literariness, and interest in the story (see also Cohen, Weimann-Saks, and Mazor-Tregerman 2017). Green (2004), on the other hand, presented participants with a story set in the context of a US college fraternity reunion, which was told from the perspective of a homosexual alumnus. They found that readers with a fraternity background and/or familiarity with the social stigma of homosexuality were more transported into the narrative than others. This suggests that more subjective and malleable identity markers perhaps allow greater potential for personal relevance than more objective demographic characteristics.

As outlined in a theoretical proposal by Kuzmičová (2016), the effect of literature can also be enhanced when a story is set in a locale or other general context identical or similar to the one in which one happens to be reading. This is personal relevance based on more or less short-term locative contingencies, that is, at the opposite end of the spectrum from stable personality trait matching. Vaughn et al. (n.d.) found indeed that when a story was read in a story-congruent season of the year, readers' transportation scores were significantly higher compared to a control group who read the same story in an incongruent season. Prentice et al. (1997) also found that students read an implausible story more critically if it was set at their university campus compared to when it was set at another campus, but attempts at replicating this finding were inconclusive (Wheeler, Green, and Brock 1999).

Notably, for all domains, personal relevance is also a matter of degree in the sense that a given condition can be relevant to the reader either directly, via firsthand experience, or indirectly, via secondhand experience. While it may not suffice to have secondhand experience of neurotic or extroverted persons to be more profoundly affected by corresponding story characters, Green's (2004) finding, for instance, applied to readers who reported just having homosexual friends or family members. In cases of subject matters for which secondhand familiarity is powerful enough, their perceived intensity and emotional valence may be distinctive. In itself, belonging to one or the other personality profile or biological gender is ideally only sometimes, but not always, a source of intense experience. Meanwhile, a homosexual orientation may be harder to abstract away from everyday experience given pervasive social prejudice. Moreover, attending a college fraternity reunion as gay is the sort of circumscribed event in which sexual orientation may become especially experientially salient. In sum, for personal relevance to make significant difference, it should probably tap into matters important to the reader and the story alike. Bortolussi, Dixon, and Sopčák (2010), for instance, note that gender similarity effects may have been absent in their study because the female protagonists in the stimulus stories were not portrayed as facing inequality issues. Thus, gender did not stand out as a salient theme. As Gerrig and Mumper (2017) additionally point out, any effect of similarity will necessarily further vary as the salience of a given matter changes over the course of a longer story.

3.2. Emotional Valence and Personal Relevance

It is no coincidence, then, that empirical studies exploring personal relevance from a more specifically aesthetic viewpoint mainly resort to stimuli where the potential source of relevance is less easily captured in mere trait or demographic categories. Rather, these studies look into personal relevance relative to powerful "affective" (Sikora, Kuiken, and Miall 2011) or "existential" (Miall and Kuiken 1999) themes. Such themes are predicted to become salient in a reader's mind due to specific fictional situations and concomitant emotions and sensory images. The more familiar the reader is with a real-life situation, the more rounded and imagery-rich their vicarious experience through self-referencing (Braun and Cupchik 2001), and the more salient a given theme (see Sikora, Kuiken, and Miall 2011 for a more nuanced account of these dynamics).

A peculiar feature of the situations and themes thus observed is that their emotional valence is largely negative. Negative emotions, or perhaps more accurately, mixed emotions arising from the portrayal of intense experiences, are considered the main source of aesthetic effect across art forms. This has led researchers to articulate, for example, the distancing-embracing model of the enjoyment of negative emotions (Menninghaus et al. 2017), the PEFiC model of character appreciation based on a distancing-involvement tradeoff (Hoorn and Konijn 2003), or the idea that fiction-elicited sadness, albeit enhanced by relevant firsthand experience, is pleasingly "unadulterated with anxiety" (Goldstein 2009). All these proposals account for the attraction of negative feelings and experiences in art beyond tragedy by identifying mechanisms of emotional distancing occurring simultaneously with empathy and other story-elicited affect.

Various experimental paradigms have been used to study personal relevance with respect to complex negative experiences. Sikora, Kuiken, and Miall (2010, 2011), for instance, collected qualitative data based on Samuel Taylor Coleridge's *The Rime of the Ancient Mariner* while also soliciting background information on the participants. They found that firsthand experience of personal loss, given a certain lapse of time after the traumatic event, deepened participants' self-implication regarding mortality themes in the text. In mixed quantitative-qualitative designs, Koopman (2015a; 2015b; 2016) exposed readers to narratives of extreme experiences such as depression, child loss, or grief more generally, and found emergent effects of personal relevance insofar that personal experience of depression led to increased donating to a related charity (Koopman 2015a), and that personal experiences of either depression or grief led to more direct reflective thought (Koopman 2015b; Koopman 2016) and empathy (Koopman 2016).

The workings of subtler forms of relevant negative experience were captured in a study of readers' remindings conducted by Larsen and László (1990; László and Larsen 1991). These authors had respondents in Denmark and Hungary, which were divided by the Iron Curtain at the time of the experiment, read a Hungarian short story portraying an incident of arbitrary power abuse. Subjects were asked to encode the occurrence and content of remindings elicited by the story as well as to rate the story on a variety of items. Although there was no overt indicator of setting or locally flavored narrative style, the two groups' responses differed. Compared to the Danish participants, the Hungarians perceived the story as possibly taking place closer to themselves in time and space (Larsen and László 1990). As for remindings, the Hungarian participants' "cultural proximity" resulted in "the generation of a larger proportion of personally experienced, contextually rich, and vividly remembered events" (László and Larsen 1991: 23). Furthermore, readers' appreciation of the text was inversely related to the valence of these events, that is, particularly enhanced by remindings of negative personal experiences.

In the latter experiment, not all remindings were negative, despite the negative theme that sparked them. Therman (2008) ran a remindings study using a more neutral story that also allowed for nostalgic or other positive emotions and memories to arise. Perfecting previous coding systems for the analysis of readers' remindings, she devised a taxonomy wherein lived experience, when subject to reminding, is coded as either repeated or single, and either ordinary or special. In Therman's data, remindings of repeated and/or ordinary experiences appear to be more commonly associated with positive rather than negative emotions. They outnumber by far other experience categories, but they are not sufficient for arousing either the reader's interest in the text or a deep, conscious feeling of personal relevance. Again, it is by way of connecting single, special, emotionally charged experiences to the central theme (mental illness within the family) that firsthand experience is found to be functional for Therman's outcome variable, that is, the reader's understanding of higher-order meanings conveyed by the story.

To date, closer treatment of positively valenced personal relevance can only be found in studies with lower resemblance to naturalistic reading scenarios. Sperduti et al. (2016), for instance, report a study where subjects rated the intensity of their experience while being exposed to video clips labeled as either true or fictional. The authors found that participants only rated their experience as more intensive in the truth (as opposed to fiction) condition when the clips depicted contents corresponding to their previous personal experience, and only if the emotional valence of the contents was positive (as opposed to negative). It is proposed that this finding indicates a particular emotion up-regulation mechanism (see also Menninghaus et al. 2017), activated in the observed encounters with negative contents in fiction. In a study conducted by Tsunemi and Kusumi (2011) participants were given a task before reading a short story: one group had to generate perceptually rich personal memories, thus activating self-schema, whereas the other group had to play a word game, a task unrelated to the self. When the researchers compared how much time the participants needed to read the story, they found that reading times increased for those who had generated perceptual memories. This effect was attributed to greater situation model elaboration, that is, more cognitive resources being used for keeping track of perceptual information in the text. However, it was only present when the content of the personal memories happened to resemble the content of the story. Valence was not measured, but the perceptual memories cited in the report were largely positive.

Finally, it should be noted that the potential effects of valence are acknowledged in theoretical accounts of perceived similarity (Hoorn and Konijn 2003; Andringa 2004), inasmuch as recognition of one's own shortcomings in a fictional character is likely to have different effects compared to identification with a character's positive qualities.

This section reviewed the documented functionality versus nonfunctionality of personal relevance across two interconnected domains: the domain of more "basic" variables such as psychological traits, gender demographics, or physical location, and the domain of more specific, complex, and intense (negative) experiences. The next and final section briefly explicates how personal relevance or perceived similarity can also become excessive in reading and how such excesses are manifested.

4. Effects of Too Much Personal Relevance

The subject matter of a text may sometimes be experienced too personally, with the consequence that the reader's response becomes more self centered than text centered. This phenomenon has been identified in psychology and communication (Sujan, Bettman, Baumgartner 1993) and empirical literary studies (Therman 2008; Sikora, Kuiken, and Miall 2011) alike. Sujan, Bettman, and Baumgartner (1993), for instance, found that when autobiographical memories are activated, people experience higher intensity of affect but pay less attention to the features of the text presented. Similarly, Mick (1992) found a curvilinear ("inverted J") relationship between message recall and self-related meanings, indicating that self-referencing facilitates memory up to a certain point, beyond which it becomes detrimental to memory. Participants in Bálint and Tan's (2019) study also described feelings of too much similarity to the protagonist, with a distancing effect. However, this dynamic was reported to be enjoyable and inherent to the narrative experience.

As suggested above, the likelihood of overly personal reading can be a matter of individual disposition and reading style. Some readers are more prone than others to projecting their life and self-schema onto text (Hynds 1989; Charlton, Pette, and Burbaum 2004; Todd 2008). In empirical literary studies, a notion of *optimal distance* between literary subject matter and the reader's current life has been proposed (Oatley 1999a; Sikora, Kuiken, and Miall 2010; Sikora, Kuiken, and Miall 2011). The difficult task is determining when someone reading for aesthetic and leisure purposes has strayed too far—when personal relevance and the reader's self-referencing have indeed overridden the text.

Focusing on variability in readers' remindings, Therman (2008) identifies a category of so-called *irrelevant remindings*. A clear-cut example of an irrelevant reminding provided by Therman is a reader being reminded by a literary story of a particular chore that needs to be done at home. While roughly complying with the definition of anticipatory self-referencing (Krishnamurthy and Sujan 1999), this kind of reminding presumably has little conscious implication for the reader's self- or story-schema in a longer term. *Distractive remindings*, on the other hand, is a term used by Therman (2008) for text-elicited associations to a phenomenon that the reader cares strongly about (e.g., religion), which nevertheless lack plausible support in the story.

Sikora, Kuiken, and Miall (2011) propose two other terms for excessive or borderline self-referencing based on a cluster analysis of verbal protocols recorded in response to narrative poetry. *Autobiographical assimilation* responses consist of simile-like juxtapositions between a reader's life events and events rendered in the narrative, without recourse to further abstraction. The authors consider autobiographical assimilation aesthetically inadequate due to the reader's intensive self-reflection replacing any attention to the text's language and sensory imagery. Another response category, *autobiographical diversion*, refers to a tendency in the reader to recall physical environments resembling those rendered in the stimulus text. Autobiographical diversion is accompanied by elaborate sensory imagery that is based on the reader's remembered past and wholly decoupled from the text. Therman's (2008) and Sikora, Kuiken, and Miall's (2011) concepts all capture varieties of one and the same excess phenomenon. The text comes to serve as a springboard for unrelated or inadequately related self-referencing, however pleasing it may be to the reader.

Another possible manifestation of excessive personal relevance is the reader's systematic nonengagement with or avoidance of certain textual features or the text altogether. Sikora, Kuiken, and Miall (2010) report that, in the same study in which readers were exposed to *The Rime of the Ancient Mariner*, the experience of severe personal loss had no positive effect on self-modification through reading the poem, if the loss occurred less than two years prior. In other words, readers for whom the text was excessively personally relevant because their memories of personal loss were too fresh systematically avoided picking up certain aesthetic cues in the text.

In a similar vein, Oatley (1999a) observes that readers' personal memories have maximum self-modification potential when they show neither too much nor too little emotional distance from the remembered event, a factor distinct from but certainly contingent on the passing of time. However, Koopman's (2014) survey of reading behavior in distressing life periods found no inverse association between loss recency and reading to cope, and a linear effect of loss gravity on reading to cope (see also Charlton, Pette, and Burbaum 2004). This suggests that there may be additional factors codetermining whether reading about human plights in fiction will provide solace during personal crises, leave no particular mark at all, or perhaps aggravate the reader's condition.

5. Conclusion

Personal relevance is a form of narrative experience involving increased self-referencing oriented toward the recognition and appreciation of salient self-related information in the narrative. This article brings together two seemingly opposing approaches to reading (van Peer, Hakemulder, and Zyngier 2012), the general-psychological and the subjectively relativist, in a review of the empirically proven effects of personal relevance and related phenomena in response to stories.

A great variety of literature can elicit self-referencing. The findings together indicate that readers engage with literature through the lens of their self-schema independent of the type of literature. Through the cognitive process of self-referencing, readers involuntarily compare story content as well as character features to the information stored in the representation of their own selves. An activated self-schema in turn can lead to a variety of subjective experiences, such as personal relevance, perceived similarity, or wishful identification, or in extreme cases, detachment from the narrative. These qualities of reading can help explain why readers experience different levels of empathy (Koopman 2015a; Koopman 2015b), insight (Miall and Kuiken 1995; Koopman 2014), self-reflection (Charlton, Pette, and Burbaum 2004), text-reflection (Halász 1991; Koopman 2016), overall appreciation (Larsen and László 1990) and engagement (Bálint and Tan 2019). As for situational factors, personal crises (Charlton, Pette, and Burbaum 2004; Koopman 2014) or the self-schema instability associated with particular life stages (Andringa 2004) seem to increase the experiential potential of self-referencing.

Importantly, there is direct evidence against the traditional preconception (Wimsatt and Beardsley 1949) that self-referencing is a mark of lesser aesthetic training in the individual (Charlton, Pette, and Burbaum 2004) or literary complexity in the text (Cupchik, Oatley, and Vorderer 1998). Furthermore, the findings reviewed here suggest that large-scale similarities between reader and character, such as gender or sexual orientation, may not per se be enough for relevance effects to arise, and that emotional valence may have a role to play in the process alongside thematic saliency. For example, a same-sex adaptation of *Romeo and Juliet* is likely to affect viewers familiar with the stigma of homosexuality to a greater extent than same-sex adaptations of plays where the protagonists' love relationship does not transgress social norms (thematic saliency) or where its repercussions are less tragic (emotional valence).

Personal relevance can enhance engagement with complex narratives and facilitate reading. In light of the decline of volitional reading among young adults and of the alleged crisis of literature as an academic discipline, the recent rediscovery of literature's beneficial effect on, for example, empathy (Djikic, Oatley, and Moldoveanu 2013; Kidd and Castano 2013) has attracted considerable attention. It is also being translated into intervention programs (EmpathyLab 2016). However, it is unlikely that any particular literary story will exert the same affective and potentially edifying power indiscriminately on all readers. As Caracciolo (2014) notes, all narrative experiences tap into one's experiential background, that is, one's unique repertoire of past experiences — emotional, social, sensory, or other. If there is a strong discrepancy between the story and the reader's experiential background, little emotional or other impact can arise.

At a time when society in a large part of the world is becoming increasingly diverse, it can be helpful for literature educators, reading promoters, and care providers relying on literature to note available evidence of the role of personal relevance. Experiencing personal relevance could help students relate to seemingly distant cultures and acknowledge universal human experiences. Research desiderata that would facilitate new literary pedagogies and that we envision as important steps toward more complex understanding of reader response include an in-depth exploratory study and a psychometric instrument measuring the experience of personal relevance in literary reading along the dimensions identified in this review.

References

Andringa, Els. 2004. "The Interface between Fiction and Life: Patterns of Identification in Reading Autobiographies." *Poetics Today* 25, no. 2: 205–40.

Andsager, Julie L., Victoria Bemker, Hong-Lim Choi, and Vitalis Towell. 2006. "Perceived Similarity of Exemplar Traits and Behavior Effects on Message Evaluation." *Communication Research* 33, no. 1: 3–18.

Apsler, Robert, and David O. Sears. 1968. "Warning, Personal Involvement, and Attitude Change." *Journal of Personality and Social Psychology* 9, no. 2: 162–66.

Bálint, Katalin, and Ed S. Tan. 2019. "Absorbed Character Engagement: From Social Cognition Responses to the Experience with Fictional Constructions." In *Screening Characters*, edited by Aaron Taylor and Johannes Riis, 209–29. New York, N.Y.: Routledge.

Bilandzic, Helena, and Rick W. Busselle. 2011. "Enjoyment of Films as a Function of Narrative Experience, Perceived Realism, and Transportability." *Communications* 36, no. 1: 29–50.

Booker, M. Keith, ed. 2010. *Cultural Theory*. Vol. 3 of *The Encyclopedia of Literary and Cultural Theory*. Malden, MA: Wiley-Blackwell.

Bortolussi, Marisa, Peter Dixon, and Paul Sopčák. 2010. "Gender and Reading." *Poetics* 38, no. 3: 299–318.

Bower, Gordon H., and Stephen G. Gilligan. 1979. "Remembering Information Related to One's Self." *Journal of Research in Personality* 13, no. 4: 420–32.

Braun, Ingrid K., and Gerald C. Cupchik. 2001. "Phenomenological and Quantitative Analyses of Absorption in Literary Passages." *Empirical Studies of the Arts* 19, no. 1: 85–109.

Burke, Michael, Anežka Kuzmičová, Anne Mangen, and Theresa Schilhab. 2016. "Empathy at the Confluence of Neuroscience and Empirical Literary Studies." *Scientific Study of Literature* 6, no. 1: 6–41.

Burnkrant, Robert E., and H. Rao Unnava. 1989. "Self-Referencing: A Strategy for Increasing Processing of Message Content." *Personality and Social Psychology Bulletin* 15, no. 4: 628–38.

Burnkrant, Robert E., and H. Rao Unnava. 1995. "Effects of Self-Referencing on Persuasion." *Journal of Consumer Research* 22, no. 1: 17–26.

Cacioppo, John T., Richard E. Petty, and Joseph A. Sidera. 1982. "The Effects of a Salient Self-Schema on the Evaluation of Proattitudinal Editorials: Top-Down versus Bottom-Up Message Processing." *Journal of Experimental Social Psychology* 18, no. 4: 324–38.

Caracciolo, Marco. 2014. *The Experientiality of Narrative: An Enactivist Approach*. Berlin: De Gruyter.

Caracciolo, Marco. 2016. "Cognitive Literary Studies and the Status of Interpretation: An Attempt at Conceptual Mapping." *New Literary History* 47, no. 1: 187–207.

Caracciolo, Marco, and Thom van Duuren. 2015. "Changed by Literature? A Critical Review of Psychological Research on the Effects of Reading Fiction." *Interdisciplinary Literary Studies* 17, no. 4: 517–39.

Charlton, Michael, Corinna Pette, and Christina Burbaum. 2004. "Reading Strategies in Everyday Life: Different Ways of Reading a Novel Which Make a Distinction." *Poetics Today* 25, no. 2: 241–63.

Chen, Meng, Robert A. Bell, and Laramie D. Taylor. 2016. "Narrator Point of View and Persuasion in Health Narratives: The Role of Protagonist-Reader Similarity, Identification, and Self-Referencing." *Journal of Health Communication* 21, no. 8: 908–18.

Cohen, Jonathan, Dana Weimann-Saks, and Maya Mazor-Tregerman. 2018. "Does Character Similarity Increase Identification and Persuasion?" *Media Psychology* 21, no. 3: 506–28.

Collinson, Ian. 2009. *Everyday Readers: Reading and Popular Culture*. London: Equinox.

Conway, Martin A. 2005. "Memory and the Self." *Journal of Memory and Language* 53, no. 4: 594–628.

Culler, Jonathan. 1980. "Prolegomena to a Theory of Reading." In *The Reader in the Text: Essays on Audience and Interpretation*, edited by Susan R. Suleiman and Inge Crosman, 46–66. Princeton, NJ: Princeton University Press.

Cupchik, Gerald C., Keith Oatley, and Peter Vorderer. 1998. "Emotional Effects of Reading Excerpts from Short Stories by James Joyce." *Poetics* 25, no. 6: 363 – 77.

Decety, Jean, Stephanie Echols, and Joshua Correll. 2010. "The Blame Game: The Effect of Responsibility and Social Stigma on Empathy for Pain." *Journal of Cognitive Neuroscience* 22, no. 5: 985 – 97.

de Graaf, Anneke. 2014. "The Effectiveness of Adaptation of the Protagonist in Narrative Impact: Similarity Influences Health Beliefs through Self-Referencing." *Human Communication Research* 40, no. 1: 73 – 90.

Djikic, Maja, Keith Oatley, and Mihnea C. Moldoveanu. 2013. "Reading Other Minds: Effects of Literature on Empathy." *Scientific Study of Literature* 3, no. 1: 28 – 47.

EmpathyLab 2016. *EmpathyLab Pioneer Schools: Evaluation Report 2016.* www.empathylab.uk /empathylab-school-trial (accessed April 25, 2017).

Escalas, Jennifer E. 2007. "Self-Referencing and Persuasion: Narrative Transportation versus Analytical Elaboration." *Journal of Consumer Research* 33, no. 4: 421 – 29.

Eyal, Keren, and Alan M. Rubin. 2003. "Viewer Aggression and Homophily, Identification, and Parasocial Relationships with Television Characters." *Journal of Broadcasting and Electronic Media* 47, no. 1: 77 – 98.

Fialho, Olivia, Sonia Zyngier and David Miall. 2011. "Interpretation and Experience: Two Pedagogical Interventions Observed." *English in Education* 45, no. 3: 236 – 53.

Fuller, Danielle, and DeNel Rehberg Sedo. 2012. "Mixing It Up: Using Mixed Methods Research to Investigate Contemporary Cultures of Reading." In *From Codex to Hypertext: Reading at the Turn of the Twenty-First Century*, edited by Anouk Lang, 234 – 51. Amherst: University of Massachusetts Press.

Gerrig, Richard J., and Micah L. Mumper. 2017. "How Readers' Lives Affect Narrative Experiences." In *Cognitive Literary Science: Dialogues between Literature and Cognition*, edited by Michael Burke and Emily T. Troscianko, 239 – 58. Oxford: Oxford University Press.

Goldstein, Thalia R. 2009. "The Pleasure of Unadulterated Sadness: Experiencing Sorrow in Fiction, Nonfiction, and 'In Person.'" *Psychology of Aesthetics, Creativity, and the Arts* 3, no. 4: 232 – 37.

Green, Melanie C. 2004. "Transportation into Narrative Worlds: The Role of Prior Knowledge and Perceived Realism." *Discourse Processes* 38, no. 2: 247 – 66.

Halász, László. 1991. "Emotional Effect and Reminding in Literary Processing." *Poetics* 20, no. 3: 247 – 72.

Hoeken, Hans, Matthijs Kolthoff, and José Sanders. 2016. "Story Perspective and Character Similarity as Drivers of Identification and Narrative Persuasion." *Human Communication Research* 42, no. 2: 292 – 311.

Hoffner, Cynthia. 1996. "Children's Wishful Identification and Parasocial Interaction with Favorite Television Characters." *Journal of Broadcasting and Electronic Media* 40, no. 3: 389 – 402.

Hoffner, Cynthia, and Martha Buchanan. 2005. "Young Adults' Wishful Identification with Television Characters: The Role of Perceived Similarity and Character Attributes." *Media Psychology* 7, no. 4: 325 – 51.

Hoffner, Cynthia A., and Elizabeth L. Cohen. 2012. "Responses to Obsessive Compulsive Disorder on Monk among Series Fans: Parasocial Relations, Presumed Media Influence, and Behavioral Outcomes." *Journal of Broadcasting and Electronic Media* 56, no. 4: 650 – 68.

Hoorn, Johan F., and Elly A. Konijn. 2003. "Perceiving and Experiencing Fictional Characters: An Integrative Account." *Japanese Psychological Research* 45, no. 4: 250 – 68.

Hynds, Susan. 1989. "Bringing Life to Literature and Literature to Life: Social Constructs and Contexts of Four Adolescent Readers." *Research in the Teaching of English* 23, no. 1: 30 – 61.

Igartua, Juan-José, and Isabel Barrios. 2012. "Changing Real-World Beliefs with Controversial Movies: Processes and Mechanisms of Narrative Persuasion." *Journal of Communication* 62, no. 3: 514 – 31.

Jose, Paul E. 1989. "The Role of Gender and Gender Role Similarity in Readers' Identification with Story Characters." *Sex Roles* 21, no. 9–10: 697–713.

Keen, Suzanne. 2010. *Empathy and the Novel.* Oxford: Oxford University Press.

Kidd, David C., and Emmanuele Castano. 2013. "Reading Literary Fiction Improves Theory of Mind." *Science* 342, no. 6156: 377–80.

Kiesler, Charles A., Barry E. Collins, and Norman Miller. 1969. *Attitude Change: A Critical Analysis of Theoretical Approaches.* New York: Wiley.

Klein, Stanley B., and Judith Loftus. 1988. "The Nature of Self-Referent Encoding: The Contributions of Elaborative and Organizational Processes." *Journal of Personality and Social Psychology* 55, no. 1: 5.

Komeda, Hidetsugu, Kohei Tsunemi, Keisuke Inohara, Takashi Kusumi, and David N. Rapp. 2013. "Beyond Disposition: The Processing Consequences of Explicit and Implicit Invocations of Empathy." *Acta Psychologica* 142, no. 3: 349–55.

Koopman, Emy. 2011. "Predictors of Insight and Catharsis among Readers Who Use Literature as a Coping Strategy." *Scientific Study of Literature* 1, no. 2: 241–59.

Koopman, Emy. 2014. "Reading in Times of Loss: An Exploration of the Functions of Literature during Grief." *Scientific Study of Literature* 4, no. 1: 68–88.

Koopman, Emy. 2015a. "Empathic Reactions after Reading: The Role of Genre, Personal Factors and Affective Responses." *Poetics*, no. 50: 62–79.

Koopman, Emy. 2015b. "How Texts about Suffering Trigger Reflection: Genre, Personal Factors, and Affective Responses." *Psychology of Aesthetics, Creativity, and the Arts* 9, no. 4: 430–41.

Koopman, Emy. 2016. "Effects of 'Literariness' on Emotions and on Empathy and Reflection after Reading." *Psychology of Aesthetics, Creativity, and the Arts* 10, no. 1: 82–98.

Koopman, Eva Maria (Emy), and Frank Hakemulder. 2015. "Effects of Literature on Empathy and Self-Reflection: A Theoretical-Empirical Framework." *Journal of Literary Theory* 9, no. 1: 79–111.

Krishnamurthy, Parthasarathy, and Mita Sujan. 1999. "Retrospection versus Anticipation: The Role of the Ad under Retrospective and Anticipatory Self-Referencing." *Journal of Consumer Research* 26, no. 1: 55–69.

Kuiken, Don, David S. Miall, and Shelley Sikora. 2004. "Forms of Self-Implication in Literary Reading." *Poetics Today* 25, no. 2: 171–203.

Kuzmičová, Anežka. 2014. "Literary Narrative and Mental Imagery: A View from Embodied Cognition." *Style* 48, no. 3: 275–93.

Kuzmičová, Anežka. 2016. "Does It Matter Where You Read? Situating Narrative in Physical Environment." *Communication Theory* 26, no. 3: 290–308.

Larsen, Steen F., and János László. 1990. "Cultural-Historical Knowledge and Personal Experience in Appreciation of Literature." *European Journal of Social Psychology* 20, no. 5: 425–40.

László, János, and Steen F. Larsen. 1991. "Cultural and Text Variables in Processing Personal Experiences while Reading Literature." *Empirical Studies of the Arts* 9, no. 1: 23–34.

Mar, Raymond A., Keith Oatley, Maja Djikic, and Justin Mullin. 2011. "Emotion and Narrative Fiction: Interactive Influences before, during, and after Reading." *Cognition and Emotion* 85, no. 5: 818–33.

McKeever, Robert. 2015. "Vicarious Experience: Experimentally Testing the Effects of Empathy for Media Characters with Severe Depression and the Intervening Role of Perceived Similarity." *Health Communication* 30, no. 11: 1122–34.

Menninghaus, Winfried, Valentin Wagner, Julian Hanich, Eugen Wassiliwizky, Thomas Jacobsen, and Stefan Koelsch. 2017. "The DISTANCING–EMBRACING Model of the Enjoyment of Negative Emotions in Art Reception." *Behavioral and Brain Sciences*, no. 40: e347.

Miall, David S. 2011. "Emotions and the Structuring of Narrative Responses." *Poetics Today* 32, no. 2: 323–48.

Miall, David S., and Don Kuiken. 1995. "Aspects of Literary Response: A New Questionnaire." *Research in the Teaching of English* 29, no. 1: 37–58.

Miall, David S., and Don Kuiken. 1999. "What is Literariness? Three Components of Literary Reading." *Discourse Processes* 28, no. 2: 121–38.

Mick, David Glen. 1992. "Levels of Subjective Comprehension in Advertising Processing and Their Relations to Ad Perceptions, Attitudes, and Memory." *Journal of Consumer Research* 18, no. 4: 411–24.

Oatley, Keith. 1999a. "Meetings of Minds: Dialogue, Sympathy, and Identification, in Reading Fiction." *Poetics* 26, no. 5: 439–54.

Oatley, Keith. 1999b. "Why Fiction May Be Twice as True as Fact: Fiction as Cognitive and Emotional Simulation." *Review of General Psychology* 3, no. 2: 101–17.

Peplow, David, Joan Swann, Paola Trimarco, and Sara Whiteley. 2015. *The Discourse of Reading Groups: Integrating Cognitive and Sociocultural Perspectives*. New York: Routledge.

Petty, Richard E., and John T. Cacioppo. 1979. "Issue Involvement Can Increase or Decrease Persuasion by Enhancing Message-Relevant Cognitive Responses." *Journal of Personality and Social Psychology* 37, no. 10: 1915–26.

Prentice, Deborah A., Richard J. Gerrig, and Daniel S. Bailis. 1997. "What Readers Bring to the Processing of Fictional Texts." *Psychonomic Bulletin and Review* 4, no. 3: 416–20.

Preston, Stephanie D., and Frans B. M. de Waal. 2002. "Empathy: Its Ultimate and Proximate Bases." *Behavioral and Brain Sciences* 25, no. 1: 1–20.

Rhine, Ramon J., and Laurence J. Severance. 1970. "Ego-Involvement, Discrepancy, Source Credibility, and Attitude Change." *Journal of Personality and Social Psychology* 16, no. 2: 175–90.

Robinson, Jenefer. 2007. *Deeper than Reason: Emotion and Its Role in Literature, Music, and Art*. Oxford: Clarendon Press.

Rogers, T. B., N. A. Kuiper, and W. S. Kirker. 1977. "Self-Reference and the Encoding of Personal Information." *Journal of Personality and Social Psychology* 35, no. 9: 677–88.

Seilman, Uffe, and Steen F. Larsen. 1989. "Personal Resonance to Literature: A Study of Remindings while Reading." *Poetics* 18, no. 1–2: 165–77.

Sikora, Shelley, Don Kuiken, and David S. Miall. 2010. "An Uncommon Resonance: The Influence of Loss on Expressive Reading." *Empirical Studies of the Arts* 28, no. 2: 135–53.

Sikora, Shelley, Don Kuiken, and David S. Miall. 2011. "Expressive Reading: A Phenomenological Study of Readers' Experience of Coleridge's *The Rime of the Ancient Mariner*." *Psychology of Aesthetics, Creativity, and the Arts* 5, no. 3: 258–68.

Sperduti, Marco, Margherita Arcangeli, Dominique Makowski, Prany Wantzen, Tiziana Zalla, Stéphane Lemaire, Jérôme Dokic, Jérôme Pelletier, and Pascale Piolino. 2016. "The Paradox of Fiction: Emotional Response toward Fiction and the Modulatory Role of Self-Relevance." *Acta Psychologica* no. 165: 53–59.

Sujan, Mita, James R. Bettman, and Hans Baumgartner. 1993. "Influencing Consumer Judgments Using Autobiographical Memories: A Self-Referencing Perspective." *Journal of Marketing Research* 30, no. 4: 422–36.

Swann, Joan, and Daniel Allington. 2009. "Reading Groups and the Language of Literary Texts: A Case Study in Social Reading." *Language and Literature* 18, no. 3: 247–64.

Therman, Cecilia. 2008. "Remindings, Understanding, and Involvement: A Close Reading of the Content and Context of Remindings." In *New Beginnings in Literary Studies*, edited by Jan Auracher and Willie van Peer, 352–71. Newcastle: Cambridge Scholars Press.

Todd, Zazie. 2008. "Talking about Books: A Reading Group Study." *Psychology of Aesthetics, Creativity, and the Arts* 2, no. 4: 256–63.

Tsay, Mina, and K. Maja Krakowiak. 2011. "The Impact of Perceived Character Similarity and Identification on Moral Disengagement." *International Journal of Arts and Technology* 4, no. 1: 102–10.

Tsunemi, Kohei, and Takashi Kusumi. 2011. "The Effect of Perceptual and Personal Memory Retrieval on Story Comprehension." *Psychologia* 54, no. 3: 119–34.

van Peer, Willie, Frank Hakemulder, and Sonia Zyngier. 2012. *Scientific Methods for the Humanities*. Amsterdam: John Benjamins.

Vaughn, Leigh Ann, Zhivka Petkova, Sarah J. Hesse, Lindsay Trudeau, and Nora E. McCaffrey. n.d. "Transportation into Narrative Worlds: The Role of Processing Fluency." Unpublished manuscript. Portable Document Format, last revised 2010.

Wheeler, Christian, Melanie C. Green, and Timothy C. Brock. 1999. "Fictional Narratives Change Beliefs: Replications of Prentice, Gerrig, and Bailis (1997) with Mixed Corroboration." *Psychonomic Bulletin and Review* 6, no. 1: 136–41.

Wimsatt, William K., and Monroe C. Beardsley. 1949. "The Affective Fallacy." *Sewanee Review* 57, no. 1: 31–55.

How Does Leisure Reading Affect Social Cognitive Abilities?

Micah L. Mumper and Richard J. Gerrig
Stony Brook University

Abstract   Research evidence supports the claim that engagement with works of fiction may benefit readers' social cognitive abilities of empathy and theory of mind. However, there is little direct evidence to support claims about the causal mechanisms underlying the positive influence of leisure reading. Simulation theory has emerged as the most common explanatory mechanism. We summarize simulation theory and indicate ways in which the theory requires a more concrete instantiation. To provide a contrast to simulation theory, we offer three accounts of the origins of the emotional content of readers' narrative experiences. Our goal is to highlight the diversity of processes that contribute to readers' affective responses. Finally, we consider how ordinary processes of learning and memory might explain changes in readers' social cognition.

Keywords   social cognition, discourse processes, simulation theory, leisure reading, fiction

Contemporary scholars often suggest that narrative experiences have the potential to impart positive social benefits to readers (Hakemulder 2000; Hogan 2011; Mar and Oatley 2008; but see Currie 2016; Keen 2007). The majority of research focuses on two social cognitive abilities: empathy and theory of mind. We begin this article with a review of evidence in favor of the claim that narrative experiences yield positive changes in social cognition. Next, we ask how and why readers may experience such benefits. Simulation theory has emerged as the most common explanatory mechanism (Currie 1995; Goldman 2006; Mar and Oatley 2008; Oatley 1999, 2016). This theory

Poetics Today 40:3 (September 2019)   DOI 10.1215/03335372-7558080
© 2019 by Porter Institute for Poetics and Semiotics

suggests that readers understand characters' emotions and cognitions by simulating the depicted events (Mar et al. 2006; Mar, Oatley, and Peterson 2009). We suggest that researchers need to provide more specifics about the time course of the processes that constitute simulation. One important component of the simulation account is that readers infer characters' emotions (Currie 1995, Mar and Oatley 2008; Oatley and Gholamain 1997). We describe three alternative processes that lead readers to experience emotions in narrative contexts. Finally, we suggest how the content of narratives may affect readers' social cognition through ordinary processes of learning and memory.

To support our analyses, we draw examples from the novel *Housebreaking* (Pope 2015). The novel presents six months in the intersecting lives of two families, the Mandelbaums (Benjamin Mandelbaum, his father Leonard, and his estranged wife Judy) and the Martin-Murrays (Audrey Martin, her husband Andrew Murray, and their daughter Emily Martin-Murray). *Housebreaking* offers insights into the drama behind the seeming serenity of the American suburbs. For us, however, what matters most is that *Housebreaking* provides ready examples of the types of narrative content that readers regularly encounter.

1. Evidence That Experiences with Fiction Affect Social Cognition

Scholars have undertaken several types of research to support the claim that readers' experiences of fiction have a positive impact on empathy and theory of mind. Some of these studies rely on correlations between readers' reports of lifetime reading and measures of social cognition. These studies typically document stronger social cognitive abilities in people who read more fiction compared to nonfiction. Other studies ask participants to read one or more brief narratives or expository works. These studies document immediate changes in social cognition. We provide a brief review of this range of research for empathy and theory of mind.

Correlational studies generally support the claim that readers' lifetime experiences with narrative fiction, compared to nonfiction, have a larger positive association with their empathic abilities (Mar et al. 2006; Mar, Oatley, and Peterson 2009; Miall and Kuiken 1995; van Schooten and De Glopper 2003; Waytz et al. 2015) and theory of mind (ToM) abilities (Bischoff and Peskin 2014; Fong, Mullin, and Mar 2013; Mar et al. 2006; Mar, Oatley, and Peterson 2009; Tamir et al. 2016). For example, Mar et al. (2006) measured participants' reading history using their revised version of the Author Recognition Test (ART; Mar et al. 2006). In the ART, participants select names of authors from a list containing both real fiction and nonfiction authors and foils. Psychometric investigations of the ART suggest that it is a valid measure of lifetime reading (Moore and Gordon 2015; Rain and Mar 2014). Mar et al. correlated participants' ART scores with a self-report measure of empathy, the Interpersonal Reactivity Index (IRI; Davis 1983). In the IRI, participants select how well a given statement describes them (e.g., "I sometimes try to understand my friends better by imagining how things look from their perspective"). Mar et al. reported a positive correlation between fiction ART scores and participants' tendencies to become absorbed in a story (one of the subscales of the IRI). This correlation did not emerge for the nonfiction ART scores.

Mar et al. also correlated participants' ART scores with a commonly used ToM measure, the Mind-in-the-Eyes task (MIE; Baron-Cohen et al. 2001). In the MIE task, participants view thirty-two black-and-white photos of eyes, and must select the one of four adjectives that best describes what the person is feeling or thinking, such as "joking," "flustered," "desire," or "convinced." After controlling for the shared variance between fiction and nonfiction reading habits, Mar et al. found that MIE performance positively correlated with fiction reading and negatively correlated with nonfiction reading.

We conducted a meta-analysis (a quantitative statistical analysis) to assess the consistency of such correlations over multiple studies (Mumper and Gerrig 2017). The meta-analysis revealed that lifetime fiction reading had a small positive correlation with empathy and ToM measures. That is, across all the studies we analyzed, as the amount of fiction participants read increased, their empathy and ToM scores also tended to increase by a small amount. We also found nonfiction reading to be positively correlated with empathy and ToM, although the effects were numerically smaller.

Researchers have also designed studies to demonstrate that particular narrative experiences can have an impact on empathy (e.g., Bal and Veltkamp 2013; Djikic, Oatley, and Moldoveanu 2013; Koopman 2016; Stansfield and Bunce 2014) and theory of mind (e.g., Black and Barnes 2015; Djikic, Oatley, and Moldoveanu 2013; Kidd and Castano 2013; Stansfield and Bunce 2014). In such studies, researchers assign participants a certain type of text to read (e.g., fiction or nonfiction). Subsequently, participants complete a measure of empathy or ToM. For example, Bal and Veltkamp (2013) assigned participants either a fiction or nonfiction story and measured empathy using the IRI. Bal and Veltkamp found that fiction readers, but not nonfiction readers, experienced empathic growth immediately after reading the text.

In a study on ToM, participants randomly assigned to read award-winning literary fictions performed better on the MIE compared to participants assigned to read nonfiction and those who read no texts (Kidd and Castano 2013). In addition, participants who read literary works outperformed participants assigned to read popular fiction, suggesting that the aesthetic and stylistic properties of the narrative work matter. However, an attempt to replicate such results in a large-scale study failed to document any differences in MIE performance regardless of the texts participants read (Panero et al. 2016). Panero et al. concluded that, while the impact of lifetime fiction reading appears to be robust, experimental results tend to be moderated by individual differences, such as transportation into the narrative, trait openness, and trait empathy. Despite the inconsistent literature, a meta-analysis of the experimental studies did find that participants who read fictional texts tend to slightly outperform those assigned to nonfictional texts on empathy and ToM measures (Dodell-Feder and Tamir 2018).

2. Simulation Theory and Narrative Impact

We turn now to causal explanations for narrative impact. Based on the research evidence, these causal explanations should include some notion of how readers' experiences of individual narratives might accumulate, over time, toward changes in empathy and theory of mind. Consider the following scene from *Housebreaking* in which seventeen-year-old Emily struggles to regain consciousness from a bad drug episode:

> She could hear them, understand them. But she couldn't speak to them. Bile came spilling out of her, black and thick. She fought to stay conscious even as she vomited. She wavered, falling back. It was impossible to come awake. She couldn't do it. It was an enormous stone on top of her. To struggle against it was pointless. (Pope 2015: 308)

Why might readers' experience of passages like this one ultimately affect their social cognition? To address the question, we begin by reviewing what stands as the most prominent causal model: simulation theory.

Simulation theory provides the modal explanation for the observed social benefits of narratives (e.g., Currie 1995; Mar and Oatley 2008; Oatley 2016; but see Carroll 2001). According to this theory, readers undertake simulations to understand what that character is thinking and feeling. Kieran (2003: 4) provided an informative statement of the theory:

> Simulation is a mental operation that consists in allowing the belief-desire system to run 'off-line', disconnected from its normal sensory inputs and behavioral outputs and from the simulator's own beliefs and desires, yet taking into account the situation of another person (Currie 1995). While run off-line, the simulator's belief-desire system nevertheless continues to operate in an otherwise normal way, generating inferences and causing emotional responses, thereby telling her what mental state she would be in were she in the other's situation.

Consider readers' experience of the passage in which Emily tries to regain consciousness. According to simulation theory, readers understand her emotional experience by substituting their own beliefs (e.g., that they are unimpaired) with Emily's beliefs (e.g., that she is struggling to remain conscious). Readers run that simulated input through their belief-desire system. If readers imagine feeling scared, they attribute that emotion to Emily. Since this simulation is run "off-line," readers do not feel scared themselves, precluding some of the typical behavioral responses associated with fear. That is, the outputs of the simulation process are dissociated from their usual role in guiding individuals' behavior. Rather, these outputs yield predictions about the mental states of the target.

Theorists have suggested that the process and products of simulation are central for readers' cognitive and emotional responses to narratives (e.g., Currie 1995; Oatley and Gholamain 1997; Mar and Oatley 2008; Oatley 2016). For instance, Bal and Veltkamp (2013: 2) claimed that "by reading a story, people imagine a narrative world that is similar to our own world. In this narrative world, people imagine how it is to see through the eyes of other people, by imagining and actually experiencing the thoughts and feelings of characters in a story. Hence, imaginative processes, evoked by fictional narrative experience, make people more empathic." Similarly, Mar, Oatley, and Peterson (2009: 408) asserted:

> While reading fiction, the simulation of social experience that occurs might engage the same social-cognitive processes employed during real-world social comprehension (e.g., mental inference, tracking of goals, emotion recognition). Repeated simulation of this kind, then, could lead to a honing of these social and empathic processes, which in turn could be applied to other contexts outside of reading. Another possibility is that readers of fiction learn concrete social information from books, acquiring knowledge about human psychology.

Although researchers frequently cite simulation as a causal mechanism, the concept has never been associated with concrete claims about what types of processes embody simulation and how those processes unfold in time. We can make a contrast to other theories of narrative processing that do, in fact, aspire to be wholly explicit with respect to the processes that underlie readers' narrative experiences (for reviews, see McNamara and Magliano 2009; O'Brien, Cook, and Lorch 2015). For example, the seminal *construction-integration model* characterizes text processing as the interplay between processes of construction and integration (Kintsch 1998). Construction refers to the spontaneous activation of information in readers' memories based on featural and semantic overlap with information in a narrative. The integration process maintains a coherent discourse representation by connecting the products of the construction process with prior information. Theories like the construction-integration model, along with the empirical research that supports its predictions, make plain what is missing from statements about simulation. They prompt the question: Does simulation easily map onto one of the mental processes articulated and supported in extant theories, or is it a competing theory that makes unique processing claims? We believe it is incumbent upon simulation theorists to connect simulation to existing process accounts. They should draw out the relevant contrasts and provide unique hypotheses.

Let us consider one example of what it would mean to make simulation theory more concrete. Based on the literature, it remains unclear whether readers simulate narrative content spontaneously or strategically: Do readers inevitably experience simulations of characters' thoughts and emotions as a product of automatic processes or must they choose to expend effort to do so? If theorists wish to claim that simulation is automatic, they must explain what processes make simulation possible and how these relate to other automatic processes (such as construction and integration). If theorists wish to claim that readers deploy simulation strategically, they have the added task of explaining what circumstances trigger readers' impulse to engage in simulation.

In the next section, we describe processes other than simulation that may evoke emotions in readers. We note in advance that our intention is not to say that simulation theory is necessarily wrong. Rather, our goal is to undertake an analysis of other processes that might give rise to literary impact.

3. Processes that Affect Readers' Emotional Experiences

Theorists have argued that social benefits accrue to readers because they simulate characters' thoughts and emotions. Becoming a proficient simulator "trains us to extend our understanding toward other people, to embody (to some extent) and understand their beliefs and emotions" (Mar and Oatley 2008: 181). In this article, we have chosen to focus on characters' emotions to describe processes other than simulation that might imbue readers' experiences with affect. To begin, we note that there are many instances in which texts explicitly state what emotions the characters feel. Consider a moment in *Housebreaking* where Benjamin runs into his estranged wife Judy for the first time since their separation: "He'd lived with this woman for most of his life, but now he felt nervous being in the same room with her" (Pope 2015: 82). We must count such instances as a first example of circumstances in which the process of simulation is not necessary. In this section, we outline three process accounts of people's affective responses to narratives. We note that these are not competing hypotheses. Rather, each process we describe likely contributes to readers' experiences.

3.1. Memory-Based Processing

Our first suggestion emerges from the literature on text processing. We begin by noting an important distinction between strategic and automatic inferences. Strategic inferences represent circumstances in which readers engage in conscious effort, whereas automatic inferences do not require such effort (for reviews, see McNamara and Magliano 2009; O'Brien, Cook, and Lorch 2015). Consider the moment in *Housebreaking* in which Andrew plays a tennis match with his younger colleague, Sampson. They make a bet on the game:

"Loser buys dinner?"

"I wasn't planning on dinner," said Andrew, "but sure, why not." (Pope 2015: 151)

Ultimately, Andrew loses the match. At the moment Sampson declares "Game" for the final time, readers could very well expend strategic effort to imagine how Andrew is feeling. They might take a moment to contemplate times at which they have lost contests or bets and the emotions that have followed such losses.

However, most research on inference-making has focused on the types of inferences that readers encode without engaging strategic effort. A prominent theoretical position, memory-based processing, suggests that readers' automatic inferences most often arise from an ordinary memory process called *resonance* (O'Brien and Cook 2015; Gerrig and O'Brien 2005; McKoon and Ratcliff 1992, 2015). Resonance is a fast and passive process whereby narrative information cues access to both earlier portions of the narrative and broader information in long-term memory. Thus, when readers experience Andrew's loss at the end of the tennis match, cues from the text will resonate through memory to yield some collection of representations. Because resonance is not a goal-directed process, many of those memories will not be directly relevant to Andrew's situation (e.g., they might be memories about tennis or other situations of loss). Even so, the bulk of memory traces cued by Andrew's unfolding defeat (assuming readers identify with Andrew) will likely be tagged with negative affect. As such, readers' representation of the moment is likely to be encoded with some indication of distress. To provide a more concrete instantiation of that claim, we draw on psychological research.

To begin, we review a classic study on predictive inferences. Consider this sentence: "The director and cameraman were ready to shoot close-ups when suddenly the actress fell from the 14th story" (McKoon and Ratcliff 1986: 83). McKoon and Ratcliff conducted a series of experiments to determine what inferences readers encode as part of their representations of this very brief story. These experiments suggest that, rather than making the specific inference that the actress will die, readers encode the broader expectation that "something bad will happen." That broader inference quite likely reflects the diversity of memory traces that emerge via the resonance process in response to the sentence — including both readers' own mishaps as well as fictional and nonfictional accounts of others' accidents. The outcomes of these accidents will vary along a continuum of severity. However, the majority of these long-term memories will quite certainly support the general inference that "something bad will happen."

Readers' inference that "something bad will happen" does not require them to simulate the actress's fate. Rather, the inference arises from information encoded in readers' memory representations. The same processes will function in the context of inferences about emotions. Information in narratives will resonate through readers' memories to yield information about emotions. Thus, readers are likely to infer distress in response to Andrew's loss without having to simulate how he might be feeling. In empirical research, narratives that include features suggestive of certain emotions reliably result in readers making appropriate emotional inferences (Gygax and Gillioz 2015). Arriving at a similar conclusion, cognitive literary theorist Hogan (2003: 156) cited a "central principle of classical Indian aesthetics . . . that artistic works communicate emotion through their '*dhvani*' or suggestiveness. Dhvani includes all the associations that cluster around anything that a reader encounters in a work of literature or a viewer encounters in a performance." Hogan argues that dhvani works through the mechanism of priming. In cognitive models, however, *priming* refers specifically to circumstances in which a current experience makes associated information more accessible in memory. Therefore, we invoke *resonance* as the distinct memory process that brings about the priming that yields automatic inferences.

In fact, the emotions that accompany people's experiences are often an important component of their representations of these events (Rubin and Umanath 2015). Memory for emotional events is typically better than memory for more neutral events (for a review, see Talmi 2013). As such, we might imagine that readers would be likely to recall instances when they suffered losses and how they felt when that happened. Consider Damasio's (1994) somatic marker hypothesis, which describes the brain mechanisms that allow people to acquire knowledge of "'what it feels like' to be in a given situation" (Bechara and Damasio 2005: 341): "For example, imagining the loss of a large sum of money . . . re-activates the pattern of somatic state belonging to an actual prior experience of money loss" (341). Hogan (2003: 156) noted that the Sanskrit philosopher Abhinavagupta made the same claim a "millennium ago": "According to him, all our experiences leave traces in our memory. These traces bear with them the emotions we felt at the time." In this context, it seems quite possible that people will reactivate the same somatic patterns when reading that Andrew lost his tennis match as they did for actual losses.

Note that, on this account, the emotion that emerges through resonance is not automatically bound to the character. We have suggested that readers quite likely will encode "distress" as part of their representation of the episode of Andrew's loss. Similarly, we have suggested that readers may experience somatic states consistent with earlier losses. Nonetheless, these conclusions do not imply that readers will have also encoded the inference that Andrew himself is experiencing distress. Theorists who identify simulation as an important mechanism for readers' inferences about characters' emotions often cite the similarity of brain activation for "real-life" and narrative experiences: "Imagined settings and characters evoked by fiction literature likely engage the same areas of the brain as those used during the performance of parallel actions and perceptions. . . . There is clearly a shared neural basis for attempting to make sense of real people and for processing fictional representations of persons" (Mar and Oatley 2008: 180). However, it is also quite likely that the similarity of brain activation emerges because narrative experiences reactivate somatic patterns through memory processes. In that sense, readers can feel emotions without ever inferring whether a character feels the same way.

3.2. Emotion Appraisal

Our second suggestion for the origins of readers' emotional responses emerges from appraisal theories of emotions. Wondra and Ellsworth (2015) provided a comprehensive extension of such theories to people's experiences of vicarious emotions (i.e., emotions for others). They suggested that the emotions people feel for others emerge from appraisals along the same dimensions that generate emotions in first-person appraisals, such as pleasantness (how agreeable the person finds the situation), anticipated effort (the amount of effort the person needs to handle a situation), self-Other responsibility (how responsible the person is for the situation), situational control (how much the situation is under the person's control), and certainty (how convinced the person is about what will happen next). Consider this example:

> Imagine that your friend got sick following an international vacation that the two of you took together. You are waiting with your friend in the hospital to hear the results of a test for malaria. Both you and your friend think that a positive test result would be awful (low pleasantness appraisal) and that your friend was extremely unlucky (high situational control appraisal). Your friend feels fairly sure that the

test will come back positive (moderate certainty appraisal) and feels sad. If you also feel confident that the test will be positive, then you will feel sad with your friend. . . . If, however, you feel that you have no idea what the test result will be (low certainty appraisal), then you will feel scared for your friend. (Wondra and Ellsworth 2015: 418)

We suggest that this account extends directly to circumstances of readers and characters. Readers likely use exactly the same appraisal processes that function pervasively in everyday life to feel emotions on behalf of characters.

Wondra and Ellsworth emphasized that appraisal processes will sometimes yield matches and sometimes yield mismatches between an actor and an observer. A match occurs if an observer feels an emotion on behalf of an actor that the actor is also feeling, whereas a mismatch occurs when the observer feels an emotion on behalf of an actor that the actor does not feel. Wondra and Ellsworth indicated that social psychologists have devoted considerable attention to empathy (circumstances in which people experience emotions that match someone else's) but have mostly ignored the nonmatching cases. Their theory provides a strong contrast to canonical accounts of empathy. Most theories of empathy focus on the actor's emotional state as the primary cause for the empathic response (e.g., mirror-neuron theories of empathy; Gallese 2003; Iacoboni 2009). According to these theories, if an individual fails to perceive the actor's emotion, or the actor displays no emotion, no empathic response should occur. In contrast, according to the appraisal theory, empathy occurs in the special case in which an observer appraises the situation in the same way as an actor.

Consider a moment from *Housebreaking* in which Benjamin returns home after Thanksgiving dinner to his presumably empty house:

As Benjamin opened the door, the dog raced ahead of him into the kitchen. The house was drafty and ice cold. He flipped the light switch and saw that the back door was wide open. His mind whirled. Had he left it open? No. He hadn't been in the backyard in a month, not since the last warm days of October.

Someone's home, he thought. (Pope 2015: 96)

Benjamin comes home to find his house in disarray (low pleasantness appraisal), and he is uncertain about what exactly has happened (low certainty appraisal). Given these appraisals, it would be reasonable to infer that Benjamin will experience fear. However, Wondra and Ellsworth's account suggests that readers would be making their own appraisals of Benjamin's situation. If they are uncertain about what has happened, they should also feel scared on behalf of Benjamin. In contrast, if readers feel slightly more certain that Benjamin has been robbed, then they may instead primarily feel sad on his behalf. In fact, depending on what exact appraisals individual readers make, they may feel a range of emotions for Benjamin from scared to sad to angry. On this view, matches between readers' and characters' emotions do not reflect the operation of a special process such as simulation. Rather, they arise because appraisal processes sometimes yield matches and sometimes mismatches.

3.3. Narrative Participation

Readers may also experience emotions as a consequence of the way in which they become immersed in narrative worlds. Consider an episode in *House-breaking* in which Andrew is cruising a Hartford park. He stops his car and becomes involved in a conversation with a boy who asks repeatedly to join Andrew in his car. Andrew ultimately unlocks the door and the boy gets in. We suspect that, as the scene unfolds, most readers will encode some sort of mental warning (e.g., "Don't!"). This type of mental content suggests that people often react to narratives with the same types of emotional responses they would encode if the events were unfolding in real life (Allbritton and Gerrig 1992; Gerrig 1993; Gerrig and Jacovina 2009). Because these mental contents reflect cognitive and emotional engagement, we have called them *participatory responses*.

To specify the categories and content of participatory responses, Bezdek, Foy, and Gerrig (2013) conducted a pair of experiments. In each experiment, participants viewed a series of suspenseful excerpts from narrative movies. Bezdek, Foy, and Gerrig asked participants to think aloud—to say whatever came to mind—as they watched each excerpt. Consider a sample of participants' responses to an excerpt from the film *Munich* (dir. Steven Spielberg, 2005). While watching the excerpt, viewers learn that a phone has been rigged to explode when it is answered by a suspected terrorist. However, when the phone rings, the terrorist's daughter approaches the phone. Participants expressed great distress:

1. Wait no! Oh it's the girl! No! Hang up!
2. Noo, no, Oh my god please, no no no don't get that. Don't get it don't get it don't get it.

The girl has no idea that her life is in danger. In that sense, the participants' emotions are very much their own.

In some cases, the emotional content of readers' participatory responses will likely match a character's emotional responses. For example, in *House-breaking*, Benjamin hopes that his estranged wife, Judy, will allow him to celebrate Thanksgiving with her and their two children. We suspect that most readers will prefer that Judy let Benjamin attend. At first, Judy refuses Benjamin's request, but ultimately she relents:

"Judy, about Thanksgiving—"
"I don't want to fight about that. You can come. It'll be good for the kids." (Pope 2015: 84–85)

When Judy allows Benjamin to attend, readers obtain the outcome they desire. Thus, readers are likely to experience positive affect.

If we return to Andrew's adventure in the park, we find circumstances in which readers' participation likely yields emotional responses that will be dissimilar to the character's responses. We've already claimed that readers likely offer Andrew a mental warning—one that Andrew does not heed. Andrew and the stranger have a sexual encounter, after which he discovers that his wallet has been stolen: "As [Andrew] buttoned his pants, he realized his wallet was missing. He checked his suit coat, his overcoat, the seat the floor.... Nothing, of course" (170). When this happens, we suspect that most readers will find this negative outcome rather easy to assimilate (as a function of their past mental advice) and, in addition, experience positive affect because the character was punished for ignoring their advice (Jacovina and Gerrig 2010). Thus, readers' participation may lead them to experience a type of happiness that is officially at odds with the character's emotion (were they to infer that emotion).

Note that, for both of these examples, we have outlined what we imagine will be the most frequent response to these narrative events. The extent to which readers participate in fictional events and the content of their participation will certainly vary (Mumper and Gerrig 2017). If a particular reader doesn't believe that Benjamin should have the privilege of sharing Thanksgiving with his family, then Judy's ultimate agreement will yield a different emotional response. The general claim is that readers' own participation will often lead to intense emotions as a function of, for example, their preferences for how narrative events should unfold (Rapp and Gerrig 2002, 2006).

We have presented three explanations for how readers' experiences of narrative events may be imbued with emotional content. The first emerges from text processing research that has demonstrated how resonance processes make readers' memory traces accessible. On this view, readers' representations will include the emotions that have accompanied similar events that have fallen within readers' purview. The second explanation emerges from appraisal theories of emotions. On this view, readers feel emotions on behalf of characters by appraising the characters' situations. The third explanation arises from the theory that readers participate in narratives. These emotional responses are very much the readers' own responses as a function, for example, of what they wished to happen at a particular narrative juncture. All three mechanisms allow that characters' and readers' emotions sometimes match and sometimes mismatch.

We have articulated these explanations as alternatives to simulation. However, as we noted, these three explanations are not in competition. We believe that all three function as readers' narrative experiences unfold. If it were to be given a more rigorous analysis, simulation could be an additional explanation. Still, we believe that simulation is not necessary to bring about changes in readers' social cognitive abilities. In the final section of this article, we consider how other processes, such as the emotional responses to which we have devoted the current section, might act on the products of readers' experiences to yield those changes.

4. What Do Readers Learn From Narratives?

In his analysis of the importance of narrative content, Oatley (2016: 624) made two relevant claims. First, he suggested that readers acquire expertise: "When we read fiction, we become more expert in its subject matter: understanding people and their intentions." Second, he suggested that readers experience pluralism: "Fiction invites us to engage in many circumstances, and to experience many emotions in relation to many kinds of people." We agree with Oatley's assertions, but argue that their scope is too narrow. We believe that readers acquire a broad range of information from narrative worlds. In the next section, we explore how readers experience the types of behaviors in which characters engage and the consequences of those behaviors. Finally, we describe how readers' narrative experiences may help reinforce various components of theory of mind.

4.1. Behaviors and Consequences

Consider one of the central storylines of *Housebreaking*, Audrey's extramarital affair with Benjamin. What is noteworthy is that the affair occurs with scant moral turmoil. Benjamin confesses his high-school crush on Audrey: "I thought about kissing you all the time." Audrey asks, "Do you still want to kiss me?" and he announces, "I'd like that" (Pope 2015: 59). Moments later, the two begin a sexual relationship. Readers already know that Audrey and her husband Andrew have not been intimate for "a year and a half" (57). Of perhaps greater importance, readers learn that Audrey seeks the carnal escape of her sexual relationship with Benjamin to help her cope with a major trauma. We suspect that most people who read *Housebreaking* will not fault Audrey for having the affair. To what extent might the experience of this particular fictional narrative have an influence on readers' real-world judgments?

The general answer to this question is that readers' experiences will change the store of memories against which they construct behavioral norms. According to norm theory (Kahneman and Miller 1986), people rarely store norms directly in memory. Rather, norms emerge at a particular moment as a product of the same types of memory processes that yield inferences. Specifically, new experiences serve as probes that resonate through long-term memory to yield related information. Norms are constructed as a weighted aggregate of that sample of memory traces. Suppose that Jessica has read *Housebreaking*. She learns that a real-life friend has engaged in an affair. To the extent that the resonance process yields information from *Housebreaking*, Jessica might be more likely to reach the unconscious judgment that her friend's affair was "normal." Research on the impact of fiction on social behavior has been dominated by the hypothesis that narrative experiences will make people better. Yet the research literature provides strong indications that fiction's impact is not inevitably prosocial (Currie 2016; Hakemulder 2000). Let's suppose that most people initially disapprove of extramarital affairs. Even so, depending on the moral context of such fictional affairs over the lifetime of people's reading, individuals' attitudes toward infidelity could change in either direction (toward more comfort or more discomfort).

We have been focusing on characters' behaviors to make the point that experiences of fictional narratives will almost certainly change readers' storehouse of potential behaviors in response to situations. However, it is equally important that readers learn the consequence of those behaviors. We take our lead from Bandura (1986), whose social cognitive theory (SCT) describes the psychological mechanisms through which people learn vicariously by observing the consequences of models' behavior. In classic learning theory of the type originated by Skinner (1969), organisms learn by experiencing direct consequences (i.e., reinforcement or punishment) for their own behaviors. Bandura provided a series of classic demonstrations to argue that people's behavior is often shaped through vicarious reinforcement or punishment. For example, Bandura, Ross, and Ross (1961) demonstrated that children were more likely to engage in aggressive behavior when they observed aggressive models whose behavior was rewarded or at least not punished.

Bandura (2009) laid out the implications of SCT for people's consumption of media. His critical claim was that people quite often learn through experiences of both fictional and nonfictional narratives. Media presentations (broadly construed) provide an unlimited number of opportunities for people to observe behaviors and their consequences. Bandura's theory has had a consistent impact on the study of media effects (for a review, see Valkenburg, Peter, and Walther 2016). Consider a study by Taylor, Alexopoulos, and Ghaznavi (2016) that provided a content analysis of sexual interactions in one hundred television shows set in workplaces. Taylor, Alexopoulos, and Ghaznavi coded for several features of the interactions, including the gender of the character who initiated sexual contact and the nature of the contact. They also coded for the consequences of the behaviors. Their analyses revealed that "a clear majority of sexual behaviors were met with either reciprocation or no response at all" (Taylor, Alexopoulos, and Ghaznavi 2016: 486). They reached a distressing conclusion: "Although SCT emphasizes the influence of discernible consequences of characters' actions on viewers' learning, the absence of any meaningful response may also have an effect on viewers. . . . It is possible that the depiction of sexual talk and behavior in the workplace without any consequences may make such behaviors seem normative" (486). This study illustrates the relevance of SCT to theoretical analyses of the social consequences of readers' experiences of fictional narratives.

Despite this conclusion, to our knowledge, none of the theorists who conceptualize the impact of fiction on readers' social lives have explored the implications of social cognitive theory. In table 1, we provide several instan-

Table 1 Examples from *Housebreaking* of characters' behavior and resulting consequences.

Behavior	Consequence
To signal his romantic interest, Andrew gives Audrey white roses.	Audrey responds passionately to the gesture.
To demonstrate his virility, eighty-four-year-old Leonard tries to do push-ups	He has a stroke.
Benjamin drives drunk.	He arrives safely at his destination.
Benjamin calls his son at college.	His son doesn't want to talk and yells at him.
Audrey waits for the doctor to read her son's MRI scan.	Her son dies of internal bleeding in his head.
Emily goes to a drug dealer's house and blacks out.	She is sexually assaulted and pictures of the assault are distributed at school.
Andrew has a sexual encounter with a coworker.	He is forced to resign from his job.
Emily gets caught with pills.	She gets grounded.
Emily's friend attempts to break into a house.	The security alarm goes off and scares him away.
Sampson demands more interesting work at the law firm.	His demands are met.

ces from *Housebreaking* that link characters' behaviors to the consequences of those behaviors. For example, the table notes that Audrey behaves passively as she waits in the emergency room with her son Daniel: "She had waited by his side those two hours, making small talk, *laughing*, while the whole time, he was bleeding inside his head, his life draining out of him; and she had done nothing" (Pope 2015: 137). Audrey's inaction is linked to Daniel's death. We suspect that *Housebreaking* readers could quite likely change their emergency room behavior because of their various experiences of the tragic consequences of Audrey's inaction.

We hypothesize that most readers will have experienced a large number of fictional works in which good behavior is rewarded and bad behavior is punished. We know, at least, that readers typically prefer fictional narratives in which that pattern obtains (e.g., Raney 2004). As such, we may reasonably wonder whether the relationship between avid reading and empathy could largely be explained in the context of social cognitive theory. Simply put, the fictional works readers enjoy likely provide compelling demonstrations that virtue is (most often) rewarded.

4.2. Theory of Mind

As we noted earlier, our meta-analysis suggested that lifelong reading is associated with improved performance on one measure of theory of mind (ToM; Mumper and Gerrig 2017). To explain narratives' effect on ToM, researchers typically make causal claims that refer to readers becoming proficient at simulating characters' minds to infer their mental states (Djikic, Oatley, and Moldoveanu 2013; Fong, Mullin, and Mar 2013; Mar et al. 2006; Mar, Oatley, and Peterson 2009; Mar and Oatley 2008). In this section, by contrast, we draw on ToM research to suggest more direct ways in which readers' experiences of literature might affect ToM.

To begin with, developmental research emphasizes that ToM has several components that children acquire over the course of several years (Wellman, Fang, and Peterson 2011). For example, around age two, typically developing children are able to succeed on a laboratory task that tests them for their knowledge that two people can have different desires about the same object. However, it is not until around age six that most children are able to understand that people can display emotions different from those they are genuinely feeling. Between these ages, children also acquire the understanding that what they believe, know, or feel might very well differ from what other people believe, know, or feel.

Researchers have repeatedly attempted to accelerate children's acquisition of the various components of ToM. Hofmann et al. (2016) conducted a meta-analysis of such training studies for ToM. The meta-analysis demonstrated that "overall, ToM training procedures were effective in improving children's ToM skills" (Hofmann et al. 2016: 207). They also provided a summary of the methods deployed in the studies: "All the training procedures prompted children to reason about alternative perspectives or mental states in one way or another. Some studies did so by engaging children in explicit discussion of mental states. Others did so by putting children in situations that implicitly required them to adopt an alternative perspective or mental state" (207). For example, to train three- to four-year-old children in ToM, Guajardo and Watson (2002) created a procedure in which children heard and discussed narratives that illustrated false belief, deception, and differences between appearance and reality (e.g., a story in which a pig repeatedly tricked a wolf so that the wolf would not eat her). We suggest that works of narrative fiction provide adults with abundant opportunities to experience informal ToM training.

Consider one salient episode from *Housebreaking*. In the section of the book that narrates the events through Benjamin's perspective, Emily Martin-Murray appears at the door to his home. After a period of erratic behavior, she rushes up the stairs and hides in the bathroom in Benjamin's father's bedroom. Benjamin reflects, "Why had she locked herself in the bathroom? He couldn't make sense of anything she was doing" (Pope 2015: 118). It is only when events are retold from Emily's perspective that her goal becomes plain. Readers learn that, when Emily had previously robbed Benjamin's house, she had discovered a stash of narcotics in the bathroom's medicine cabinet left over from when Benjamin's mother was dying from cancer. Emily's goal is to get renewed access to the medicine cabinet so she can steal more drugs. The retelling of this episode provides readers with a salient reminder that people often have different knowledge of the world.

The episode also has the potential to provide training with respect to other elements of ToM. For instance, Emily quite plainly desires to make off with the stash of drugs. We suspect that most readers will encode a preference that Emily fail in this outcome. Thus, readers who experience compassion for Emily may strongly desire that she *not* achieve her goals. When Emily finds "the stash," she opens a bottle of Ativan that has five remaining pills: "She popped all five, like Tic Tacs" (256). Emily is quite happy; we suspect that readers will not share her happiness. As she leaves the bathroom, the novel engages in an explicit discussion of emotions: "When she opened the door, [Benjamin] was standing directly in front of her, a worried expression on his face—worry and something else too. *Fear*. She saw it in his eyes. He was frightened of her. This exhilarated her, made her want to go further" (256). At this moment, we suspect that readers' responses are more aligned with Benjamin than with Emily. Once again, the novel makes plain the types of differences that are relevant to ToM.

Furthermore, *Housebreaking* narrates the same events from multiple perspectives. Its readers might obtain, therefore, particularly rich lessons in ToM. Even so, it would be difficult to find any extended work of fiction in which narrators did not, for example, distribute knowledge unequally or explore differences among characters' beliefs and emotions. We suggest that those pervasive moments have great potential to provide informal training for the components of ToM. Zunshine (2006) has also argued that literary experiences help train ToM, but her analysis most often focuses on readers' ability to puzzle out characters' mental states with respect to texts that have complex patterns of high-order intentions. Although some of her claims for ToM training may be correct, we suspect that benefits accrue to readers largely because narratives provide straightforward evidence to reinforce the diverse components of theory of mind.

5. Conclusions

Our goal for this article has been to explore how readers' experiences of novels like *Housebreaking* may bring about changes in social cognition. We have expressed some skepticism toward simulation theory, because we find the theory to be poorly specified. The theory's proponents would do well to provide more concrete accounts of how and when simulation occurs. We provided three alternative accounts of the origins of readers' emotional experiences, citing theory and data to support the claim that these processes are already at work. We suggested ways in which experiences of fiction may expand readers' repertoires of behavior but, additionally, that the behaviors in which they choose to engage may be influenced by the consequences of characters' behaviors. Finally, we described how fiction provides abundant evidence that people do not inevitably share, for example, the same knowledge and emotions. Readers may largely remember works of fiction like *Housebreaking* for their dramatic events. Nevertheless, these narrative experiences quite likely accumulate to change readers' responses to their everyday social world.

References

Allbritton, David W., and Richard J. Gerrig. 1991. "Participatory Responses in Text Understanding." *Journal of Memory and Language* 30, no. 5: 603–26.
Bal, P. Matthijs, and Martijn Veltkamp. 2013. "How Does Fiction Reading Influence Empathy? An Experimental Investigation on the Role of Emotional Transportation." *PLoS ONE* 8, no. 1: e55341.

Bandura, Albert. 1986. *Social Foundations of Thought and Action: A Social Cognitive Theory*. Englewood Cliffs, NJ: Prentice-Hall.

Bandura, Albert. 2009. "Social Cognitive Theory of Mass Communication." In *Media Effects: Advances in Theory and Research*, 2nd ed., edited by Jennings Bryant and Mary Beth Oliver, 94–124. Mahwah, NJ: Lawrence Erlbaum.

Bandura, Albert, Dorothea Ross, and Sheila A. Ross. 1961. "Transmission of Aggression through Imitation of Aggressive Models." *Journal of Abnormal and Social Psychology* 63, no. 3: 575–82.

Baron-Cohen, Simon, Sally Wheelwright, Jacqueline Hill, Yogini Raste, and Ian Plumb. 2001. "The 'Reading the Mind in the Eyes' Test Revised Version: A Study with Normal Adults, and Adults with Asperger Syndrome or High-Functioning Autism." *Journal of Child Psychology and Psychiatry* 42, no. 2: 241–51.

Bechara, Antoine, and Antonio R. Damasio. 2005. "The Somatic Marker Hypothesis: A Neural Theory of Economic Decision." *Games and Economic Behavior* 52, no. 2: 336–72.

Bezdek, Matthew A., Jeffrey E. Foy, and Richard J. Gerrig. 2013. "'Run For It!': Viewers' Participatory Responses to Film Narratives." *Psychology of Aesthetics, Creativity, and the Arts* 7, no. 4: 409–16.

Bischoff, Theanna, and Joan Peskin. 2014. "Do Fiction Writers Have Superior Perspective Taking Ability?" *Scientific Study of Literature* 4, no. 2: 125–49.

Black, Jessica E., and Jennifer L. Barnes. 2015. "The Effects of Reading Material on Social and Non-Social Cognition." *Poetics* 52: 32–43.

Carroll, Noel. 2001. *Beyond Aesthetics: Philosophical Essays*. Cambridge: Cambridge University Press.

Currie, Gregory. 1995. *Image and Mind: Film, Philosophy and Cognitive Science*. Cambridge: Cambridge University Press.

Currie, Gregory. 2016. "Does Fiction Makes Us Less Empathic?" *Teorema* 35, no. 3: 47–68.

Damasio, Antonio R. 1994. *Descartes' Error: Emotion, Rationality and the Human Brain*. New York: Putnam.

Davis, Mark H. 1983. "Measuring Individual Differences in Empathy: Evidence for a Multidimensional Approach." *Journal of Personality and Social Psychology* 44, no. 1: 113–26.

Djikic, Maja, Keith Oatley, and Mihnea C. Moldoveanu. 2013. "Reading Other Minds: Effects of Literature on Empathy." *Scientific Study of Literature* 3, no. 1: 28–47.

Dodell-Feder, David, and Diana I. Tamir. 2018. "Fiction Reading Has a Small Positive Impact on Social Cognition: A Meta-Analysis." *Journal of Experimental Psychology: General* 147, no. 11: 1713–27.

Fong, Katrina, Justin B. Mullin, and Raymond A. Mar. 2013. "What You Read Matters: The Role of Fiction Genre in Predicting Interpersonal Sensitivity." *Psychology of Aesthetics, Creativity, and the Arts* 7, no. 4: 370–76.

Gallese, Vittorio. 2003. "The Roots of Empathy: The Shared Manifold Hypothesis and the Neural Basis of Intersubjectivity." *Psychopathology* 36, no. 4: 171–80.

Gerrig, Richard J. 1993. *Experiencing Narrative Worlds: On the Psychological Activities of Reading*. New Haven: Yale University Press.

Gerrig, Richard J., and Matthew E. Jacovina. 2009. "Reader Participation in the Experience of Narrative." *Psychology of Learning and Motivation*, no. 51: 223–54.

Gerrig, Richard J., and Edward J. O'Brien. 2005. "The Scope of Memory-Based Processing." *Discourse Processes* 39, nos. 2–3: 225–42.

Goldman, Alvin. 2006. "Imagination and Simulation in Audience Responses to Fiction." In *The Architecture of the Imagination: New Essays on Pretense, Possibility, and Fiction*, edited by Shaun Nichols, 41–56. Oxford: Clarendon Press.

Guajardo, Nicole R., and Anne C. Watson. 2002. "Narrative Discourse and Theory of Mind Development." *Journal of Genetic Psychology* 163, no. 3: 305–25.

Gygax, Pascal, and Christelle Gillioz. 2015. "Emotion Inferences during Reading: Going beyond the Tip of the Iceberg." In *Inferences during Reading*, edited by Edward J. O'Brien,

Anne E. Cook, and Robert F. Lorch Jr., 122–39. Cambridge: Cambridge University Press.

Hakemulder, Jèmeljan. 2000. *The Moral Laboratory: Experiments Examining the Effects of Reading Literature on Social Perception and Moral Self-Concept.* Philadelphia: John Benjamins.

Hofmann, Stefan G., Stacey N. Doan, Manuel Sprung, Anne Wilson, Chad Ebesutani, Leigh A. Andrews, Joshua Curtiss, and Paul L. Harris. 2016. "Training Children's Theory-of-Mind: A Meta-Analysis of Controlled Studies." *Cognition*, no. 150: 200–212.

Hogan, Patrick Colm. 2003. *Cognitive Science, Literature, and the Arts: A Guide for Humanists.* New York: Routledge.

Hogan, Patrick Colm. 2011. *What Literature Teaches Us about Emotion.* New York: Cambridge University Press.

Iacoboni, Marc. 2009. "Imitation, Empathy, and Mirror Neurons." *Annual Review of Psychology* 60, no. 1: 653–70.

Jacovina, Matthew E., and Richard J. Gerrig. 2010. "How Readers Experience Characters' Decisions." *Memory and Cognition* 38, no. 6: 753–61.

Kahneman, Daniel, and Dale T. Miller. 1986. "Norm Theory: Comparing Reality to Its Alternatives." *Psychological Review* 93, no. 2: 136–53.

Keen, Suzanne. 2007. *Empathy and the Novel.* New York: Oxford University Press.

Kidd, David Comer, and Emanuele Castano. 2013. "Reading Literary Fiction Improves Theory of Mind." *Science* 342, no. 6156: 377–80.

Kieran, Matthew. 2003. "In Search of a Narrative." In *Imagination, Philosophy, and the Arts*, edited by Matthew Kieran and Dominic Lopes, 69–87. New York: Routledge.

Kintsch, Walter. 1998. *Comprehension: A Paradigm for Cognition.* Cambridge: Cambridge University Press.

Koopman, Eva Maria. 2016. "Effects of 'Literariness' on Emotions and on Empathy and Reflection after Reading." *Psychology of Aesthetics, Creativity, and the Arts* 10, no. 1: 82–98.

Mar, Raymond A., and Keith Oatley. 2008. "The Function of Fiction is the Abstraction and Simulation of Social Experience." *Perspectives on Psychological Science* 3, no. 3: 173–92.

Mar, Raymond A., Keith Oatley, Jacob Hirsh, Jennifer dela Paz, and Jordan B. Peterson. 2006. "Bookworms versus Nerds: Exposure to Fiction versus Non-fiction, Divergent Associations with Social Ability, and the Simulation of Fictional Social Worlds." *Journal of Research in Personality* 40, no. 5: 694–712.

Mar, R. A., Keith Oatley, and Jordan B. Peterson. 2009. "Exploring the Link between Reading Fiction and Empathy: Ruling out Individual Differences and Examining Outcomes." *Communications* 34: 407–28.

McKoon, Gail, and Roger Ratcliff. 1986. "Inferences about Predictable Events." *Journal of Experimental Psychology: Learning, Memory, and Cognition* 12, no. 1: 82–91.

McKoon, Gail, and Roger Ratcliff. 1992. "Inference during Reading." *Psychological Review* 99, no. 3: 440–66.

McKoon, Gail, and Roger Ratcliff. 2015. "Cognitive Theories in Discourse-Processing Research." In *Inferences during Reading*, edited by Edward J. O'Brien, Anne E. Cook, and Robert F. Lorch Jr., 42–67. Cambridge: Cambridge University Press.

McNamara, Danielle S., and Joe Magliano. 2009. "Toward a Comprehensive Model of Comprehension." *Psychology of Learning and Motivation*, no. 51: 297–384.

Miall, David S., and Don Kuiken. 1995. "Aspects of Literary Response: A New Questionnaire." *Research in the Teaching of English* 29, no. 1: 37–58.

Moore, Mariah, and Peter C. Gordon. 2015. "Reading Ability and Print Exposure: Item Response Theory Analysis of the Author Recognition Test." *Behavior Research Methods* 47, no. 4: 1095–109.

Mumper, Micah L., and Richard J. Gerrig. 2017. "Leisure Reading and Social Cognition: A Meta-Analysis." *Psychology of Aesthetics, Creativity, and the Arts* 11, no. 1: 109–20.

Oatley, Keith. 1999. "Why Fiction May Be Twice as True as Fact: Fiction as Cognitive and Emotional Simulation." *Review of General Psychology* 3, no. 2: 101–17.

Oatley, Keith. 2016. "Fiction: Simulation of Social Worlds." *Trends in Cognitive Sciences* 20, no. 8: 618–28.

Oatley, Keith, and Mitra Gholamain. 1997. "Emotions and Identification: Connections between Readers and Fiction." In *Emotion and the Arts*, edited by Mette Hjort and Sue Laver, 263–81. New York: Oxford University Press.

O'Brien, Edward J., and Anne E. Cook. 2015. "Models of Discourse Comprehension," In *The Oxford Handbook of Reading*, edited by Alexander Pollatsek and Rebecca Treiman, 217–31. New York: Oxford University Press.

O'Brien, Edward J., Anne E. Cook, and Robert F. Lorch Jr., eds. 2015. *Inferences during Reading*. Cambridge: Cambridge University Press.

Ortony, Andrew, Gerald L. Clore, and Allan Collins. 1990. *The Cognitive Structure of Emotions*. Cambridge: Cambridge University Press.

Panero, Maria Eugenia, Deena Skolnick Weisberg, Jessica Black, Thalia R. Goldstein, Jennifer L. Barnes, Hiram Brownell, and Ellen Winner. 2016. "Does Reading a Single Passage of Literary Fiction Really Improve Theory of Mind? An Attempt at Replication." *Journal of Personality and Social Psychology* 111, no. 5: 46–54.

Pope, Dan. 2015. *Housebreaking*. New York: Simon and Schuster.

Rain, Marina, and Raymond A. Mar. 2014. "Measuring Reading Behavior: Examining the Predictive Validity of Print-Exposure Checklists." *Empirical Studies of the Arts* 32, no. 1: 93–108.

Raney, Arthur A. 2004. "Expanding Disposition Theory: Reconsidering Character Liking, Moral Evaluations, and Enjoyment." *Communication Theory* 14, no. 4: 348–69.

Rapp, David N., and Richard J. Gerrig. 2002. "Readers' Reality-Driven and Plot-Driven Analyses in Narrative Comprehension." *Memory and Cognition* 30, no. 5: 779–88.

Rapp, David N., and Richard J. Gerrig. 2006. "Predilections for Narrative Outcomes: The Impact of Story Contexts and Reader Preferences." *Journal of Memory and Language* 54, no. 1: 54–67.

Rubin, David C., and Sharda Umanath. 2015. "Event Memory: A Theory of Memory for Laboratory, Autobiographical, and Fictional Events." *Psychological Review* 122, no. 1: 1–23.

Skinner, Burrhus F. 1969. *Contingencies of Reinforcement: A Theoretical Analysis*. New York: Meredith.

Stansfield, John, and Louise Bunce. 2014. "The Relationship between Empathy and Reading Fiction: Separate Roles for Cognitive and Affective Components." *Journal of European Psychology Students* 5, no. 3: 9–18.

Talmi, Deborah. 2013. "Enhanced Emotional Memory: Cognitive and Neural Mechanisms." *Current Directions in Psychological Science* 22, no. 6: 430–36.

Tamir, Diana I., Andrew B. Bricker, David Dodell-Feder, and Jason P. Mitchell. 2016. "Reading Fiction and Reading Minds: The Role of Simulation in the Default Network." *Social Cognitive and Affective Neuroscience* 11, no. 2: 215–24.

Taylor, Laramie D., Cassandra Alexopoulos, and Jannath Ghaznavi. 2016. "Touchy Subjects: Sex in the Workplace on Broadcast, Cable, and Internet Television." *Sex Roles* 75, nos. 9–10: 476–89.

Valkenburg, Patti M., Jochen Peter, and Joseph B. Walther. 2016. "Media Effects: Theory and Research." *Annual Review of Psychology* 67, no. 1: 315–38.

van Schooten, Erik, and Kees de Glopper. 2003. "The Development of Literary Response in Secondary Education." *Poetics* 31, nos. 3–4: 155–87.

Waytz, Adam, Hal E. Hershfield, and Diana I. Tamir. 2015. "Mental Simulation and Meaning in Life." *Journal of Personality and Social Psychology* 108, no. 2: 336–55.

Wellman, Henry M., Fuxi Fang, and Candida C. Peterson. 2011. "Sequential Progressions in a Theory-of-Mind Scale: Longitudinal Perspectives." *Child Development* 82, no. 3: 780–92.

Wondra, Joshua D., and Phoebe C. Ellsworth. 2015. "An Appraisal Theory of Empathy and Other Vicarious Emotional Experiences." *Psychological Review* 122, no. 3: 411–28.

Zunshine, Lisa. 2006. *Why We Read Fiction: Theory of Mind and the Novel*. Columbus: Ohio State University Press.

II. EMPATHY AND LITERARY ETHICS

"Some Powerful Rankling Passion": An Interdisciplinary Exploration of Emotion Regulation Strategies in Joanna Baillie's Passion Plays

M. Soledad Caballero and Aimee Knupsky
Allegheny College

Abstract   The article considers how Joanna Baillie's concept of "sympathetick curiosity" informs contemporary discussions about emotion regulation. By focusing on Baillie's *De Monfort* (1798) and *Orra* (1812), the article argues that regulatory flexibility is a learned skill that can be improved by actively engaging sympathetic curiosity. Baillie insisted that her plays had pedagogical value and that having audiences watch them would help them learn how to avoid the destructive nature of the passions. Working with Bonanno and Burton's (2013) model of regulatory flexibility, the article demonstrates the importance not just of inherent differences in emotion regulation but also of learning opportunities individuals engage to develop it. In particular, the article presents a model of how people learn through narrative simulation, drawing on the work of Romantic writers and current critics as well as cognitive psychologists and neuropsychologists. Consideration is then given to how watching protagonists' manifestations of and responses to an unfolding passion helps audiences learn to develop their regulatory flexibility.

Keywords   emotion regulation, Baillie, sympathetic curiosity, learning, cognitive humanities

Poetics Today 40:3 (September 2019)   DOI 10.1215/03335372-7558094

Scholars in both Romantic studies and cognitive psychology have made a strong argument for the idea that people learn from narrative.[1] Building on this scholarship, we propose a cognitive humanities perspective on how that learning takes place, grounded in the work of Joanna Baillie and theorists exploring the psychology of fiction. We argue that sympathetic curiosity triggers imagination, which leads to learning. Drama provides the cues and triggers necessary to engage viewers in simulation so that they learn from it as from real-world experiences but at a safe, aesthetic distance. Just as with real-world experience, simulation via narrative provides iterative practice, so that it is the accumulation of experiences that lead to learning rather than any single engagement with one text. To exemplify this learning process, we integrate Baillie's ([1798] 2001a) concept of sympathetic curiosity with psychological models of emotion regulation; we then consider how her plays *De Monfort* (1798) and *Orra* (1812) offer us an opportunity to expand our regulatory flexibility skills.

1. Sympathetic Curiosity: Our First Propensity, Our First Teacher

In her 1798 *Introductory Discourse*, Baillie defines the concept of sympathetic curiosity as "that strong sympathy which most creatures, but humans above all, feel for others of their kind, nothing has become so much an object of man's curiosity as himself" (Baillie [1798] 2001a: 67). Here, "sympathy" reads almost as a synonym for "curiosity." Indeed, the connection between what makes people potentially curious but not sympathetic or, conversely, sympathetic but not curious is the balance Baillie seeks as she argues for the educational value of drama. Specifically, the human "propensity" for sympathetic curiosity is the driving motivation from which people learn about themselves in relation to others. This inherently social learning can be fostered through instruction in various forms, the drama primary among them. According to Baillie, "the Drama improves us by the knowledge we acquire of our own minds, from the natural desire we have to look into the thoughts, and observe the behaviors of others (Baillie [1798] 2001a: 90). Baillie is interested in educating her viewers about the nature and management of emotions, those "primary passions" that made up her life's work.

For Baillie, sympathetic curiosity functions like a feedback loop, creating a space for drama, the stage, and the dramatist to focus audience attention on characters' vulnerability while not actually being vulnerable. Sympathetic curiosity allows viewers to project the "what might have been" about them-

---

1. For extensive reviews of narrative and its impacts, see Keen (2007, 2011), Oatley (2011), Richardson (2011), and Zunshine (2006).

selves while not being *in* the passion, thus giving room to focus on the Other and at the same time to *imagine* themselves in that distress. Sympathetic curiosity enables imaginative foreshadowing. Baillie was invested in distilling the primal passions, what she called "the most powerful passions," to offer a classification of their development (Baillie [1798] 2001a: 92). She wanted her audience to observe their evolution, to understand how to avoid them, and to recognize how to control them by watching moments of failure exhibited by the protagonists of her plays. People learn as they observe others, think about them, and think about themselves in their place. Because of sympathetic curiosity, humans are pliable enough to observe with sympathy and receive a lesson about the passion of the actor on stage. Since the mechanism Baillie illuminates depends on the process of imagination, the "as if" moments on stage, Baillie's ideas about sympathetic curiosity are in conversation with con-temporaneous debates about the power of the imagination.

2. Imagination as Bridge: From Curiosity to Simulation

For Baillie, imagination is essential to the idea that people learn from nar-rative, because it entails thinking about one's self in another's place, thus forming a bridge between sympathetic curiosity and the educational efficacy of drama. Indeed, it has always had a primary role in learning for Romantic philosophers, just as imagery has for contemporary scholars in cognitive psychology and neuroscience.[2] Nevertheless, for Romantic thinkers, a key question was, How can imagination function as a source of learning in the real world when it is so closely tied to "flights of fancy," which may encourage escape from the struggles of that real world? Imagination became a touch-stone in debates about the dangers or benefits of art, highlighting the way that, in either case, imagination was a conduit of influence and learning. Concern centered on whether narrative engaged sympathy and empathy as ends in themselves rather than as motivators for action and appropriate behavior. For example, critics of the gothic novel, such as Hannah Moore, thought that the genre was dangerous: that it would lead women astray, because they would spend time enjoying the escape and thus ignore their duties.

A parallel version of this debate centered on sensibility—specifically, whether overactive sensibility (as sparked by works of fiction) would lead to

2. Note the important distinctions between imagination for Romantic thinkers and imagery for cognitive psychologists. For Romantic thinkers, imagination is what allows us to use imagery; for the majority of cognitive psychologists, imagination is one function of imagery. However, for our purposes, we focus on the fact that each concept allows for simulation and thus use them to inform one another.

pathology (i.e., sexual, moral, and religious looseness).[3] Contemporary scholars like Sha (2009a, 2009b) point to the nineteenth-century emphasis on
finding a balance between a "wild" or unfettered use of imagination, which
could overwhelm the senses and lead to self-destruction, and the potential
use of structured and guided imagination for the moral and public good (see
Beer 1992; Burwick 1996; Klein 1996; McFarland 1986). The struggle to
"redeem" imagination was motivated by trying to understand its uses in
scientific and literary production. How then to treat a quality or "faculty"
necessary to the common good while also recognizing its potential dangers to
the soul and to the social body?[4] Was imagination passive or active? Were
people in charge of imagination, and where might that imagination reside?
Of course, the debate itself is redundant. After all, "even when diseased, the
imagination's hold over the body paradoxically gave it powers of transformation" (Sha 2009b: 199).[5]

Among Romantic thinkers, William Wordsworth may have presented
the most well-known conceptualization of the function of imagination in his
preface to the *Lyrical Ballads*. While not specifically using the word *imagination*,
Wordsworth ([1802] 1994: 449–50) discusses how poetry functions as an
imaginative process: it "is the spontaneous overflow of powerful feelings: it
takes its origin from emotion recollected in tranquillity: the emotion is con-
templated till, by a species of reaction, the tranquillity gradually disappears,
and an emotion, kindred to that which was before the subject of contemplation, is gradually produced, and does itself actually exist in the mind." Wordsworth's conception of imagination as a kind of reactivation of perception
foreshadowed the topic of debate in cognitive and neuroscientific explorations
of imagery.

To understand whether imagination plays a role in learning, imagery must
be understood as a bidirectional, cognitive process, one in which perceptual
information is transformed and stored as knowledge or knowledge is accessed
and transformed back into a perceptual-like experience. Empirical debates
about the nature and function of imagery began before William James's (1890)
thesis on the topic and largely focused on whether thought was composed of
symbolic, abstract manipulations or involved more one-to-one re-creations
of perceptual experience (Finke and Shepard 1986; Pinker and Kosslyn

3. Much has been written on the Gothic novel and gender dynamics. See Clemens (1999);
Duncan (1992); Hoeveler (1998); Kilgour (1995); Massé (1992); Punter (1996); Richter (1996);
Wallace (2013); Watt (1999); and Williams (1995). For more on women and reading, see Gonda
(1996) and Pearson (1999). For more on the social influence of women's writing, see Gilbert and
Gubar (2000) and Mellor (2002).
4. For more on varying constructions of the Romantic imagination, see Richardson (2013).
5. For an extensive discussion of narrative and empathy, including the benefits and "danger" of
"emotionally engaged reading practices," see Keen (2011: 25).

1983; Richardson 1983; Shepard and Metzler 1971; Yuille and Catchpole 1977). Bringing these two possibilities together, Paivio (1970, 1972) developed the dual-process model of knowledge, arguing that learned information was stored in both a symbolic, linguistic code and a perceptual-like, analog visual code. Later neurological investigations into the physiological processes of imagery provided additional evidence for the analog conception (Farah 1984, 1995; Kosslyn, Ganis, and Thompson 2001). Ultimately, both cognitive and neuroscientific investigations converged on the notion that imagery is a kind of perception in reverse, echoing Wordsworth's conception of imagination as a re-creation of experience. In fact, in his work on grounded cognition, Barsalou (1999, 2010) describes "perceptual symbol systems" that function as productive simulators (read imagery) of experience.[6]

2.1. Narrative as Simulator

Baillie's idea that learning is triggered by sympathetic curiosity and that drama is a powerful place for learning anticipated the ongoing debates about the educational value and efficacy of narrative. In trying to answer the question of how people learn from fiction, we are attempting to elucidate a sociocognitive process—that is, a process in the brain of a person who is situated within the motivations and constraints of the social and historical world. We are emboldened in our endeavor by Romantic critics who held that the imagination fosters scientific projects and serves as a bridge—between the various sciences, the sciences and the arts, the known and the unknown, and the brain and the "mind" (Savarese 2013; Sha 2009a, 2009b). Imagination in a literary sense provides the metaphors by which we search and, thus, a good framework for thinking about the cognitive processes of imagery and learning. Our following theorization of fictional learning is informed by Baillie's centuries-old work as well as current literary critics, cognitive psychologists, and neuroscientists. We invoke a series of constructs that treat fiction as a *simulation* (see Mar 2011; Oatley 2011).[7] As Oatley specifies, in fiction, or drama, or narrative, the focus is not on textual characters' emotions but on those of the audience. As he argues, "it is we [the audience] who puts these events together, constructing them into something meaningful for ourselves, and experiencing the resulting emotions" (Oatley 2011: 112). The audience's active re-creation

6. For recent neuroimaging studies illustrating the overlap of perception and imagery during narrative engagement, see Mar (2011) and Speer et al. (2009).
7. See Schacter and Addis (2007) for a related conception of simulation: the constructive episodic simulation hypothesis.

and engagement with the work enables fiction to function as an emotional simulator.[8]

Once grounded in the notion of simulation, we can draw on that metaphor for its features and functions, in particular, the way that simulators are used to practice and learn about little-known or unexplored contexts while remaining at a safe physical distance.[9] Fiction as simulation reaps the rewards of emotional activation, real-time problem solving, and feedback about our decisions without requiring readers or viewers to endure the real-world consequences. Oatley (2011: 119) calls this the "theory of sympathetic emotion," positioning it as a "fascination" and remarking that it makes us "want to know more" — especially about events such as "accidents, fallings-in-love, fights and other assaults, betrayals, injustices, falls from grace, sufferings of loss." Oatley's theory is a direct descendant of Baillie's sympathetic curiosity. Baillie ([1798] 2001a: 69) asks us, "If man is an object of so much attention to man, engaged in ordinary occurrences of life, how much more does he excite his curiosity and interest when placed in extraordinary situations of difficulty and distress?" But for Baillie, there is more in it for us than just "fascination," and she would argue that we "want to know more" about how people themselves might hold up in such circumstances.

We contend, then, that sympathetic emotion is subsumed by sympathetic curiosity put in service of learning. The spirit of sympathetic curiosity lives on in contemporary cognitive explorations of fiction; Oatley (2011: 156) notes that "fiction offers very particular kinds of truth, of what we human beings are like, and what we are up to in our interactions with each other." Simulation through fiction compels people to think about themselves in a narrative social world in the same way that sympathetic curiosity drives the desire for self-knowledge on the stage or in the real world.

2.2. Drama as Simulator

The stage has always been a site of simulation. In particular, Levy (1997, 2005) reexamines drama's pedagogical value and emphasizes the close ties between the practices of drama and education. As he notes, historically, "live theatre was the closest we could get to practice for life. . . . Theatre, like a pilot's simulator, could give a child, in a predictable, compressed, and *repeatable* form, a preview of the moral dilemmas he or she would encounter in real

---

8. For examinations of how readers actively and automatically "fill in the gaps," see Oatley (2011), Polichak and Gerrig (2002), and Sha (2009a; 2009b).
9. Recent work by Zhou, Majka, and Epley (2017) has shown that success at figuring out the thoughts and feelings of others is greater via simulation than via inferring perspective, suggesting that narrative's function of simulation may be even more important than its role in developing empathy and theory of mind.

life and practice living through them correctly and honorably" (Levy 1997: 66). Much of his work centers on delineating ideas over time about how drama teaches. Among these, he emphasizes that theater teaches because it supports repetition and memorization, allows the acting out of moral lessons and decisions, engages pleasure (imagination and play), and is embodied. He also concludes that viewers learn through drama because the audience is malleable and receptive to the lessons and is distanced enough to consider the problems presented on the stage from an undistracted perspective. Finally, of concern to Levy is "what remains" after an audience leaves the theater. Specifically, he suggests that the residue is "a kind of sympathetic resonance," like "shadow tracks of emotion," a suggestion convergent with cognitive neuroscientific explanations of memory formation (Levy 2005: 25).[10] Over a century before Levy's theorization, this notion of a long-lasting residue was central to Baillie's project about what an audience would take away from her plays and incorporate into the actions and decisions of their own lives.

Ultimately, Levy (1997: 71) surmises that drama educates by "training [people] to experience more deeply, more vividly, and more fully; to discern distinctions, nuances, suggestions, and intimations not available through the uneducated faculty." This claim for the educational value of theater aligns with the vision Baillie laid out for *Plays on the Passions* as well as Romantic theories of imagination (see Burwick 1990; Coleridge [1815–17] 1985; Hazlitt [1826] 2010; and Weinstein 1971). Baillie's "one emotion at a time" approach is also in line with contemporary methods for studying emotion (see Le Doux 2012; Oatley 2011). Because of its attempt to systematically pursue the passions with a scalpel-like precision, Baillie's work is ripe with research questions for affective science. We suggest that Baillie was grafting the structure of an empirical approach onto the power of narrative to educate emotionally. Hers is the precursor to interdisciplinary investigations of emotional education through drama. What stands at the heart of learning from narrative is that the reader/audience/viewer is re-creating and engaging with the scenes and situations presented to their ear, eye, and body.

3. How We Learn from Narrative: A Cognitive-Humanities Proposal

Memory is central to the process of learning, and fundamental to our argument is Schank and Berman's (2002) idea that memory is story. The source

---

10. For example, the idea of "shadow tracks" could be interpreted as neuronal activation capable of creating or strengthening pathways in a connectionist model of memory. See McClelland (2000).

of stories is not important: they can be about one's own experiences, they can be stories told by others, and they can be stories that people read or watch. Schank and Berman (2002: 302) argue that people treat all these stories as "functionally similar," all having an equivalent impact on memory and, thus, on learning. The way humans organize, think about, and benefit from this repository of stories is through what they call "indexing" (288), which occurs when people look for points of similarity or connection among the stories, then fusing them together.

Overall, the process of building memory with stories illustrates how people can learn from narrative.[11] Turning narrative into memories via the process of indexing, people know how to act in or understand new events and how to plan, make judgments, and solve problems (Schank and Berman 2002: 293). People create and tell stories to teach themselves and others. Often, people hear nothing that makes them confront the unexpected. But there are times of "expectation failure" when anticipated events don't materialize, "right decisions" lead to tragedy, new acquaintances reveal unfamiliar experiences, or the unimaginable occurs. This is when learning is the strongest and most long-lasting, perhaps because "these expectation failures lead us to examine our beliefs and sometimes build on them or change them" (294). Stories are inherently pedagogical; "whether or not the listeners understand or receive the lesson we mean to teach, the utterance is meant to inform" (289). The intent to inform does not equal an automatic learning outcome, but for Baillie, sympathetic curiosity is the motivating balm that primes humans for the lesson.

Indexing stories as memory, i.e., knowledge, cultivates people's sociocognitive capabilities and enhances greater skill at finding "the right stories at the right times," which eventually helps people distill the learned essence of these common experiences.[12] In this manner, Baillie's passion plays allow people to index those stories, connect them to their own experiences, and help them to learn over time. People become more skilled as they fuse their stories and others' into a richer representation of the world.[13] Learning through story is a powerful mechanism, because it is an implicit, automatic process compared to more effortful, explicit learning encountered in other contexts. Stories teach even when people don't "think" they are "learning."

11. For examples of the rich cognitive and neuroscientific examination of the function of sharing stories and autobiographical memory, see Alea and Bluck (2003); Marsh and Tversky (2004); McAdams and McLean (2013); and Miller, deWinstanley, and Carey (1996).
12. Herbert and Burt (2004) describe this distillation as a transfer from specific, time-stamped episodic memory to generalized semantic memory.
13. For recent evidence that we treat the memories of others as our own and use our own memories to understand the motivations of others, see Brown et al. (2015), Rabin and Rosenbaum (2012), and Spreng and Mar (2012).

3.1. Transportation and the In-Between

If memory is built from shared stories, what motivates or facilitates that sharing? One answer to this question involves "transportation,"[14] which Green and Brock (2002) argue is inherently reliant upon imagery.[15] According to their transportation-imagery model, stories that persuade do so because they invoke imagery or relate to readers' beliefs. Imagery activates the indexing of memory and depends on the transportable nature of a story, and transportation depends on aspects of readers' history (imagery ability and absorption), the text (quality or kind), and the context (investment in imagery). Central to the role of transportation in learning from narrative are the conditions it creates for readers. Specifically, transportation creates a kind of "psychological distance" from reality, allows for a loss of public self-awareness, offers the possibility of change, and precipitates *some* level of emotional response (325–26).

Among these components of the transportation-imagery model, we think it paramount to emphasize imagination's capacity to create psychological distance, because this distance is a cornerstone of Baillie's theory that we learn from emotion when we are not in the "throes" of it. Baillie ([1798] 2001a: 74) writes, "With limbs untorn, with head unsmitten, with senses unimpaired by despair, we know what we ourselves might have been on the rack, on the scaffold, and in the most afflicting circumstances of distress." Baillie wanted her audience to imagine without suffering, to simulate without immediate consequences. Others have also noted how writers strive to create this balance between lived emotional responses and re-creation in the reading process, or what Wordsworth ([1802] 1994: 449) called the "spontaneous overflow of powerful feelings" that is "recollected in tranquillity." Oatley (2011) refers to this as "aesthetic distance," and Gerrig (1993) refers to it as the "paradox of fiction."

In all these descriptions, readers' attention lands not quite on themselves and not wholly on the characters on the page or on the stage. In other words, "instead of focusing on one's own identity the reader may 'become' the story characters, or feel as if she is experiencing narrative events" (Green and Brock 2002: 326). This emotional in-between provides a mechanism by which people can disrupt the social bias Oatley discusses, i.e., the actor-observer bias (Jones 1976; Jones and Nisbett 1971) that prevents identification with

14. Transportation as a psychological concept was described by Gerrig (1993). Green and Brock (2000) developed the measurement commonly used to assess it.

15. While there might not be a parallel concept in literary critical discussions for "transportation," writers have this goal in mind when they attempt to "move the reader" by utilizing craft techniques like point of view, direct or indirect or free indirect discourse, plot arcs, metaphor, characterization, setting, personification, allusion, etc.

others.[16] Because of this bias, people explain the behaviors of others in terms of innate characteristics, while they make sense of their own behavior differently, by focusing on its context. When people engage in fiction, they can expand beyond this system of identification. So fiction can be superior to learning from real-life experience, because it dismantles the cognitive biases with which individuals view and judge others. The question, then, is not *do* people learn from fiction, but *how* do they learn from fiction?

3.2. Side Participation

To learn from fiction, people simulate its narrative or, as Polichak and Gerrig (2002: 72) explain, when motivated by the story of another person, they become active or "side participants" in that story. We propose that side participants live in the "emotional in-between." As Polichak and Gerrig indicate, the neurological experience is "produced through the same processes that yield similar effects in conversation and other interactions with people" (72). Thus, readers and viewers apply everyday conversational and other real-world skills. As side participants, readers and viewers experience what Polichak and Gerrig refer to as *participatory responses* (p-responses), acting "as if" the story were happening to them. Perhaps because of sympathetic curiosity, engagement entails learning. They can also try to solve the problems facing protagonists; such p-responses are "a reader's attempt to strategically gather evidence from a narrative that will allow them to more confidently predict outcomes" (78). Watching Baillie's plays, the audience searches for clues for how protagonists might achieve a goal, in the process developing sociocognitive skills.

Similarly, readers and audiences can experience a replotting p-response by thinking about what might have been. Baillie ([1798] 2001a) describes people's ability to learn from these "if only" responses. In particular, she notes that "tracing the progress of passion" in a narrative "points out to us those stages in the approach of the enemy, when he might have been combatted most successfully" (94). Finally, the impact of a narrative can take place long after people have engaged with it. Evaluatory p-responses occur when readers think about and synthesize the overall message of a narrative. These kinds of responses can "impact people's beliefs about the world and the way they themselves ought to behave" and "may influence the reader's decisions" (Polichak and Gerrig 2002: 79). Each of these p-responses is a moment when people are engaging and enhancing their ability to learn and to regulate emotions.

16. For the gendered version of this bias, see Barrett and Bliss-Moreau (2009). For a neuroscience account of the bias, see Lee and Siegle (2012).

3.3. Curiosity as Connection

At first glance, the process by which people learn through narrative seems relatively simple, powerful, and consistent. However, there are limitations. For example, Schank and Berman (2002) argue that stories have the greatest impact when people are interested, see similarities between themselves and the characters, and are willing or compelled to recognize limitations in their own knowledge. Do these findings imply that personal experience equals interest? Such a conclusion further suggests that people who do not see any points of contact between someone else's story and their own "simply will not understand the theme or any point of the story" so that they "may not even know that [they] heard it" (Schank and Berman 2002: 304). Baillie ([1798] 2001a) would respond by insisting that sympathetic curiosity makes humans inherently care. Paralleling Baillie's claim and drawing on contemporary cognitive psychology, literary theorist Zunshine (2010) emphasizes this innate curiosity, calling theory of mind a "hungry adaptation" and maintaining that interest is automatically engaged when humans try to interpret the thoughts and feelings of others. Notably, Baillie was especially careful and detailed in her stage directions and scripts, adopting recognized gestures of the time and creating morally ambiguous characters, neither all evil nor all good, to promote audience identification with protagonists. Indeed, Baillie's emphasis on the primary passions implies that she considered these to be what we might now call "basic" emotions, thus universal enough to be a generalized frame of reference. While there is some debate about whether emotions are "innate," any story that taps into these common experiences, as Oatley (2011) notes, is going to provide an inherent connection between audiences and characters to make them want to care, to hear, and ultimately, to learn.[17]

By storing experiences of narrative through the process thus described, people learn how to read new emotional contexts, what strategies might help in these contexts, and how to respond to the feedback they receive. As Richardson (2011: 670) notes, "Imagination functions to model or simulate possible future events that, however likely, might never come to pass." This ability to displace or "transport" anticipates work on the narrative impact of fiction. As Levy (2005) comments, "emotionally we have been there — not in the general but *right there* — before" (25; emphasis added). Overall, then, a chain of events triggers learning when people engage with narrative. It may go something like this: transported readers engage imagination, which leads to participatory responding, motivating them to index the story with their own

17. For a comprehensive discussion of whether emotions are "basic," see Barrett (2006); Barrett et al. (2007); Izard (2007); and Panksepp (2007).

stories, finally resulting in learning. The narrative becomes a kind of reality, from which people learn as they do from real-world experiences but at an aesthetic distance.

4. Regulatory Flexibility: Managing One's Emotions

While previous explorations of narrative impact have questioned whether readers can develop theory of mind and empathy (Bernaerts et al. 2013; Jaén and Simon 2012; Keen 2007; Hogan 2011; Leverage et al. 2011; Oatley 2011; Vermeule 2010; Zunshine 2006), Mumper and Gerrig (2017) provide a conclusive argument that narrative fiction does indeed impact these sociocognitive skills. We pursue this avenue further by addressing another primary sociocognitive process, namely regulatory flexibility. In the remainder of this essay, we do so by considering how the narrative learning processes described above can be put to work in audiences watching Baillie's plays, ultimately leading to enhanced regulatory flexibility. Regulatory flexibility is an emotion regulation model proposed by Bonanno and Burton (2013, 2016).

Emotion regulation includes physiological, cognitive, and social processes used to decrease, maintain, or increase emotional response.[18] One way of thinking about regulating emotion is to consider how to disrupt it at different moments in its development. Gross (1999, 2015) outlines the possibilities. Preemptive regulation strategies are used to avoid people, contexts, or environments that may trigger emotion in the first place. If avoidance is not possible in an emotionally charged environment, other modification strategies come into play. These strategies aim to prevent an emotion from fully developing by either altering the physical environment or by changing how a person thinks about the situation. Ways to alter the physical environment to decrease its volatility include changing topics, suggesting alternative activities, or directly confronting the situation. If such physical change is impossible, inappropriate, or unsuccessful, the individual may try to alter his or her cognitive engagement with it in one of several diverse ways: through distraction, rumination, or reevaluation (reappraisal) of the situation.

Clearly, humans are perpetually driven to regulate emotion, which perhaps explains the complexities of modeling these processes. Given the number of factors impacting emotion regulation, we ask, How do individuals successfully navigate this complex process? Bonanno and Burton (2013) provide a model of regulatory flexibility and contend that emotion regulation abilities vary,

---

18. Scholarship on emotion regulation is vast and multifaceted. Key investigations include Aldao, Sheppes, and Gross (2015); Cheung, Gardner, and Anderson (2015); Koole and Veenstra (2015); Sheppes et al. (2011); Tamir (2011); Troy, Shallcross, and Mauss (2013); and Zaki and Williams (2013).

depending on sensitivity to context, availability of a repertoire of strategies, and responsiveness to feedback (591). Individual differences in emotion regulation, then, can be a result of variations in flexibility across these three components. Consequently, inherent differences in emotion regulation and learning opportunities individuals engage to develop it are equally important.[19] Through sympathetic curiosity, we expect improved self-knowledge and, hence, enhanced regulatory flexibility.

4.1. Context Sensitivity

Context sensitivity is a component of regulatory flexibility akin to "reading a room." It is a collection of abilities, including the capacity to accurately detect and interpret facial cues, body language, and—important to nineteenth-century theorists—gestures of emotion (see Siddons 1807). Context sensitivity also entails the ability to discern relevant environmental cues and to monitor situational contexts and interpersonal goals. What is required of people in the emotional environment? What are others expecting? What emotional activity would be appropriate? Given the considerable variability in these cues, context sensitivity will operate effectively to the extent that cues in the environment are present, complete, and interpretable. Moreover, context sensitivity is a top-down process, influenced by one's personal emotional state and goals.[20] Consequently, a controlled, detached, and close dissection of external cues surrounding the unfolding of emotion, such as Baillie provides for audiences, is key to the development of strong context sensitivity. Watching one of Baillie's plays, the audience may look carefully at how her protagonists express an emotion, focus on the posture of others toward them, and wonder at their motivations and compulsions. Analyzing the factors surrounding protagonists' fall into passion, viewers may increase their perception of cues in interactions with others.

4.2. Emotion Regulation Repertoire

However, recognizing the swell of emotion in oneself and others is useful only to the extent that one has strategies to manipulate its progression, therefore necessitating the full range of regulation strategies. If the ability to read the room defines context sensitivity, the repertoire component of the model is

19. Bonanno and Burton (2016) emphasize the importance of thinking about emotion regulation as a multiprocess skill that develops over time and changes (for better and sometimes worse) across the life span.

20. Bonanno and Burton (2016) note the importance of the perception of how controllable a situation is in determining flexibility. Of course, this ignores the possibility that there may be structural factors (i.e., power dynamics) that limit what would be perceived as "appropriate" in an emotional situation for one person versus another.

made up of people's emotional regulation skills. How has the audience learned to respond to the imminent threat of passion? How have they observed others reacting in times of stress? In assessing repertoire, Bonanno and Burton (2013, 2016) urge theorists to consider not just the number of regulatory strategies available but also their diversity and sustainability. Successful regulatory flexibility requires a multitude of responses to emotion. Viewers of Baillie's passion plays witness the variety in regulation strategies adopted by characters, thus expanding their repertoires and increasing overall regulatory flexibility. Moreover, since Baillie presents the consequences of reliance upon a limited number of regulation strategies in her protagonists, the audience improves their own regulation flexibility by witnessing the failure of others.

4.3. Responsiveness to Feedback

The final component in Bonanno and Burton's (2013, 2016) conception of regulatory flexibility is responsiveness to feedback, which highlights the iterative nature of the emotion regulation process. Specifically, Bonanno and Burton (2013: 601) define *responsiveness* as "the ability to monitor feedback about the efficacy of the regulatory strategy that has been enacted and to maintain or adjust that strategy, end the strategy, or select a new regulatory strategy as needed." While many are adept at reading the room and have a number of regulation strategies at their disposal, unless people can determine the ongoing effectiveness of the strategy engaged, emotion regulation fails. Persistence in a regulation strategy that is no longer successful demonstrates a serious deficit in regulatory flexibility. By sustaining focus on a passion unfolding over time, Baillie gives the audience a chance to observe how protagonists evaluate the impact of their selected strategy. Has the passion been sustained, intensified, eliminated? Even when the intended outcome varies across time with the goals of the protagonists, the audience witnesses the feedback presented to them and their success or failure at interpreting and responding to it.

5. Simulating Regulatory Flexibility through the Passion Plays

As we have noted, Baillie's plays focus on one primary emotion and stage its evolution across time. While scientific experiments offer the specificity of testing regulatory flexibility, Baillie's medium provides more real-world contexts and allows audiences to experience the entirety of an emotion, to observe attempts to regulate it, and to receive pedagogical insights about how and when emotion regulation fails. In these ways, Baillie's concept of sympathetic curiosity connects directly to regulatory flexibility, since it is the means by which we learn from others' regulatory choices while not having directly experienced the emotional state itself.

In both plays we consider, Baillie provides the audience space to learn from narrative by engaging in the simulation of the events of the story—by being transported, responding as side participants, and updating or indexing their own stories with the new story. The first play focused on hatred is *De Monfort* (Baillie [1798] 2001b), which stages the titular character's attempts to manage his hatred for his childhood nemesis, Rezenvelt, and the efforts of others, particularly his sister Jane, to help him do this. Because this is a tragedy, the audience knows at the outset that De Monfort will fail; nevertheless, from a cognitive perspective, the audience will still learn, especially because learning is most powerful through expectation failures. The second play, *Orra* (Baillie [1812] 2007), is part of Baillie's third set of passion plays and centers on fear. Orra, an orphan, is pressured to marry her guardians' son but resists and tries to alter her reality. Also a tragedy, this play ends badly for Orra, but again, the audience learns about how it might regulate under circumstances utterly out of their control.[21] We demonstrate how the sympathetic curiosity invoked by Baillie serves to develop regulatory flexibility in audiences by exploring how context sensitivity, repertoire, and responsiveness to feedback can be observed in the actions of the characters in *De Monfort* and *Orra*.

5.1. Simulating Context Sensitivity

In *De Monfort*, a key moment of context sensitivity failure occurs when De Monfort's sister, Jane, travels to find her brother, learns of his hatred for Rezenvelt, and convinces him to apologize. De Monfort appears sincere in his attempts to make up with Rezenvelt and offers him his hand, noting, "I owe my spared life to your forbearance. (*Holding out his hand.*) Take this from one who boasts no feeling warmth, But never will deceive" (Baillie [1798] 2001b: 3.1.192–95). Baillie's stage directions indicate that "*Rezenvelt runs up to him with open arms*" and exclaims, "Away with hands! I'll have thee to my breast" (3.1.196–98). Then, stage directions indicate that De Monfort, "*shrinking back from him,*" cannot embrace Rezenvelt and makes an excuse, claiming that he is "not prepared" and that his "nature is of temp'rature too cold" (3.1.197–98). This meeting in front of family and friends is a high-stakes affair, in which De Monfort is expected to make peace with his enemy. However, the descriptions of De Monfort's expressions, postures, and gestures throughout the play suggest that extreme agitation drives his atten-

---

21. Troy, Shallcross, and Mauss (2013) provide evidence that the effectiveness of different emotion regulation strategies depends on whether or not a situation is perceived as controllable.

tion inward rather than outward; he is unable to read the room, to receive his enemy's embrace, or to fully grasp the effect of his cold behavior.

By the end of the scene, Jane and De Monfort "*look expressively to one another*" (3.1. 347), indicating that both are distressed. Yet the causes of their distress are different. Because Jane is context sensitive, she understands that her brother's attempted apology has failed. In contrast, De Monfort's distress is derived from his hatred of Rezenvelt rather than his failure to appease others. In fact, from the beginning of the play, De Monfort's hatred makes him unable to use context sensitivity, and these uncomfortable moments of failure stand out for the audience. For example, he is also insensitive to the death of a loved one, impatient with servants who are judging him, and overly willing to accept a stranger's story of Jane's engagement to Rezenvelt.

In contrast to De Monfort's failure at context sensitivity, Baillie foregrounds Orra's keen sense of how to read the room. Specifically, Baillie portrays Orra as an intelligent, witty character who uses sarcasm to simultaneously adhere to social conventions (i.e., to maintain context sensitivity) and defy them. When Orra enters the room "*tripping gaily, and playing with the folds of her scarf*" (Baillie [1812] 2007: 1.3.94), her behavior foreshadows her navigation of the tense environment in which she finds herself. Orra knows that something is expected of her, and she responds by ignoring it. The rest of the scene hinges on Orra's defiance of her surrogate father's command that she marry Glottenbal, his son. Orra mocks Glottenbal for losing the jousting tournament, noting that she watched with merriment at his "wondrous grace / So high in air to toss thine armed heels / And clutch with outspread hands the slippry sand" and marveled at his "dexterity" (1.3.105–108). Orra reads Glottenbal's failures and his excuses for them, and she teases him accordingly. Here, Orra uses sarcasm to obtain agency, despite her subservience as a woman and as Hughobert's ward, deftly and subtly chiding her unwanted suitor. She knows what the situation will and will not allow—outward defiance, no; subtle recriminations, yes.

Perhaps Orra's context sensitivity is due to the fact that, unlike De Monfort, Orra does not begin the play in a state of extreme passion (in this case, fear). Orra displays many moments of successful context sensitivity, translatable to the audience, as she negotiates the prevailing male hierarchy. For instance, she extracts herself from a proposal of marriage from another suitor without wounding his pride, thanking him for his offer and noting that should she ever need his strength, "to no sword but [yours] / Will I that service owe" (2.1.83–84). Still, as with De Monfort, once the passion of fear reaches its heights, Orra's context sensitivity fails, a lesson not lost on the audience. In fact, the lesson is clearer because of the juxtaposition of her skill at the beginning of the play and its ultimate deterioration.

5.2. Simulating Repertoire

In evaluating the breadth of repertoire, what is of interest is not just the number of regulatory strategies at hand but also their diversity. Although ultimately unsuccessful at regulating his hatred, De Monfort utilizes a range of strategies. For example, at the beginning of the play, he attempts to leave the city where he and Rezenvelt have been, thus removing himself from the source of his hatred. Awakening, he tells his servant how good he feels: "This pure air / Braces the listless nerves, and warms the blood: / I feel in freedom here" (Baillie [1798] 2001a: 1.2.4–6). Indeed, though others have noted that "something disturbs his mind" (1.1.67) and his friend Count Freberg observes that he finds De Monfort pale, for a brief moment De Monfort notes that he feels "free." Later, using another regulation strategy, De Monfort attempts to suppress his anger through the distraction of reading and prayer. Specifically, Jane asks if she can "pursue with [him] the study of some art, / Or noble science, that compels the mind / To steady thought progressive, driving forth / All floating, wild, unhappy fantasies" (2.2.41–45). Jane thinks she can turn his attention away from previous "unhappy fantasies" so that he can again "bless heaven" (2.2.51). While Jane initially tells her brother that together they will find a way for him to distract himself, once she knows his secret, Jane instead insists that De Monfort suppress his feelings and "repel this hideous foe" (2.2.200). In contrast to his inability to read the room and perhaps because of all the social relationships available to him, De Monfort uses a broad range of regulation strategies (including avoidance, distraction, and suppression), thus indicating to the audience what a strong repertoire might look like. Because ultimately De Monfort fails to regulate his emotion, however, the audience also learns that having a number of different strategies available to use is not enough; emotion regulation requires more.

Conversely, Orra, prompted by a need for control in an environment where she is disempowered, engages a less diverse range of regulatory strategies. Orra's primary means of regulation is distraction, especially in the form of having her lady-in-waiting Cathrina tell her ghost stories. This distraction through fantasy and storytelling, while serving as entertainment, also enables Orra to imagine a world where she is in charge rather than the men around her. When Alice, another lady-in-waiting, asks Orra about the allure of ghost stories, Orra responds, "There is a joy in fear" (Baillie [1812] 2007: 2.1.180). She wants to live in a state where "the cold blood shoots through every vein," since being afraid in dreams and in her imagination is better than "the dreadful waking" (2.1.175. 240). Because of her physical isolation, then, escape into fearful fantasy provides distraction. For Orra, distraction through controlled fear provides "joy" and suppresses the threat of the imposed fear of unwanted marriage. Similarly, when Orra explains to Theobald, a potential suitor, her desire to remain unmarried, she paints a picture of an imagined kingdom where she would rule independently of any husband. Orra further elaborates upon her ideal world, describing in vivid detail a place of women and stories where "way-worn folks, / And noble travellers, and neighb'ring friends, / Both young and old" would be welcome (2.1.115–17). Orra thus primarily regulates the fear of her actual circumstances through a distracting vision. But as the play progresses, Orra's desire for distracting stories regulates her emotion in the wrong direction, thus underscoring the risk of too few strategies, because distraction ultimately increases fear. Orra's lack of repertoire is exposed when she is banished to an abandoned, supposedly haunted castle with the midnight hour approaching. In this moment, Cathrina's ghost stories have not helped. Orra attempts instead to use a different strategy to calm herself, wishing "that my mind / Could raise its thoughts in strong and steady fervor / To HIM, the Lord of all existing things" (4.3.36–38), but she is unable to benefit from prayer. With avoidance unavailable, and because others continue insisting on her marriage, which makes suppression difficult at best, Orra is left with the choice of distraction or reappraisal. Since her abhorrence of forced marriage and violence blocks reappraisal, all she is left with is distraction to regulate emotion.

5.3. Simulating Responsiveness to Feedback

Finally, responsiveness to intra- and interpersonal feedback impacts regulatory success. De Monfort fails to respond to interpersonal feedback from the beginning of the play. Upon Rezenvelt's arrival, Count Freberg immediately notices that De Monfort seems strained: "Thy looks speak not of rest. / Thou art disturbed" (Baillie [1798] 2001a: 1.2.79). He tries to convince De Monfort, pleading "open thy heart to me" (1.2.86). But De Monfort actively rejects attempts by his friend Count Freberg to help him achieve a calmer, less overwrought state, denying that he is feeling distressed and downplaying his agitation. De Monfort acknowledges his inability to respond to interpersonal feedback, exclaiming, "That man was never born whose secret soul / With all its motley treasure of dark thoughts, / Foul fantasies, vain musings, and wild dreams, / Was ever open'd to another's scan. / Away, away! it is all delusion!" (1.2.95–99). Although he recognizes that feedback is offered by a friend, he rejects its potential to alleviate his hatred, unable to imagine that by talking through his feelings he might find relief. Later, alone in his room, De Monfort muses, "I know not how it is, my heart stands back, / And meets not this man's love.—Friends! rarest friends!" (1.1.215–16). In this moment of intrapersonal reflection, although he recognizes the feedback his friend has given him, he is unable to employ it to change strategies or adopt new ones. By witnessing such moments of both interpersonal and intrapersonal feedback, the audience can appreciate the need for such reflections and can imagine using such feedback to regulate their emotion in the future.

Interactions between Orra and the supporting characters demonstrate how a restricted repertoire can result from manipulative interpersonal feedback. In other words, interpersonal feedback can be unproductive; in Orra's case, it augments a pattern of distraction already bordering on obsession. For example, while De Monfort is offered helpful interpersonal feedback by at least two others, Orra is limited by the insidious nature of the interpersonal feedback she receives. Cathrina, under the direction of Rudigere, the villain suitor, continues plying her with ghost stories, masking a failed distraction technique as feedback. In a dire moment of fear, as Orra waits for midnight to be over so that the imagined threat of the ghost of the hunter-knight is past, Cathrina grants Orra's foolhardy request for a story about a time when Cathrina "had look'd upon the spectred dead," the very thing Orra has feared the entire night (Baillie [1812] 2007: 4.3.105). As the stage directions indicate, Orra "*eagerly*" waits for a story about that time. She is unable to benefit from effective interpersonal feedback because none is given and, thus, falls back on a failed distraction technique.

In these moments, Orra does not engage intrapersonal feedback that might have pushed back against the negative interpersonal feedback she receives. For example, after her attempt at praying fails, she exclaims, "Some powerful hindrance / Doth hold me back, and mars all thought" (4.3.46–47), and she continues to imagine the moment of contact between the ghost and herself: "O! If it look on me with its dead eyes! / If it should move its lock'd and earthy lips, / And utt'rance give to the grave's hollow sounds! / If it stretch forth its cold and bony grasp— / O horror, horror!" (4.3.49–53). By failing to recognize distraction as a counterproductive strategy in this moment, Orra shows a total failure of intrapersonal regulation. She has relinquished her ability to self-regulate and is caught therefore in an automatic and inescapable rumination on the hunter-knight. After Orra's failed attempt at prayer, the stage directions note that her body itself seems to increasingly be oppressed by fear: "*sinking lower at every successive idea, as she repeats these last four lines, till she is quite upon her knees on the ground*" (4.3.134). The audience is compelled to reflect on both interpersonal and intrapersonal feedback. The lesson is that people need to be able distinguish between effective and unproductive feedback and act accordingly.

6. Conclusions

We have discussed the role of imagination in learning, which through narrative takes place via simulation. Emphasizing convergence across fields of study, we have built an interdisciplinary bridge for thinking about narrative and the development of sociocognitive skills. We encourage scholars exploring the psychology of fiction to think about regulatory flexibility, a skill just as important as empathy and theory of mind, thus adding to the growing literature on the benefits of fictional narrative. Moreover, we have demonstrated how an interdisciplinary approach allows us to ask and answer questions that are not available to us in controlled laboratory settings. We envision ethical interdisciplinarity: exchanges across disciplines that encourage closer, bidirectional collaborations. Baillie showed us the way by casting an empirical eye on the question of learning from drama and designing, perhaps, one of the first interdisciplinary "experiments" with her passion plays. We are inspired by her methods and take comfort in her championing of the interplay between literature and the scientific method.

References

Aldao, Amelia, Gal Sheppes, and James J. Gross. 2015. "Emotion Regulation Flexibility." *Cognitive Therapy and Research* 39: 263–78.

Alea, Nicole, and Susan Bluck. 2003. "Why Are You Telling Me That? A Conceptual Model of the Social Function of Autobiography Memory." *Memory* 11, no. 2: 165–78.

Baillie, Joanna. (1798) 2001a. "Introductory Discourse." In *Plays on the Passions*, edited by Peter Duthie, 67–113. Ontario: Broadview.

Baillie, Joanna. (1798) 2001b. "De Monfort: A Tragedy." In *Plays on the Passions*, edited by Peter Duthie, 299–387. Ontario: Broadview.

Baillie, Joanna. (1812) 2007. "Orra." In *Six Gothic Dramas*, edited by Christine A. Colón, 85–154. Chicago: Valancourt.

Barrett, Lisa F. 2006. "Are Emotions Natural Kinds?" *Perspectives on Psychological Science* 1, no. 1: 28–58.

Barrett, Lisa F., and Eliza Bliss-Moreau. 2009. "She's Emotional. He's Having a Bad Day: Attributional Explanations for Emotion Stereotypes." *Emotion* 9, no. 5: 649–58.

Barrett, Lisa F., Kristen A. Lindquist, Eliza Bliss-Moreau, Seth Duncan, Maria Gendron, Jennifer Mize, and Lauren Brennan. 2007. "Of Mice and Men: Natural Kinds of Emotions in the Mammalian Brain? A Response to Panksepp and Izard." *Perspectives on Psychological Science* 2, no. 3: 297–312.

Barsalou, Lawrence W. 1999. "Perceptual Symbol Systems." *Behavioral and Brain Sciences* 22, no. 4: 577–660.

Barsalou, Lawrence W. 2010. "Grounded Cognition: Past, Present, and Future." *Topics in Cognitive Science* 2, no. 4: 716–24.

Beer, John. 1992. "Is the Romantic Imagination Our Imagination?" In *Imagining Romanticism: Essays on English and Australian Romanticisms*, edited by Deirdre Coleman and Peter Otto, 25–48. West Cornwall, UK: Locust Hill.

Bernaerts, Lars, Dirk De Geest, Luc Herman, and Bart Vervaeck, eds. 2013. *Stories and Minds: Cognitive Approaches to Literary Narrative*. Lincoln: University of Nebraska Press.

Bonanno, George A., and Charles L. Burton. 2013. "Regulatory Flexibility: An Individual Differences Perspective on Coping and Emotion Regulation." *Perspectives on Psychological Science* 8, no. 6: 591–612.

Bonanno, George A., and Charles L. Burton. 2016. "Regulatory Flexibility and Its Role in Adaptation to Aversive Events throughout the Lifespan." In *Emotion, Aging, and Health,* edited by Anthony D. Ong and Corinna E. Löckenhoff, 71–94. Washington, DC: American Psychological Association.

Brown, Alan S., Kathryn C. Caderao, Lindy M. Fields, and Elizabeth J. Marsh. 2015. "Borrowing Personal Memories." *Applied Cognitive Psychology* 29, no. 3: 471–77.

Burwick, Frederick. 1990. "The Dilemma of the 'Mad Rhapsodist' in Romantic Theories of the Imagination." *Wordsworth Circle* 21, no. 1: 10–18.

Burwick, Frederick. 1996. "Verbal and Visual Modes of Imagination." In *The Romantic Imagination: Literature and Art in England and Germany*, edited by Fredrick Burwick and Jürgen Klein, 1–16. Amsterdam: Ropodi.

Cheung, Elaine O., Wendi L. Gardner, and Jason F. Anderson. 2015. "Emotionships: Examining People's Emotion-Regulation Relationships and Their Consequences for Well-Being." *Social Psychological and Personality Science* 6, no. 4: 407–14.

Clemens, Valdine. 1999. *The Return of the Repressed: Gothic Horror from "The Castle of Otranto" to "Alien".* New York: State University of New York Press.

Coleridge, Samuel Taylor. (1815–17) 1985. "Biographia Literaria." In *Samuel Taylor Coleridge: The Major Works*, edited by H. J. Jackson, 155–482. Oxford: Oxford University Press.

Duncan, Ian. 1992. *Modern Romance and the Transformations of the Novel: The Gothic, Scott, Dickens.* Cambridge: Cambridge University Press.

Farah, Martha J. 1984. "The Neurological Basis of Mental Imagery: A Componential Analysis." *Cognition* 18, no. 1–3: 245–72.

Farah, Martha J. 1995. "Current Issues in the Neuropsychology of Image Generation." *Neuropsychologia* 33, no. 11: 1455–71.

Finke, Ronald A., and Roger N. Shepard. 1986. "Visual Functions of Mental Imagery." In *Handbook of Perception and Human Performance*, edited by Kenneth R. Boff, Lloyd Kaufman, and James P. Thomas, 1–55. New York: Wiley-Interscience.

Gerrig, Richard J. 1993. *Experiencing Narrative Worlds: On the Psychological Activities of Reading.* New Haven: Yale University Press.

Gilbert, Sandra, and Susan Gubar. 2000. *The Madwoman in the Attic: The Woman Writer and the Nineteenth-Century Literary Imagination.* New Haven: Yale University Press.

Gonda, Caroline. 1996. *Reading Daughters' Fictions 1709–1834: Novels and Society from Manley to Edgeworth.* Cambridge: Cambridge University Press.

Green, Melanie C., and Timothy C. Brock. 2000. "The Role of Transportation in the Persuasiveness of Public Narratives." *Journal of Personality and Social Psychology* 79, no. 5: 701–21.

Green, Melanie C., and Timothy C. Brock. 2002. "In the Mind's Eye: Transportation-Imagery Model of Narrative Persuasion." In *Narrative Impact: Social and Cognitive Foundations*, edited by Melanie C. Green, Jeffrey J. Strange, and Timothy C. Brock, 315–42. Mahwah, NJ: Lawrence Erlbaum.

Gross, James J. 1999. "Emotion Regulation: Past, Present, Future." *Cognition and Emotion* 13, no. 5: 551–73.

Gross, James J. 2015. "Emotion Regulation: Current Status and Future Prospects." *Psychological Inquiry* 26, no. 1: 1–26.

Hazlitt, William. (1826) 2010. "On Reason and Imagination." In *On the Pleasure of Hating*, 73–84.

Herbert, Debra M. B., and Jennifer S. Burt. 2004. "What Do Students Remember? Episodic Memory and the Development of Schematization." *Applied Cognitive Psychology* 18, part 1: 77–88.

Hoeveler, Diane L. 1998. *Gothic Feminism: The Professionalization of Gender from Charlotte Smith to the Brontës.* University Park: Pennsylvania State University Press.

Hogan, Patrick C. 2011. *Affective Narratology: The Emotional Structures of Stories.* Lincoln: University of Nebraska Press.

Izard, Carroll E. 2007. "Basic Emotions, Natural Kinds, Emotion Schemas, and a New Paradigm." *Perspectives on Psychological Science* 2, no. 3: 260–80.

Jaén, Isabel, and Julien J. Simon, eds. 2012. *Cognitive Literary Studies: Current Themes and New Directions*. Austin: University of Texas Press.

James, William. 1890. "Imagination." In *The Principles of Psychology*, 690–721. New York: Henry Holt.

Jones, Edward E. 1976. "How Do People Perceive the Causes of Behavior? Experiments Based on Attribution Theory Offer Some Insights into How Actors and Observers Differ in Viewing the Causal Structure of Their Social World." *American Scientist* 64, no. 3: 300–305.

Jones, Edward E., and Richard E. Nisbett. 1971. *The Actor and the Observer: Divergent Perceptions of the Causes of Behavior*. New York: General Learning.

Keen, Suzanne. 2007. *Empathy and the Novel*. Oxford: Oxford University Press.

Keen, Suzanne. 2011. "Introduction: Narrative and the Emotions." *Poetics Today* 32, no. 1: 1–53.

Kilgour, Maggie. 1995. *The Rise of the Gothic Novel*. New York: Routledge.

Klein, Jürgen. 1996. "Genius, Ingenium, Imagination: Aesthetic Theories of Production from the Renaissance to Romanticism." In *The Romantic Imagination: Literature and Art in England and Germany*, edited by Fredrick Burwick and Jürgen Klein, 19–62. Amsterdam: Rodopi.

Koole, Sander L., and Lotte Veenstra. 2015. "Does Emotion Regulation Occur Only Inside People's Heads? Toward a Situated Cognition Analysis of Emotion-Regulatory Dynamics." *Psychological Inquiry: An International Journal for the Advancement of Psychological Theory* 26, no. 1: 61–68.

Kosslyn, Stephen M., Giorgio Ganis, and William L. Thompson. 2001. "Neural Foundations of Imagery." *Nature Reviews*, no. 2: 635–42.

Le Doux, Joseph. 2012. "A Neuroscientist's Perspective on Debates about the Nature of Emotion." *Emotion Review* 4, no. 4: 375–79.

Lee, Kyung H., and Greg J. Siegle. 2012. "Common and Distinct Brain Networks Underlying Explicit Emotional Evaluation: A Meta-analytic Study." *Social Cognitive and Affective Neuroscience* 7, no. 5: 521–34.

Leverage, Paula, Howard Mancing, Richard Schweickert, and Jennifer M. William, eds. 2011. *Theory of Mind and Literature*. West Lafayette, IN: Purdue University Press.

Levy, Jonathan. 1997. "Theatre and Moral Education." *Journal of Aesthetic Education* 31, no. 3: 65–75.

Levy, Jonathan. 2005. "Reflections on How the Theatre Teaches." *Journal of Aesthetic Education* 39, no. 4: 20–30.

Mar, Raymond A. 2011. "The Neural Bases of Social Cognition and Story Comprehension." *Annual Review of Psychology* 62, no. 1: 103–34.

Marsh, Elizabeth J., and Barbara Tversky. 2004. "Spinning the Stories of Our Lives." *Applied Cognitive Psychology* 18, no. 5: 491–503.

Massé, Michelle A. 1992. *In the Name of Love: Women, Masochism, and the Gothic*. Ithaca, NY: Cornell University Press.

McAdams, Dan P., and Kate C. McLean. 2013. "Narrative Identity." *Current Directions in Psychological Science* 22, no. 3: 233–38.

McClelland, James L. 2000. "Connectionist Models of Memory." In *The Oxford Handbook of Memory*, edited by Endel Tulving and Fergus I. M. Craik, 583–96. New York: Oxford University Press.

McFarland, Thomas. 1986. "Imagination and Its Cognates: Supplementary Considerations." *Studies in the Literary Imaginary* 19, no. 2: 35–50.

Mellor, Anne K. 1992. *Romanticism and Gender*. New York: Routledge.

Mellor, Anne K. 2002. *Mothers of the Nation: Women's Political Writing in England, 1780–1830*. Bloomington: Indiana University Press.

Miller, Judi B., Patricia A. deWinstanley, and Pandora Carey. 1996. "Memory for Conversation." *Memory* 4, no. 6: 615–31.

Mumper, Micah L., and Richard J. Gerrig. 2017. "Leisure Reading and Social Cognition: A Meta-Analysis." *Psychology of Aesthetics, Creativity, and the Arts* 11, no. 1: 109–20.

Oatley, Keith. 2011. *Such Stuff as Dreams: The Psychology of Fiction.* Malden, MA: Wiley-Blackwell.

Paivio, Allan. 1970. "On the Functional Significance of Imagery." *Psychological Bulletin* 73, no. 6: 385–92.

Paivio, Allan. 1972. "A Theoretical Analysis of the Role of Imagery in Learning and Memory." In *The Function and Nature of Imagery,* edited by Peter W. Sheehan, 253–79. New York: Academic Press.

Panksepp, Jaak. 2007. "Neurologizing the Psychology of Affects: How Appraisal-Based Constructivism and Basic Emotion Theory Can Coexist." *Perspectives on Psychological Science* 2, no. 3: 281–96.

Pearson, Jacqueline. 1999. *Women's Reading in Britain, 1750–1835.* Cambridge: Cambridge University Press.

Pinker, Steven, and Steven M. Kosslyn. 1983. "Theories of Mental Imagery." In *Imagery: Current Theory, Research, and Application,* edited by Anees A. Sheikh, 43–71. New York: John Wiley and Sons.

Polichak, James W., and Richard J. Gerrig. 2002. "Get Up and Win! Participatory Responses to Narrative." In *Narrative Impact: Social and Cognitive Foundations,* edited by Melanie C. Green, Jeffrey J. Strange, and Timothy C. Brock, 71–96. Mahwah, NJ: Lawrence Erlbaum.

Punter, David. 1996. *The Literature of Terror, the Gothic Tradition: The New History of Gothic Fictions from 1765 to the Present Day.* New York: Longman.

Rabin, Jennifer S., and R. S. Rosenbaum. 2012. "Familiarity Modulates the Functional Relationship between Theory of Mind and Autobiographical Memory." *Neuroimage* 62, no. 1: 520–29.

Richardson, Alan. 1983. "Imagery: Definition and Types." In *Imagery: Current Theory, Research, and Application,* edited by Anees A. Sheikh, 3–42. New York: John Wiley and Sons.

Richardson, Alan. 2001. *British Romanticism and the Science of the Mind.* Cambridge: Cambridge University Press.

Richardson, Alan. 2011. "Defaulting to Fiction: Neuroscience Rediscovers the Romantic Imagination." *Poetics Today* 32, no. 4: 663–92.

Richardson, Alan. 2013. "Reimagining the Romantic Imagination." *European Romantic Review* 24, no. 4: 385–402.

Richter, David. 1996. *The Progress of Romance: Literary Historiography and the Gothic Novel.* Columbus: Ohio University Press.

Savarese, John. 2013. "Reading One's Own Mind: Hazlitt, Cognition, Fiction." *European Romantic Review* 24, no. 4: 437–52.

Schacter, Daniel, and Donna Rose Addis. 2007. "The Cognitive Neuroscience of Constructive Memory: Remembering the Past and Imagining the Future." *Philosophical Transactions of the Royal Society B* 362, no. 1481: 773–86.

Schank, Roger C., and Tamara R. Berman. 2002. "The Pervasive Role of Stories in Knowledge and Action." In *Narrative Impact: Social and Cognitive Foundations,* edited by Melanie C. Green, Jeffrey J. Strange, and Timothy C. Brock, 287–313. Mahwah, NJ: Lawrence Erlbaum.

Schlutz, Alexander M. 2009. *Mind's World: Imagination and Subjectivity from Descartes to Romanticism.* Seattle: University of Washington Press.

Sha, Richard C. 2009a. "Imagination as Inter-Science." *European Romantic Review* 20, no. 5: 661–69.

Sha, Richard C. 2009b. "Toward a Physiology of the Romantic Imagination." *Configurations* 17, no. 3: 197–226.

Shepard, Roger N., and Jacqueline Metzler. 1971. "Mental Rotations of Three-Dimensional Objects." *Science* 171, no. 3972: 701–3.

Sheppes, Gal, Susanne Scheibe, Gaurav Suri, and James J. Gross. 2011. "Emotion Regulation Choice." *Psychological Science* 22, no. 11: 1391–96.

Siddons, Henry. 1807. *Of Rhetorical Gesture and Action, Adapted to the English Drama from a Work on the Same Subject by M. Engel*. London: Printed for Richard Phillips.

Speer, Nicole K., Jeremy R. Reynolds, Khena M. Swallow, and Jeffrey M. Zachs. 2009. "Reading Stories Activates Neural Representations of Visual and Motor Experiences." *Psychological Science* 20, no. 8: 989–99.

Spreng, R. N., and Raymond A. Mar. 2012. "I Remember You: A Role for Memory in Social Cognition and the Functional Neuroanatomy of Their Interaction." *Brain Research*, no. 1428: 43–50.

Tamir, Maya. 2011. "The Maturing Field of Emotion Regulation." *Emotion Review* 3, no. 1: 3–7.

Troy, Allison S., Amanda J. Shallcross, and Iris B. Mauss. 2013. "A Person-by-Situation Approach to Emotion Regulation: Cognitive Reappraisal Can Either Help or Hurt, Depending upon the Context." *Psychological Science* 24, no. 12: 2505–14.

Vermeule, Blakey. 2010. *Why Do We Care about Literary Characters?* Baltimore: Johns Hopkins University Press.

Wallace, Diane. 2013. *Female Gothic Histories: Gender, History, and the Gothic*. Cardiff, UK: University of Wales Press.

Watt, James. 1999. *Contesting the Gothic: Fiction, Genre and Cultural Conflict, 1764–1832*. Cambridge: Cambridge University Press.

Weinstein, Mark A. 1971. "Imagination and Reality in Romantic Fiction." *Wordsworth Circle* 2, no. 4: 126–34.

Williams, Anne. 1995. *Art of Darkness: A Poetics of the Gothic*. Chicago: University of Chicago Press.

Wordsworth, William. [1802] 1994. "Preface to Lyrical Ballads, with Pastoral and Other Poems." In *William Wordsworth, Selected Poems*, edited by John O. Hayden, 431–59. New York: Penguin Books.

Yuille, John C., and Michael J. Catchpole. 1977. "The Role of Imagery in Models of Cognition." *Journal of Mental Imagery* 1, no. 1: 171–80.

Zaki, Jamil, and W. C. Williams. 2013. "Interpersonal Emotion Regulation." *Emotion* 13, no. 5: 803–10.

Zhou, Haotian, Elizabeth A. Majka, and Nicholas Epley. 2017. "Inferring Perspective Versus Getting Perspective: Underestimating the Value of Being in Another Person's Shoes." *Psychological Science* 28, no. 4: 482–93.

Zunshine, Lisa. 2006. *Why We Read Fiction: Theory of Mind and the Novel*. Columbus: Ohio State University Press.

Zunshine, Lisa, ed. 2010. "Lying Bodies of the Enlightenment: Theory of Mind and Cultural Historicism." In *Introduction to Cognitive Cultural Studies*, 115–33. Baltimore: Johns Hopkins University Press.

Adaptive Affective Cognition in Literature and Its Impact on Legal Reason and Social Practice

Marshall Alcorn and Michael O'Neill
George Washington University

Abstract   The concept of *adaptive affective cognition* is developed to explain the affective impact of Richard Wright's novel *Native Son* on the judicial reasoning of the *Brown v. Board of Education* Supreme Court case of 1954. Although research in neuroscience clearly argues that affect contributes decisively to reason, few essays examine the processes, particularity, and significance of this contribution to literary experience. The authors use historical evidence to argue that the affective impact of *Native Son* reorganized cognitive practices authorized by segregation. Adaptive affective cognition explains the paradox of how *Native Son*, while triggering racist fears with the image of the violent, angry black man, also paradoxically reduced those fears.

Keywords   affect, race, cognition, prejudice

Jerome Bruner (2003: 208–9) claims that a new understanding of segregation, conveyed by the literature of the Harlem Renaissance, helped win the *Brown v. Board of Education* Supreme Court case of 1954. Such assertions about the influence of literature on social life—that new understandings of life are triggered by emotionally charged narratives—are part of a long tradition. Plato argued that literature's affective resonance disrupted people's capacity to think rationally, but by the turn of the nineteenth century Percy Bysshe Shelley ([1840] 2002: 535) proclaimed, conversely, that the

We would like to thank Nancy Easterlin and Richard Sha for the care they took to help focus and develop this manuscript.

Poetics Today 40:3 (September 2019)   DOI 10.1215/03335372-7558108
© 2019 by Porter Institute for Poetics and Semiotics

affective power of literature was transformative; for him, poets elicit empathy for others and are therefore "unacknowledged legislators of mankind." Literary scholars are generally cautious about these very common, very old, and much overused claims. Difficult to validate and therefore to incorporate into serious scholarship, they traditionally emerge in contexts of enthusiastic subjective judgment.

Bruner was coached by the NAACP in preparation for the 1952 Delaware Educational Board case, one of five that were combined into the 1954 Supreme Court case. Based on his experience in 1952, Bruner (2003: 54) asserted that the "voices" of "Langston Hughes and Richard Wright" were "heard" in the background of the 1954 Supreme Court case.[1] Bruner, speaking as a witness for the plaintiff in the 1952 case, gave an account of the damage to self-respect inflicted by segregation, only to discover that the attorney representing Delaware's public schools chose not to cross-examine him (55). Such arguments were at that point in history too powerful to oppose.

Wright's *Native Son*, a fictional account of segregation's damage to self-respect, is dramatic and memorable. The novel features a fictional court case not markedly different from the real one Marshall presented to the Court in 1954. At the time, Wright's work was prominent in East Coast reading culture. *Native Son* had been promoted by the Book of the Month Club and had sold unusually well; furthermore, the NAACP had awarded the prestigious Spingarn Medal to Wright in 1941, the year after the novel was published. Bruner was undoubtedly correct about the court hearing Wright's voice in the background of the case; many among the judicial elite remembered Wright, and Wright's fictional case, when they tried Brown. The 1954 case was heard in the affectively charged context of Wright's novel. Wright's novel had contributed heavily to changed assumptions about segregation.

Now new research in cognitive neuroscience illuminates the affective processes set in motion by the novel and explains the impact of these processes on the legal thinking that resolved the case. Current research supports three interrelated generalizations: first, that literature increases reader empathy with others (Kidd and Castano 2013, 2017; Mumper and Gerrig 2017); second, that literature activates and works on not just cognitive processes but also bodily, kinesthetic, and affective experience that can be the ground of value assessment (Starr 2013); and third, that affect defines and redefines categories of value that are crucial for linguistic reasoning and also central to judgments of racial bias (Damasio 1995, 2000; Dolan 2002).

1. Bruner was an expert witness recruited by Thurgood Marshall and his team in the 1952 *Belton (Bulah) v. Gebhart* Delaware segregation case. Four public school segregation cases were moving forward in the courts (Kansas, Delaware, Virginia, and the District of Columbia); they were later consolidated for the Supreme Court case of *Brown v. Board of Education* in 1954.

This essay will examine the impact of *Native Son* on racial bias, using Wright's novel to explore its documented relations to important affective cultural shifts in racial awareness and legal reasoning. Our primary focus will be on testimony regarding the work's sheer affective force, particularly in its initial raw and unstructured form. Raw and unstructured forms of experience, we will argue, may be more important than the cognitive experience that follows them. Raw affective impact shifts evaluative categories that give real power to conceptual meanings. Readers often initially register the reading experience not with a systematic cognitive clarity but with the wordless experience of being profoundly moved, a sometimes inarticulate but abiding bodily phenomenon. By contrast, in conscious ratiocination, readers may pause for a second at the end of a thoughtful sentence but soon go on to other new and different meanings, sentences, and ideas. Affective moods, moreover, last longer than the experience of registering meaning in a single sentence. They persist in their influence and color, over time, the tones of meanings represented through many sentences and pages. Affective moods contribute powerfully to meanings generated by a play of thought over a lengthy period of time. Through mood, the salience of particular words becomes memorable. Concepts, linked to words, find new affective resonances and associated networks of meaning and value. Reading has personal and social impact when affect is intense and when complex experiences of cognition are brought in to play within new affective states and are allowed to develop over time, changing habitual patterns of affective response and their attendant implicit values.

Appreciative recognition of the raw power of texts can be found in responses to works as diverse as Wright's *Native Son* and Longinus's description of the Sublime, and it is seen often in everyday classroom discussions. Affective responses express experiences of value and are thus more consequential than is commonly recognized. Value determines what matters in a sea of information, and such value recognition, neuroscientific research suggests, is necessary for adaptive reasoning. Further, new experiences of value give new affective resonance to established conceptual terminology, shifting their possible terminological links within novel networks of social discourse.

We propose that literary affective cognition can move readers profoundly, subsequently facilitating cognitive, verbally coherent reorganizations of judgment and value. Our use of the phrase *adaptive affective cognition* is indebted to Daniel Stern's (1985) "implicit cognition," which signifies highly sophisticated cause-and-effect reasoning and intention in children before they develop language.[2] Developmentally, affective experience informs memory, initiates nonverbal cognition, and contributes to internalized approach/avoid maps for interacting with the environment. It does so, research suggests, independently of linguistic reason. Contemporary neuroscience adds further support to our notion of adaptive affective cognition, because findings indicate that emotion is central to human reason.[3] In short, adaptive affective cognition registers, formulates, and retains experiential values that are foundational to reason and to emergent choice and intention. Affective systems mark bodily experiences of value and orient bodies prelinguistically toward values.

According to evolutionary theory, emotions are functionally central to survival; Darwin ([1872] 2009) suggests that they evolved to promote flexible responses in organism-environment interaction. As Patrick Colm Hogan (2016: 8) defines it, "an emotion is the activation of some motivation system." For sophisticated human animals, emotion typically contributes to intention before verbal reason comes into play. Because individuals and groups must often define intentions in response to competing emotional demands, affective cognition prioritizes and selects among them, grasping patterns in motivational impulses and clarifying intentions as the body moves in the world, responding instinctively to affective signals. Such movement, moreover, is cognitively adaptive. Affective cognition is ongoing and formulates newly adaptive affective responses to a changing environment. Moreover, and especially significant here, because humans are highly social animals, groups generate shared affective intentions. At times, however, the intentions of

2. Stern (1985), a child psychologist, offers a rich account of how nonsymbolic embodied thinking operates; see also Stern et al. 1998. The phrase *affective cognition* has been used in different ways in cognitive science (Ong, Zaki, and Goodman, 2015); humanities scholars have recently begun to employ it to describe both reasoning in response to emotion and a nonlinguistic form of adaptive cognition grounded in affective evaluation. Contributors to *The Palgrave Handbook of Affect Studies and Textual Criticism* adopt similar phrasing and accounts of psychological processes (e.g., Harbus 2017; Miller 2017). *The Cognitive Emotional Brain* offers a thorough neuroscientific account of cognitive emotional interactions (Pessoa 2013). Richard Sha (2017) and Alcorn (2017) used the phrase *affective cognition* in their essays. We are indebted to Sha for the more specific use of the concept developed here.

3. The terms *affect* and *emotion* have been used differently by affect theorists. Although scholars under the influence of Brian Massumi use the terms differently than we do here, we use the term *emotion* to refer to particular primary emotions and their physiology, described first by Tomkins (2008) as nine emotions present at birth and later expanded by Ekman (2003) to include eleven more emotions, such as relief, embarrassment, contempt, and amusement. We find an understanding of primary emotions to be valuable but are suspicious of the claim that human affective experience can be defined by pure primary emotions, and thus use the term *affect* to refer to both affect and emotion as a system, or more often, as competing part-systems linked to self-regulation. Others quoted in this essay use the term *emotion* when we would use the term *affect*. See Margaret Wetherell (2012) for a useful summary and analysis of major representations of affect-emotion theories.

different social groups are in conflict. In modern culture, court cases address the competing demands of social groups with careful, systematic, and sustained deliberation. In this process, important court cases impact society and have unusual power to change group practices.

Change emerges from multiple, often opposed, interactions of individuals and groups. But a central problem for social change is that the suffering of marginalized people is often invisible. And since group identity is frequently organized around the subordination of exploited, suffering social others whose distress is unrecognized and misrepresented, the challenge for social progress is in formulating dramatic representations of this plight. Examining the impact of Wright's *Native Son*, we will sketch an understanding of a socially progressive affective functioning that responds to human suffering and, in turn, seeks remedies.

1. Social Progress and Affective Visibility

A major shift in perception and in the attendant definition of racial equality between 1896 and 1954 is key to the landmark judgments of those dates. Before the 1954 *Brown v. Board of Education* case, school segregation was legally supported by the 1896 case of *Plessy v. Ferguson*. *Plessy* assumed that comparable material conditions — equivalent access to textbooks, classroom facilities, and the like — constituted the heart of equality. By contrast, *Brown* emphasized sociological and psychological research about the inner lives of people affected by segregation. In doing so, it welcomed new stories about black lives into the courtroom, and many of these stories, most particularly the self-reports of black children, resonated powerfully with the court. As Gwen Bergner (2009: 299) summarizes it,

> The landmark 1954 Supreme Court decision in *Brown v. Board of Education* dealt a lethal blow to the "separate but equal" doctrine of segregation established by *Plessy v. Ferguson* in 1896; it did so largely on the grounds that segregation damages African American children's self-esteem. In the Court's words, "to separate [children] from others of similar age and qualifications solely because of their race generates a feeling of inferiority as to their status in the community that may affect their hearts and minds in a way unlikely ever to be undone" (*Brown v. Board of Education* 1954). Because of this psychological harm, the Court determined, African American children could never get an education equal to white children's in a segregated school, no matter how good the physical facilities or curriculum.

Chief Justice Earl Warren wrote the judgment for the ruling, declaring the Court decision unanimous. Laws supporting segregation were "inherently unequal" and therefore unconstitutional.[4] In 1896, inattentive to the internal lives of black people, *Plessy* had decreed that the separation of the races did not imply inferiority. In *Brown*, attention to the inner lives of black people generated a new story about self-esteem; replacing a previous story and ruling about material equality, it resulted in an impressive legal accomplishment.

In fact, the cultural shifts that gave a hearing to black voices had actually begun much earlier. Testifying in a different case two years before *Brown*, Bruner (2003: 54) had argued that "the American tradition of consciousness and protest" had created a new understanding of segregation, largely effected by the literature of the Harlem Renaissance. In his words, a group of African American authors writing ten years before *Brown*, including Richard Wright and James Baldwin, "had plenty to say about what it felt like to live Jim Crow" (55). Wright published *Native Son* in 1940, and that novel influenced both Baldwin and Ralph Ellison. Additionally, in 1945 Wright published the nonfictional *Black Boy*; his accounts of his experiences, as represented in both fiction and nonfiction, figured in many academic books seeking to understand racial experience. These voices became part of legal thinking because of changes in legal practice developed in 1908.

The 1954 *Brown* decision was made possible by a new form of legal practice: the Brandeis brief, first employed in 1908 by Louis Brandeis.[5] Winning a case on worker's rights, Brandeis went on to become a Supreme Court justice in 1916. The Brandeis brief allowed new forms of discourse — testimony and academic research — to circulate and support argumentation in legal deliberation. Academic research was not plentiful in 1908; by 1954, when Thurgood Marshall adopted the Brandeis brief effectively for legal reasoning in the *Brown* decision, a huge reservoir of academic discourse on race was available. Moreover, Richard Wright had himself inspired and contributed to some of it, writing an introduction to Horace Cayton and St. Clair Drake's pathbreaking 1946 sociological work, *Black Metropolis*, and influencing a host of academic literature discussing race relations and segregation.

Records also show that a number of black narratives had especially powerful affective impacts on the thinking of the justices. Kenneth and Mamie Clark's sociological study of the choices of dolls by black children from Clarendon County, South Carolina, is a well-known case in point. In their exper-

---

4. *Brown v. Board of Education of Topeka*, 74 S. Ct. 686 (1954).
5. In the 1908 Supreme Court case *Muller v. Oregon*, Brandeis argued in support of a state law restricting the hours women were allowed to work, applying research from medicine and social science to support his claims (see Sturm 1989). Brandeis, then a relatively young lawyer, submitted a brief of more than one hundred pages with only two pages of argumentation from legal precedents. Instead, Brandeis used testimony from doctors and social scientists asserting that long working hours had a negative impact on the "health, safety, morals, and general welfare of women" (Johnson 2006: 206).

iment, the Clarks handed black children four dolls, all identical except that two had a dark-colored skin and two had light-colored skin. The Clarks asked the children which dolls were "nice" and which were "bad," and "Which doll is most like you?" The results showed that the majority of black children preferred the white dolls to the black dolls, labeled the black dolls "bad," and aspired to identification with the white dolls. To the Clarks, these tests provided solid proof that enforced segregation stamped African American children with a badge of inferiority that would last the rest of their lives. Dr. Clark offered a striking example in which one young black girl is recorded as pointing to a brown doll and asserting identification, "That's nigger. I am a nigger" (NAACP Legal Defense Fund 2014).[6]

Lawyers commonly recognize that a major task of any prosecution lawyer is to have the jury or judges identify with, rather than detach from, the story told by the plaintiff. Earl Warren and his court clearly identified with the young girls in the Clarks' experiment. Chief Justice Warren, writing the Court's opinion, displayed considerable empathy for the plaintiffs. He argued that the legal separation of black children from white children gave them "a feeling of inferiority as to their status in the community that may affect their hearts and minds in a way unlikely to ever be undone."[7] Richard Wright's fictional court case of 1940 had outlined a very similar argument and had sought to develop sympathy for the black experience of segregation. Bruner, in his account of his own experience with lawyers linked to the case, argued that this capacity to identify with African American experience was very heavily influenced by African American novels.

John Semonche (2000) argues that Supreme Court cases begin as expressions of conflicts in social links. Important cases operate as focal points where social bonds among American groups are contested, judged, and reorganized. As social groups experience antagonism over rights and property, the law works not only to resolve antagonism but also to formulate new ideals for social ties. Semonche (2000: 1) observes that "the Supreme Court of the United States, which is at the apex of the country's legal system, plays a central role in explicating, reinforcing, and expanding the range of these ties." The conflict in a court case may be very specific, but the affective conflicts that generate a case are broader in scope than the conflict itself. In consequence, when the case is resolved, the diverse social affects that attend the conflict may be synthesized more expansively than those affects

6. Recent scholarship suggests that the process of identification described by Clark was more complicated than his account. But American culture had, by that time, accepted overwhelmingly, an understanding of segregation's damage to self-esteem. See Gwen Bergner (2009).
7. Bessel Van Der Kolk (2015) describes how traumatic memory remains alive in the brain as an affective threat long after the initial threat is over.

proper to the original conflict. For instance, whereas the abolition of public school segregation was the immediate result of the 1954 Supreme Court ruling in *Brown v. Board of Education*, that ruling ultimately led to the desegregation of all public facilities, including train cars, restaurants, and department stores. It is as if the court case illuminated the nature of a whole system of social practices and found them injurious.

Overturning legal precedent is a momentous event and, in the case under discussion here, both real-life and fictional narratives played a major role. In light of overwhelming evidence of harm, the moral authority of *Plessy* was superseded in the *Brown* decision of 1954. A new and socially authoritative moral value, that segregation is wrong, attests to the emotional impact of a story about children playing with dolls and fiction portraying black experience; the *Brown* decision served as an affective anchor for a host of linked concepts making new sense of segregation throughout an array of cultural discourses.

2. Literary Contributions to Legal Reason

Literature from the Harlem Renaissance increased the visibility of black experience. Toward the end of Wright's *Native Son*, the protagonist, Bigger Thomas, laments, "White folks and black folks is strangers. We don't know what each other is thinking" (Wright [1940] 1998: 362). This lack of mutual understanding enabled laws such as *Plessy* to deny the suffering of African Americans, largely because the experience of racial injustice did not circulate across social spaces and hence went unperceived. Wright's novel effectively illuminated the suffering caused by segregation, and it also gave white people reasons for wanting to stop such suffering.

We want to emphasize the importance of sheer shock response to the novel, which brings readers close to Bigger's suffering, violence, and rage. Affective cognition, in reading, begins in wordlessness and then gropes for adequate, new language to grasp the experience. Conceptual understandings of Wright's *Native Son* take many forms but repeatedly attest to initial shock and discomfort. For example, reading *Native Son* as an undergraduate in 1970, African American novelist David Bradley felt violent antipathy:

> Put simply, I hated *Native Son*. Put more accurately, I hated it with a passion. Hated it because it violated most of the principles of novelistic construction I was struggling to master. The plot was improbable, the narrative voice intrusive, the language often stilted and the characters — especially that silly little rich white tease Mary Dalton and her stupid, gigolo Communist boyfriend, Jan — were stereotypical beyond belief. At first I tried to rationalize these flaws as precisely the

"ineptitude" and "unfitness" that James T. Stewart had written about. But I couldn't get around what I hated with a passion: Bigger Thomas. (Bradley 1986, citing Stewart 1968)

Bradley ultimately changed his mind about the value of the novel and went on to edit an edition of *Native Son* later in his career.

Untrained readers respond largely to character and situation, and to them *Native Son* presents the affective-cognitive challenge of a violent black man in a violent world. For white readers, antihero Bigger triggers racial fears, and for this reason, James Baldwin, like Bradley, found Wright's practice counterproductive. He denounced *Native Son* for having an unrealistic, stereotyped central character, a black ape gone wild. However, Wright purposely creates an antihero who is the fictional embodiment of white paranoid fantasies of black violence rather than seeking to make African American males generous and harmless. Bigger, a powerfully angry and violent black man, kills the innocent and molests white women.

Through affective cognition, the novel forces white readers to reorganize their emotions and redefine their fears. As readers engage with Bigger, they come to learn that Bigger is himself harrowed by his own brutality. Fearing Bigger, they learn that Bigger fears himself. This offers opportunities for identification. Mark Bracher (2013: 239–40) points out that the novel invites a set of increasingly affectively distant perspectives on Bigger's brutality as the narrative progresses. Suffering from the remembered image of the bloody head of Mary, one of the women he has killed, Bigger rationalizes what he has done: "Hell, she made me do it. I couldn't help it" ([1940] 1998: 113). A reader may, in reading such a line, be encouraged to hate Bigger for this response. However, Wright moves gradually away from the immediacy and intensity of this image to bring the reader into a larger awareness of Bigger's experience. For instance, Mary's boyfriend, Jan, visits Bigger and confesses, "I see now that you couldn't do anything else but that . . . I'm the one who ought to be in jail for murder instead of you" (288). Still later in the novel, in the culminating court case, Bigger's Marxist lawyer Boris Max makes an extended argument that the social system is the source of Bigger's evil.

Because the novel progressively distances readers from the unsettling experience of violence, they can gain purchase on their fears, locating the cause of violence less in the character and more in the culture that has created him—a culture that the readers' everyday social fears have, in part, created. Thus, although the affective core is violent and brutal, the narrative brings the reader face to face with this core, then slowly moves away, developing an increasingly reflective and affectively complex integrative response. An immediate affective response is modulated, not simply by thought, but by affective responses to the original response. Wright, in effect, shocks with affect and then demands that the reader judge what such an experience means. For many, the final impact of the novel was to lay bare the injustice of racist practice.

Caribbean and British writer Caryl Phillips, reading at leisure on a California beach, describes his encounter with *Native Son* as a life-changing event. It was "as if an explosion had taken place inside my head. If I had to point to any one moment that seemed crucial in my desire to be a writer, it was then, as the Pacific surf began to wash up around the deck chair. The emotional anguish of the hero, Bigger Thomas, the uncompromising prosodic muscle of Wright" (Phillips 2002: 18 – 19). Phillips argues that it is, very emphatically, his identification with the "emotional anguish" of Bigger Thomas that reorganized his own system of affect. Affect here seems to serve as a trigger for a cascade of cognitive developments. The tradition in literary scholarship that ignores testimonials such as this from Phillips and lay readers alike casts aside critical frameworks for analyzing literature's affective impact.

3. Affect and the Redefinition of Value

Neuroscience shows that affect contributes to the redefinition of value as it operates in the process of reason. Writing in *Science*, R. J. Dolan (2002) synthesizes twenty years of research in response to the initial groundbreaking work of Antonio Damasio and Joseph LeDoux, arguing that reason needs to work with affective categories of value to appraise deliberative action. In his first studies, Damasio (1995, 2000) analyzed the brain damage suffered by the nineteenth-century railroad worker Phineas Gage and his corresponding change in behavior, demonstrating that reason devoid of affect lacks secure grounding in experiential values. LeDoux (1996) observes that affect precedes conscious awareness and structures what emerges as an experience of cognition.

In contrast to human cognition, machine reason need not use affect to appraise value but works with stable, quantifiable units. For instance, a smartphone can calculate the best route to take to Virginia when there is heavy traffic in downtown DC, and computers can win chess games. But many critically important forms of human reason require ongoing affective input, synthesis, and recalibration. In calculating the best route to a destination, humans also "calculate" *why*, a category informed by ongoing unconscious, prelinguistic, emotional knowing and memory. *Why* responds to a felt sense of self that keeps track of motivational impulse and seems to have at its disposal a whole lifetime of memory. The acts of reflection and reverie can also be vital for the conscious reorganization of networks of affect. Marshall may think he wants to go to Baltimore, but if he reflects on his priorities, he may find that his initial affective desire has been recoded. Crucially, information available to the mind in one temporal context is not available until a more reflective mode brings wider networks of memory into operation. Thus, affect and memory may not be immediately available to a decision-making process but may become available by shifting the mind into an imaginative or reflective mode that reassesses memory and value.

Imagination, understood thus as a complex affective-cognitive process, is crucial to ongoing action. Experience sediments affective values, but such values must be constantly recalibrated by increasingly sophisticated forms of imagination, complex acts of attention, consolidated physiological experience, and reflection. The affective categories of value we develop at age fourteen must give way to more complex values at age forty. Though not fully conscious, changes in affective values are constant and ongoing. Dolan (2002: 1191) claims that this

> ability to ascribe value to events in the world [is] a product of evolutionary selective processes ... evident across phylogeny. ... Value in this sense refers to an organism's facility to sense whether events in its environment are more or less desirable. Within this framework, emotions represent complex psychological and physiological states that, to a greater or lesser degree, index occurrences of value.

Specific states are experienced in the context of larger, meaning-conferring affective networks that orient organisms in their environment. Memory thus defines and keeps in play an evolving system of value that works iteratively to appraise objects and events of the world in relation to remembered rewards.

If Wright's Bigger Thomas can mobilize white racial fears and then, by means of affective triggers, reduce those fears, the experience of reading *Native Son* reduces racial bias. If these affective experiences also contribute to long-term memory, then this reading experience marks a lasting change in attitude. But how do established and remembered fears become adjusted through a reading process? Researchers argue that our brains regularly adjust memory so that affective lessons of the past can be redefined by new affect and thus contribute to better future planning, preventing unsuitable, repetitive responses.

In many cases, people have trouble developing new responses, as studies in the neuroscience of trauma highlight.[8] Trauma resets the brain, so that memories of overwhelming experiences are not easily or not at all modified by new experience. Traumatized individuals continue to anticipate similar stressful encounters even when the old situations of combat, rape, or catas-

---

8. *Brown v. Board of Education*, 74 S. Ct. 686.

trophe are no longer present (Herman 1992; Williams et al. 2006; Van der Kolk 2014). In such cases, constantly haunted by ghosts of the past, one perceives objects not directly but as a projection of anticipated threats such that real objects may not be seen or experienced at all. In trauma, an illness determined by memory's inability affectively to adjust to new experience, biochemicals released by stress damage the operation of the amygdala and hippocampus, and real objects become habitual albeit unrealistic triggers for past fears.

Racism has a structural similarity to trauma: it is an affectively alive but, in truth, imaginary threat triggered by imagined objects: marginalized people. Threat experiences, left unprocessed by new adjustments in affective experience, generate "complex psychological and physiological states" constantly "on tap" as threat signals. Reason may seek to change this pattern of repetition, but is powerless in relation to affective demand. Changes in this fear memory require shifts not just in rational thought but in affective experience. In this sense, literary experiences with race simulate affective practices and are more important than dispassionate exercises in reasoning about race. *Native Son* changed racial values for many readers, and in this respect its impact is not so different from the use of exposure therapy to diminish traumatic memory. While generating habitual, repetitive fear, the novel simultaneously controls the contextualization of and reflection on fear so that initial appraisals of black males as threats are modified by new affective information.

4. The Case for Adaptive Affective Cognition

In 1963, Irving Howe proclaimed that "the day *Native Son* appeared, American culture was changed forever" (Howe 1963: 354). Howe argued that the novel exposed a whole system of racist thinking, "[making] impossible a repetition of the old lies. In all its crudeness, melodrama, and claustrophobia of vision, Richard Wright's novel brought out into the open, as no one ever had before, the hatred, fear, and violence that have crippled and may yet destroy our culture" (355). Paradoxically, the novel makes the old lies about race impossible precisely as it intensifies and makes visible "hatred, fear, and violence."

How does a story about a violent black man dispel racial bias? Dolan (2002: 1194) observes that the "evocation of past feeling states biases the decision making process toward or away from a particular behavioral option." Affects operate according to an approach/avoidance logic to provide organisms with an autonomic but flexible system of situational appraisal and subsequent action, and good and bad encounters with the world train memory via powerful affective encodings. Additionally, memory's durability is in relation to the intensity of affect. Adaptive affective cognition thus evolves for quick response in complex situations, foreshadowing perception. Affective systems think in terms of cause and affect; they can experiment with and offer a syntax of varied responses to similar problems.[9] Perceptual memories leave representational markers in the body and influence ongoing perception. Pleasure and pain, actions and consequences, are remembered by the body, and the body, acting in response to internal affective cues, adaptively navigates its way through the world.

The primacy of nonconscious processes influencing thought and behavior currently enjoys acceptance across an array of fields. Developmentally complex cause-effect intentional structures emerge in children as a form of implicit nonverbal knowledge. Learning through interactions with caretakers, children show, according to Stern et al. (1998: 903), "anticipations and expectations and manifest surprise or upset at violations of the expected." Stern argues that "implicit knowing is registered in representations of interpersonal events in a non-symbolic form, beginning in the first year of life" (905). Stern et al. (1998: 903) have termed this emerging domain of affective mapping of self-world encounters "implicit relational knowing"; it is organized around cause-effect interactions, recorded in implicit memory, largely unconscious, and affectively active.

These developmental claims are convergent with an embodied mind perspective in cognitive science and cognitive literary studies, which holds that the mind-brain is inextricable from the body and its functions, many of which are habituated and unconscious. In her work on human wayfinding cognition, Nancy Easterlin (2012: 37) challenges dominant assumptions that "thought is predominantly language based." She cites Merlin Donald's account of the evolution of presymbolic thought through other modalities. Reason, Donald (1993: 353) argues, operates in "parallel representational channels"; these "channels" attain a "level of structured logic and concepts" and are grounded nonlinguistic forms of experience. "Words and sentences," he says, "define and clarify knowledge that resides elsewhere, in foundational semantic processes that we share with other primates" (2001: 277).

This account of unconscious cognition is consistent with Antonio Damasio's (2000: 109) discussion of "dispositional representations" contributing to decision making "in embodied human thought." Damasio documents cases of people who lose the ability to use language yet still retain a sophisticated capacity for cognition and reason. If Donald is correct, our brains utilize

9. Aristotle argued long ago that this interior mental life works with something like representation that is not quite a language (MacCready-Flora 2014; Alcorn 2017).

several different channels in decision making, one being rational thought. But many decisions must be fast and intuitive, having evolved for quick response to bodily cues in situations where delays in response can mean death.

Novels work, of course, through the medium of language, but literary language, with its stylistic choice and narrative focus, can represent concrete situations that trigger affect and then amplify that affect by means of selective attention to triggering objects. Caryl Phillips's (2002) account of a new sense of purpose engendered by his reading of *Native Son* suggests that for him, Wright's novel operated as an intense experience that reformulated an existing system of affective cognition; racial fears are changed by being more fully exposed and thus understood. Similarly, Howe's description of the impact of *Native Son* upon a racist norm in American social life asserts that it worked to reformulate existing dispositional representations. For readers like Phillips and Howe, the novel not only made black experience visible but was a "sublime" experience. As Longinus (1890: VII:4) argues, sublime experience is difficult, "indeed impossible to withstand, for the memory of it is strong and hard to efface." In effective literature, style triggers affective experience through its many modes of direct and indirect communication.

Experiences described as sublime have a powerful reorganizing affective force, pushing everyday cognition aside. Experiences of fear, loss, or hope impact cognitive function with immediacy and intensity. The force of uncontrollable affect colors cognition and mingles new affective valences with new cognitive representations.[10] It pushes the reader to new modes of perception; new modes of perception then trigger new reflections that bring a large domain of affect into new systems of meaning and impacting memory. The memory, "strong and hard to efface," persists and reorients a new flow of interlinked meanings that emerge linguistically in thought and discourse.

Mary Helen Immordino-Yang and Antonio Damasio (2007: 40) argue that "the neurobiological evidence suggests that the aspects of cognition that we recruit most heavily in schools, namely learning attention, memory, decision making and social functioning are both profoundly affected by and subsumed within the processes of emotion; we call these aspects emotional thought." Focusing on the transfer of knowledge from the structured and programmatic school environment to real-world decision making, their work suggests that affect is not some addition to thought but a physical brain state necessary for certain kinds of cognitive practices. Students may memorize many facts

10. Psychiatrist Wilfried Bion (1962) has argued that although people think to solve problems, the rationality of many thoughts is diverted by powerful affects of love, hate, and a desire to not know. Problem-solving cognition begins but is often undone by affective demands pulling cognitive links in irrational directions.

for classroom testing, but these facts may contribute nothing to real problem-solving responses to real-world events, which are experienced in terms of their affective impact. That is in fact what makes them "problems." Problems of race, for example, are clearly one area in which a rote memory solution offered by structured school learning is not easily transferred to real-world decision making. Paula Ioanide (2015: 3) argues that to combat racist thought, we need to do emotional work on the affective practices that support racist agendas.

Literary experience offers opportunities for emotional work, but the information gained from such emotional work does not always enter into or remain in memory as a resource for reason. In order for new information to contribute to processes of reason, it must be internalized in memory as working information available for cognition. Some information registered by the mind that should be used as evidence for reason never enters into consciousness and working memory. Based on his work with patients suffering from anosognosia, V. S. Ramachandran (1995, 1999) argues that, in states of denial, special brain processes are necessary to make emotionally discordant information thinkable. We suggest that the affective experience of *Native Son* functions to generate old affective habits of thought and then repeatedly puts new affective pressure on such habits. Minds already stuck in habituated patterns of racial bias anticipate and repeat their bias both before and while, they read the novel. The novel generates change by means of affective pressure and conflict. It increases the reader's confrontation with conflicting information and brings habitual affective bias into sharp and ongoing affective contradiction. In the context of the novel's well-organized and repeated cognitive and affective conflict, new processes of affect, generated by processes of attention, reverie, and reflection and modes of internalization, similar to REM memory processing, reorganize existing affective habits (Alcorn 2013). This internalization process relies on affective experiences of reading becoming integrated within more complex and habituated patterns of affect already existing in the reader. This process of internalization and integration, which we argue is essential to the experience of the novel, is described in part by G. Gabrielle Starr (2013) in her account of aesthetic experience.

Starr's empirical research at the NYU Center for Brain Imaging suggests that literary experience, with its affective and reflective dimensions, internalizes new experience and reorders affective habits. She observes, "Aesthetic experience starts with sensations or imagery, which we analyze perceptually and semantically and which engage processes of memory as well as of emotion; these sensations and images also have evolving reward value" (Starr 2013: 24). Objects and events marked with reward value impact affect, generate motivation, and hold in memory expectations of value. *Native Son* generates habits and memories of racial bias and replaces those affective habits with a capacity for white people to recognize the value of the racial Other, thus contributing to an "evolving reward value." White readers' habits of fantasy, of imagery and affect, are put into motion and, as meaningful experiences derived from the text impact these images and affects, new practices of affect and imagery evolve. Starr suggests that "mental images" — referring not to pictorial representations but to images across sensory modalities, in accord with neuroscientific terminology — "can serve to integrate a variety of information and expand our ways of knowing" (78).

Literature offers us an opportunity to expand not simply our thinking but our bodily access to new experiences, including the affective reorganization of irrational racial fear. Alexa Weik von Mossner (2014: 122) argues that "in Wright's novels fear, and its more sustained relative anxiety, tend to precede and sometimes cause other negative and potentially dangerous emotions" (see also Warnes 2006: 40). Fear circuits are part of an affective system that calibrates action in the world. This system controls behavior, sending "low road" signals of threat directly to the amygdala, thus generating immediate reactive response, such as fight, flight, or freeze, and bypassing thought-generating cortical regions (LeDoux 1994; Myers and Davis 2012). Fear memories stored in long-term memory continue to generate fear behavior, unless they are reconsolidated or their trigger capacity is blocked by newer, competing memories. Just as exposure therapy for trauma has the capacity to modulate traumatic fear, so also simulated exposure therapy for racial fears can change those biased affects. As old fears are reactivated and put to rest through affective reconsolidation, new possibilities for cognition emerge.

In its entirety, *Native Son* works on the "fear circuits" of the racialized brain and complicates those circuits by bringing, slowly and repeatedly, problem-solving thought to bear upon fear cues, operating thus as a kind of exposure therapy for ineffective anxiety triggers. Long-term affective memories must be reactivated, worked on, and redefined in effective aesthetic experience that generates and then works with powerful emotion. Such processing, through reflection, fantasy, and imagination, allows the memory reconsolidation mechanisms of the brain to rework entrenched fears, holding in place particular markers for the fear circuit.

Wright scholars have long observed the systemic and cyclical functioning of fear in *Native Son*: people fear Bigger, but his violence is caused by the system that they themselves perpetuate, and thus reduction of violence requires a change in the system that produces it (Fanon [1952] 2008; Weik von Mossner 2014; Warnes 2007). As Frantz Fanon noted in 1952, Bigger himself carries white fear inside, a portion of his fear of himself. If that fear is not contained by Bigger, it will spill out into the world and fill it. Wright's achievement is that he enables at least some white readers to carry Bigger's fears, and in so doing, diminish their own fears. Weik von Mossner (2014: 122) argues that "*Native Son, The Outsider* and 'Islands of Hallucination' encourage us to think critically about the role of the surrounding socio-cultural conditions in the development of such protracted forms of negative emotion and related feelings of powerlessness." Critical thoughts about race often require not just a logical process of thought, but something more — emotional work. Affects must be generated, and affects must be held in mind through a process of consciously and nonconsciously dwelling affectively with their implications. The more intensely affects can be generated, the more effectively existing systems of affect can be shifted.

Porayska-Pomsta et al. (2013: 107) observe, "Emotions are crucial to learning, but their nature, the conditions under which they occur, and their exact impact can be challenging, because emotions are subjective, fleeting phenomena that are often difficult for learners to report accurately and for observers to perceive reliably." Our analysis of the affective impact of *Native Son* suggests that the emotion triggered by *Native Son* has both a powerful and a memorable impact that can be easily observed in the strong emotionally negative responses to the work and in the powerful claims about the work's impressive reformulations of self-purpose. Responses to the work also suggest that the global impact of the novel generates, impacts, and reconsolidates memories and values in such a way as to reformulate racial bias. This process is not directly observable, but nonetheless observations can be made about its operation. The affective appeal of the novel must trigger habitual racial responses but then rework them in relation to new socially simulated experiences. As Suzanne Keen (2010: 69) observes, literature can "disarm readers of some of the protective layers of cautious reasoning that may inhibit empathy" (see also Kidd and Castano 2013, 2017). Our analysis of *Native Son* argues that increased empathy may indeed be an effect of reading the novel but that such an effect requires complex arousal of interlinked affective states: first those that support racist thought and second those that can conflict with the initial assessment. Finally, engaged modes of reverie must work on affective memory to process conflict so that new appraisal systems can emerge and circulate as cognitive representations.

5. Conclusion

Affect is not a random collection of intensities, as Brian Massumi and other poststructuralist affect theorists purport. Affect is organized, orienting a biological organism toward a complex environment in which it must either adapt or die. Because adaptation requires shifts in affective cues, scattered observations about it may imply randomness. But evolutionary theory and empirical evidence suggest that our bodies organize affect according to a more or less adaptive logic. Unfortunately, social groups sometimes organize affect to exclude the suffering of other groups, which, while adaptive for groups in power, is maladaptive for society as a whole. In such cases, work needs to be done to bring recognition of invisible suffering into social circulation. Because affect is systematic in its response to predictable experiences of pain and reward, oppressed people have "gut" experiences of oppression that can be represented by wrenching, emotionally powerful narratives. Resonant literary narratives, and the teaching of them, is critical to the healthy social life of communities and nations.

Some scholars fear that attention to affect forecloses possibilities for formulating reasoned intention and creating projects for social justice. For instance, Ruth Leys (2011: 437) argues that affect theorists, in both poststructuralist and neuroscience camps, posit affect as "independent of, and in an important sense prior to, ideology—that is, prior to intentions, meanings, reasons, and beliefs—because they are nonsignifying, autonomic processes that take place below the threshold of conscious awareness and meaning." The argument of this paper reverses Leys's worry. It is precisely because affect is prior to thought and an appraisal of conditions of suffering that it must be primary in projects for social justice. Bodies move with affects and register them before minds make sense of experience with language. The practice of sociocultural critique must explore ideological signification as it emerges not from intention and deliberative reason but from multiple sites of affective contact.

References

Alcorn, Marshall. 2013. *Resistance to Learning: Overcoming the Desire Not to Know in Classroom Teaching*. New York: Palgrave Macmillan.
Alcorn, Marshall. 2017. "Affect and Intention in Rhetoric and Poetics." In Wehrs and Blake 2017: 299–324.
Bergner, Gwen. 2009. "Black Children, White Preference: The Doll Tests and the Politics of Self-Esteem." *American Quarterly* 6, no. 2: 299–332.
Bion, Wilfried. 1962. *Learning from Experience*. London: William Heinemann.
Bracher, Mark. 2013. *Literature and Social Justice: Protest Novels, Cognitive Politics, and Schema Criticism*. Austin: University of Texas Press.
Bradley, David. 1986. "On Re-Reading Native Son." *New York Times*, December 7.
Bruner, Jerome. 2003. *Making Stories: Law, Literature, Life*. Cambridge, MA: Harvard University Press.
Cayton, Horace, and St. Clair Drake. (1945) 2015. *Black Metropolis: A Study of Negro Life in a Northern City*. Chicago: University of Chicago Press.
Damasio, Antonio. 1995. *Descartes' Error: Emotion, Reason, and the Human Brain*. New York: Harper Collins.

Damasio, Antonio. 2000. *The Feeling of What Happens: Body and Emotion in the Making of Consciousness*. New York: Mariner Books.

Darwin, Charles. (1872) 2009. *The Expression of Emotions in Man and Animals*. New York: Penguin Classics.

Dolan, R. J. 2002. "Emotion, Cognition, and Behavior." *Science* 298, no. 5596: 1191–94.

Donald, Merlin. 1993. *The Origins of the Human Mind*. Cambridge, MA: Harvard University Press.

Donald, Merlin. 2001. *The Evolution of Human Consciousness*. New York: W W Norton.

Easterlin, Nancy. 2012. *A Biocultural Approach to Literary Theory and Interpretation*. Baltimore: Johns Hopkins University Press.

Ekman, Paul. 2003. *Emotions Revealed: Recognizing Faces and Feelings to Improve Communication and Emotional Life*. New York: Henry Holt.

Fanon, Frantz. (1952) 2008. *Black Skin, White Masks*. New York: Grove Press.

Harbus, Antonina. 2017. "Medieval English Texts and Affects: Narratives as Tools for Feeling." In Wehrs and Blake 2017: 299–324.

Herman, Judith. 1992. *Trauma and Recovery: The Aftermath of Violence from Domestic Abuse to Political Terror*. New York: Basic Books.

Hogan, Patrick Colm. 2016. "Affect Studies and Literary Criticism." *Oxford Research Encyclopedia of Literature*. Oxford: Oxford University Press.

Howe, Irving. 1963. "Black Boys and Native Sons." *Dissent*, no. 10: 353–68.

Immordino-Yang, Mary Helen, and Antonio Damasio. 2007. "We Feel, Therefore We Learn: The Relevance of Affective and Social Neuroscience to Education." *Mind, Brain, and Education* 1, no. 1: 3–10.

Ioanide, Paula. 2015. *The Emotional Politics of Racism: How Feelings Trump Facts in an Era of Colorblindness*. Stanford, CA: Stanford University Press.

Johnson, John W. 2006. "Brandeis Brief." In *The Oxford Companion to the Supreme Court of the United States*, edited by Kermit Hall, 100–101. New York: Oxford University Press.

Kandel, Eric. 2012. *Age of Insight: The Quest to Understand the Unconscious in Art, Mind, and Brain from Vienna 1900 to the Present*. New York: Random House.

Keen, Suzanne. 2010. "Narrative Empathy." In *Toward a Cognitive Theory of Narrative Acts*, edited by Frederick Luis Aldama, 61–94. Austin: University of Texas Press.

Kidd, David Comer, and Emanuele Castano. 2013. "Reading Literary Fiction Improves Theory of Mind." *Science* 342, no. 6156: 377–80.

Kidd, David Comer, and Emanuele Castano. 2017. "Different Stories: How Levels of Familiarity with Literary and Genre Fiction Relate to Mentalizing." *Psychology of Aesthetics, Creativity, and the Arts* 11, no. 4: 474–86.

LeDoux, Joseph. 1994. "Emotion, Memory, and the Brain." *Scientific American* 270, no. 6: 50–57.

LeDoux, Joseph. 1996. *The Emotional Brain: The Mysterious Underpinnings of Emotional Life*. New York: Simon and Schuster.

Leys, Ruth. 2011. "The Turn to Affect: A Critique." *Critical Inquiry* 37, no. 3: 434–72.

Longinus. (1st century AD) 1890. "On the Sublime," translated by H.L. Havell. London: Macmillan. Project Gutenberg ebook. www.gutenberg.org/files/17957/17957-h/17957-h.htm.

MacCready-Flora, Ian. 2014. "Aristotle's Cognitive Science: Belief, Affect and Rationality." *Philosophy and Phenomenological Research* 89, no. 2: 394–435.

Massumi, Brian. 2002. *Parables for the Virtual: Movement, Affect, Sensation*. Durham, NC: Duke University Press.

Miller, Brook. 2017. "Affect Studies and Cognitive Approaches to Literature." In Wehrs and Blake 2017: 113–33.

Mumper, Micah L., and Richard J. Gerrig. 2017. "Leisure Reading and Social Cognition: A Meta-Analysis." *Psychology of Aesthetics, Creativity, and the Arts* 11, no. 1: 109–20.

Myers, Karyn M., and Michael L. Davis. 2012. "Mechanisms of Fear Extinction." *Molecular Psychiatry* 12, no. 2: 120–50.

NAACP Legal Defense Fund. 2014. "Brown at 60: The Doll Test." www.naacpldf.orn/brown -at-60-the-doll-test.

Ong, Desmond C., Jamil Zaki, and Noah D. Goodman. 2015. "Affective Cognition: Exploring Lay Theories of Emotion." *Cognition*, no. 143: 141–62.

Pessoa, Luiz. 2013. *The Cognitive Emotional Brain: From Interactions to Integration*. Cambridge, MA: MIT Press.

Phillips, Caryl. 2002. *A New World Order*. New York: Vintage International.

Porayska-Pomsta, Koska, Sidney D'Mello, Cristina Conati, and Ryan S.J. Baker. 2013. "Knowledge Elicitation Methods for Affect Modelling in Education." *International Journal of Artificial Intelligence in Education* 22, no. 3: 107–40.

Ramachandran, Vilayanur Subramanian. 1995. "Anosognosia in Parietal Lobe Syndrome." *Conscious Cognition* 4, no. 1: 22–51.

Ramachandran, Vilayanur Subramanian. 1999. *Phantoms in the Brain: Probing the Mysteries of the Human Mind*. New York: Harper Books.

Semonche, John E. 2000. *Keeping the Faith: A Cultural History of the U.S. Supreme Court*. Lanham, MD: Rowman and Littlefield.

Sha, Richard. 2017. "The Turn to Affect: Emotions without Subject, Causality without Demonstrable Cause." In Wehrs and Blake 2017: 259–98.

Shelley, Percy Bysshe. (1840) 2002. "A Defense of Poetry." In *Shelley's Poetry and Prose*, 2nd ed., edited by Donald H. Reiman and Neil Fraistat, 509–38. New York: Norton.

Starr, G. Gabrielle. 2013. *Feeling Beauty: The Neuroscience of Aesthetic Experience*. Cambridge, MA: MIT Press.

Stern, Daniel N. 1985. *The Interpersonal World of the Infant: A View from Psychoanalysis and Developmental Psychology*. New York: Basic Books.

Stern, Daniel N., Louis W. Sander, Jeremy P. Nahum, A. M. Harrison, Karlen Lyons-Ruth, Alexander C. Morgan, Nadia Bruschweiler-Stern, and Edward Z. Tronick. 1998. "Non-Interpretive Mechanisms in Psychoanalytic Therapy: The 'Something More' than Interpretation." *International Journal of Psychoanalysis* 79, no. 5: 903–21.

Stewart, James T. 1968. "The Development of the Black Revolutionary Artist." In *Black Fire: Anthology of Afro-American Writing*, edited by Leroi Jones and Larry Neal, 11–18. Baltimore: Black Classic Press.

Sturm, Philippa. 1989. "Brandeis and the Living Constitution." In *Brandeis and America*, edited by Nelson Dawson, 98–119. Lexington: University Press of Kentucky.

Tomkins, Silvan. 2008. *Affect Imagery Consciousness: The Complete Edition*. New York: Springer.

Van der Kolk, Bessell. 2014. *The Body Keeps the Score: Brain Mind and Body in the Healing of Trauma*. New York: Viking.

Warnes, Andrew. 2007. *Richard Wright's Native Son: A Routledge Study Guide*. London: Routledge Press.

Wehrs, Donald, and Thomas Blake, eds. 2017. *The Palgrave Handbook of Affect Studies and Textual Criticism*. New York: Palgrave Macmillan.

Weik von Mossner, Alexa. 2014. *Cosmopolitan Minds: Literature, Emotion, and the Transnational Imagination*. Austin: University of Texas Press.

Wetherell, Margaret. 2012. *Affect and Emotion: A New Social Science Understanding*. London: Sage Press.

Williams, Leanne, Andrew H. Kemp, Kim Felmingham, Matthew Barton, Gloria Oliveri, Anthony Peduto, Evian Gordon, and Richard A. Bryant. 2006. "Trauma Modulates Amygdala and Medial Prefrontal Responses to Consciously Attended Fear." *NeuroImage* 29, no. 2: 347–57.

Witmer, Helen, and Ruth Kotinsky. 1952. *Personality in the Making: The Fact-Finding Report of the Mid-Century White House Conference on Children and Youth*. New York: Harper Brothers.

Wright, Richard. (1940) 1998. *Native Son*. New York: Perennial.

Can—and Should—Literary Study Develop Moral Character and Advance Social Justice? Answers from Cognitive Science

Mark Bracher
Kent State University

Abstract Drawing on empirical studies, the article argues that developing moral character and advancing social justice through literary study is both eminently feasible and profoundly ethical, and that claims to the contrary are based on faulty notions of the psychological bases of morality and justice. The article explains how certain literary texts together with certain pedagogical practices can achieve these ends by training students to recognize two key but routinely overlooked facts about other people—their profound sameness and interconnectedness with oneself and their ultimate blamelessness for negative life outcomes, behaviors, and character traits—as well as a key fact about themselves: that they are inherently compassionate, as manifested by their compassionate impulses and the gratification they get from helping others in need.

Keywords social justice, moral character, cognitive science, compassion

Once upon a time, in an era of bold feminism and vibrant Marxist criticism, the conviction was widespread among literature scholars and teachers that literary study could and should be a significant force for social change.[1] And in an even earlier age, that of critics such as F. R. Leavis, the assumption that literature could make one a better person seemed eminently plausible if not self-evident. Today, however, discussions of the purposes of literary study

---

1. For strong statements of this conviction, see Fetterley (1978: viii); Lentricchia (1983: 10); Schweickart (1986: 39); Eagleton (1983); and Jameson (1982).

Poetics Today 40:3 (September 2019) DOI 10.1215/03335372-7558122

tend to soft-pedal these aims, ignore them, or, in some cases, even denounce them. The special section in *Profession*, for example, titled "How We Teach Now" (2009), drawn from the 2008 Modern Language Association (MLA) Presidential Forum on that topic, has no discussion of how the teaching of literature might enhance either moral character or social justice, even though several of the papers treat at some length a recent book by Stanley Fish arguing that we can't do either and shouldn't try. A decade later, presenters in the 2017 MLA Convention session titled "Why Teach Literature?" gave nary a mention to either of these aims. These glaring omissions are symptomatic of the profession today, further indicated by the absence of serious engagement with the issue in any number of recent books exploring the uses of literature and the purposes of literary study, including two self-proclaimed "manifestos": Marjorie Garber's 2003 *A Manifesto for Literary Studies* and Rita Felski's 2008 *Uses of Literature*.

This is not to say that the goals of building character and advancing social justice through the study of literature have been completely abandoned by literature teachers and scholars. Marshall Gregory, Mark Edmundson, Elizabeth Ammons, and others have argued for the character-building and/or justice-promoting effects of literary study,[2] but affirmations such as these are rare, and they are even more rarely advanced with evidentiary support. The causes of this avoidance are no doubt multiple and include such things as institutional inertia and professional identity investments, but two appear to be particularly significant. First, many teachers fear that trying to change students' minds, brains, or behaviors is unethical. Second, there seems to be an even wider fear that the study of literature may be incapable of producing the kinds of changes in students' hearts and minds that would be necessary to effect significant character development or social change. This fear is understandable in light of the absence of compelling evidence that people who devote their lives to the study of literature — i.e., literary scholars — are morally superior to members of other professions or that social justice was significantly enhanced by the Marxist and feminist literary criticism of the 1970s and 1980s.

Many literature teachers, then, either share or cannot refute the position that Stanley Fish asserts in *Save the World on Your Own Time*: that the goals of

2. Marshall Gregory's *Shaped by Stories: The Ethical Power of Narrative* (2009) and Mark Edmundson's *Why Read?* (2004) and *Why Teach?* (2013) advance important claims about literature as a vehicle for personal growth and character building. And on the social justice front, Elizabeth Ammons's *Brave New Words: How Literature Will Save the Planet* (2010), and Jeffrey Williams and Heather Steffen's collection, *The Critical Pulse: Thirty-Six Credos by Contemporary Critics* (2012), include heartening affirmations of what Gerald Graff (2012, 137), opposing such affirmations, calls "teaching for social justice."

character development and social change are both unfeasible and unethical for educators to pursue. For many, Fish's position is unassailable. Hence Gerald Graff, in his "Credo of a Teacher," summarily dismisses "teaching for social justice" as one of several "descendants of sixties political pedagogy that expressly aim to turn students into radical Leftists," declaring it to be "a terrible idea," a practice that "doesn't work" and that is "unethical and unprofessional" (Graff 2012: 137).

1. The Cognitive Bases of Morality and Social Justice

Claims of unfeasibility are often bolstered by anecdotes of bad people (e.g., Nazis) who were supposedly avid consumers of literature. Thus, many literature teachers and scholars, sharing Fish's (2008: 55) incontestable observation that "readers of Henry James or Sylvia Plath or Toni Morrison can be as vile and as cruel and as treacherous as anyone else," jump, like Fish, to the invalid conclusion that "moral capacities (or their absence) have no relationship whatsoever to the reading of novels" (11). But if most literary study at present is not making students more moral, that doesn't mean that it is incapable of doing so. If, in fact, literary study is currently doing little to foster character development and promote social justice, this failure may be due to the way literature is being read and taught rather than to any inherent limitations of literary study itself. A better understanding—informed by cognitive science—of the nature of character and of its relation to social justice suggests that, contrary to the claims of skeptics like Fish, literary study is actually ideally suited to shaping moral character traits that lead to greater social justice.

The belief that character development and social justice cannot be promoted by literary study is based on the common assumption that knowledge and skills—which education can develop, and which Fish and most other educators believe it should develop—have little or nothing to do with character, morality, or social justice. This assumption is simply wrong. As the philosopher Amélie Rorty (1993: 30–31) explains in "What It Takes to Be Good," morality is a function of "a vast array of psychological and characterological capacities, abilities, and skills that vary independently of one another and need to be developed and sustained." And literature, Rorty maintains, has an important role to play in this development (38). In a similar vein, Gregory (2009: 23) points out that "the fact that stories . . . cue our capacities for feeling, believing, and judging . . . inevitably raises questions about their potential influence on character, for what is character other than the particular configuration of our own ways of feeling, believing, and judging?" Martha Nussbaum (1995: 92) avers, similarly, that reading literature can serve the development of certain capabilities and habits of perception, judgment, and feeling that are prerequisites for social justice.

Rorty, Gregory, and Nussbaum provide little evidence in support of their claims. But significant evidence has emerged in recent years from cognitive science that engagement with literature can develop social justice – advancing moral character traits in two basic ways: by improving people's social cognition and by fostering healthy development of their identities. Recent empirical research has established that improvements in social cognition are key to improved character. Such research has revealed that bad character and bad behaviors — including social policies and other collective actions that are harmful and unjust to individuals and groups — result from cognitive deficiencies in perceiving crucial information about other people. Studies of chronically aggressive individuals, for example, have demonstrated that in many instances one key component of their aggressive character is their inability to accurately assess the intentions behind other people's actions. This leads them to attribute a hostile intention, and hence a threat, where none exists, causing them to respond to the illusory threat with aggression (see Dodge 1980; Hudley and Graham 1993; Epps and Kendall 1995; Huesmann 1998). Similarly, a number of studies have found that rapists are often inept at reading women's signals of refusal or distress (see Scully 1990; McDonnell and McFall 1991).

Other research has demonstrated that refusal to provide personal assistance to others in need or to support social policies that help them is often due to the faulty judgment that the needy are somehow to blame for their distress, which leads to the conclusion that they don't deserve assistance (Weiner 1995, 2006). This judgment is embodied in most negative stereotypes (see Sherman et al. 2005; Wittenbrink, Gist, and Hilton 1997; Reyna et al. 2005; and Henry, Reyna, and Weiner 2004), and it can also influence perceptions and judgments in which no specific stereotype is involved.

Research has further shown, moreover, that neglect of the needy and other forms of harm can be reduced by the development of cognitive capabilities that produce more adequate perceptions and judgments of other people, thus changing character in ways that also enhance social justice. One program reduced anger and aggression by helping individuals develop more adequate cognitive schemas for assessing the causes of another person's actions. This program engaged abnormally aggressive boys in activities such as role-playing and the study of facial expressions to train them how to search for, identify, and correctly interpret and categorize verbal and behavioral cues. Then, the boys read scenes of ambiguous behavior, in response to which they practiced formulating attributions of nonhostile intentions. The program also helped the boys understand how certain causal beliefs trigger aggressive behaviors and engaged them in formulating action scripts for nonhostile responses when evidence about the other person's intentions is ambiguous (Hudley and Graham 1993: 127–28). Follow-up evaluations showed that participants in this program manifested lower levels of aggression than those in a control group.

Another program reduced the subsequent offences of child molesters by 50 percent by training them in perspective-taking (see Goleman 2006: 107). Similar interventions that improve individuals' assessments of other people's situations and dispositions have been shown to lead to greater compassion and fewer punitive social practices toward stigmatized people, such as the indigent and homeless as well as murderers and drug dealers (Batson et al. 2002; Weiner 1995, 2006).

2. Improving Social Cognition through Literary Study

Such interventions demonstrate that character and morality can be improved by doing exactly what Fish and others say education should do: teaching knowledge and skills. The knowledge and skills that produce these results, however, are not the learning objectives of traditional literary pedagogy, which focuses on textual interpretation, analysis of literary techniques, and command of the canon (Fish 2008: 171).[3] Rather, the knowledge and skills that deliver these results are those that produce our perceptions and judgments of other people, which in turn determine our emotions and actions toward them, including the collective actions embodied in social policies, institutions, systems, and structures. Several key appraisals about others determine whether we feel compassion, indifference, or anger toward them, and hence whether we support social structures, institutions, and policies that help them instead of ignoring or punishing them. These include appraisals of the other's responsibility for and degree of need as well as perception of the other's sameness, or overlap, with oneself.

For example, if other people are deemed the sole or primary cause of their own condition of need, then the likelihood that we will help them is much less than if we judge them not to be responsible (see Weiner 1995, 2006, 2014; Weiner, Osborne, and Rudolph 2011). Research has conclusively demonstrated that people in general, and Americans especially, tend to overrate others' responsibility and underestimate the role that uncontrollable factors play in determining a person's behaviors, life outcomes, and indeed their very

3. It may be — as Willie van Peer has suggested, based on a 2008 study that found that science students, on average, possess greater emotional intelligence than humanities students — that traditional literary pedagogy actually inhibits the development of emotional intelligence (van Peer 2008; cited in Oatley 2011: 60).

character (see Choi, Nisbett, and Norenzayan 1999; Gill and Cerce 2017). This chronic misapprehension, which psychologists call the "fundamental attribution error," is at the root of many unjust social policies that blame the victims—including the poor, the unemployed, the homeless, the uneducated, the sick, and the incarcerated (see Ryan 1976; Bracher 2013b).

The same is true of self-other overlap: to the extent that we recognize others' common humanity or other similarities beneath surface differences, we are inclined to sympathize with, cooperate with, and assist them, whereas if we see only differences between us, we assume a more competitive—and even hostile and violent—stance toward them (see Cialdini et al. 1997: 89–92; Levy, Freitas, and Salovey 2002: 1224–25; Gaunt 2009: 734; Phillips and Ziller 1997: 427–30). Moreover, failure to apprehend other people's common humanity is often an obstacle to recognizing their suffering: people perceived as less human than ourselves are deemed less sensitive or vulnerable to sources of suffering.

If literary study can help people correct the faulty cognitive schemas that are responsible for misperceptions of others, such as the fundamental attribution error and the failure to recognize others' fundamental sameness and connectedness with ourselves—the schemas, respectively, of self-determination and social atomism—then it can in effect change people's character in ways that advance social justice. And there is mounting evidence that literary study of a certain kind can do this. The cognitive-evolutionary scholar Brian Boyd (2009: 197), among others, argues that fiction has evolved as a means of developing better social cognition, including enhanced perspective-taking and "sympathetic imagination." A related argument has been advanced by philosopher-psychologist Daniel Hutto, whose Narrative Practice Hypothesis (NPH) draws on developmental psychology to argue that humans learn to decipher the reasons for each other's actions through narrative exposure to them (Hutto 2008: xii). Stories develop skill in discerning what desires, intentions, character traits, past experiences, and present circumstances have converged to produce specific behaviors (28–29, 34–39).

Hutto focuses on children's learning, but other research indicates that literature has a similar schema-developing function for adults. Raymond Mar and Keith Oatley, for instance, conclude that reading literature facilitates readers' construction of social schemas—that is, abstractions and generalizations, or models, of social experience that then guide cognition and behavior in real life (Mar and Oatley 2008: 176–77). Likewise, David Herman (2013: 18) finds that "engagements with characters in narratives . . . have the power to remold wider understandings of persons circulating in a given culture or subculture." Narratives do so by altering our prototypical or "model persons"—that is, our "schemes for understanding persons . . . that scaffold our encounters with others" (194). In this way, literature is capable of effecting "a reorganization of thought and conduct—at both a group and an individual level" (243; see also Cook 1994; Gerrig and Rapp 2004; Miall 2006).

In this vein, I have drawn on findings concerning schema change to argue that literary study can work to replace the faulty cognitive schemas of self-determination (which gives rise to the fundamental attribution error) and social atomism (which blinds us to others' sameness or overlap with ourselves) with the corrective schemas of moral luck and solidarity, respectively, which take into account crucial information about others that the faulty schemas exclude (Bracher 2013a, 2013b). Recent empirical studies conducted by my research group have produced strong support for this hypothesis (Bracher et al. 2019), showing that literary study can enhance compassion and aid by making readers more aware of the respective truths that the two faulty schemas obscure: that human behavior, character, and life outcomes are often largely determined by forces outside people's control (the moral luck schema), and that humans are inherently and profoundly interconnected—practically, ontologically, emotionally, and neurologically—with all other human beings, including those who seem most different from oneself (the solidarity schema).

3. Promoting Identity Development through Literary Study

Literary study can also enhance character, morality, and social justice by modifying readers' identities. There is considerable evidence that identity, or sense of self, is a fundamental determinant of all human behavior, and that it is thus key to both prosocial, moral behaviors and immoral, antisocial behaviors (Bracher 2006a, 2006b, 2009; see also Burke and Stets 2009; Stets and Carter 2011; Hitlin 2003; Aquino and Reed 2002). Numerous empirical studies have found that when people's identities are threatened, their perceptions of others become more distorted, their feelings toward outgroup members become more negative, and their behavior toward such people becomes more aggressive (see, e.g., Pyszczynski, Greenberg, and Solomon 1999). In addition, certain identity contents (e.g., hyperindividuality, hypermasculinity, and nationalism) entail aggressive, antisocial actions, while other contents (e.g., kindness, compassion, cosmopolitanism) promote prosocial behaviors. In some cases, others are an integral element to one's identity— that is, compassion-producing self-other overlap constitutes a structural component. Thus, identity might be changed to promote morality and social justice by helping people do one or more of the following: (1) achieve greater

526   Poetics Today 40:3

identity security, (2) develop and invest more heavily in benign identity contents, (3) divest themselves of toxic contents, and/or (4) expand the boundaries of their identity to include more, and more diverse, others within one's sense of self (see Bracher 2006b, 2009).

While there is as yet little empirical evidence about the potential of literary study to alter students' identities in these specific ways, we know from a number of studies that literature can produce at least temporary alterations in readers' sense of self. An experiment conducted by Djikic, Oatley, and colleagues (2009) "found that the personalities—the way people saw themselves—of those who read Chekhov's story ["The Lady with the Little Dog"] changed more than those who read ... the non-fiction styled version of the story" (Oatley 2011: 161). This change occurred, Oatley surmises, because "in the Chekhov story, people were taken out of themselves, out of their usual ways of being and thinking..., and this helped to loosen up the habitual structures of selfhood" (162). Miall and Kuiken (2002: 221) conclude, similarly, that "aesthetic and narrative feelings evoked during reading interact to modify the reader."

More specifically, there appear to be a number of things literary study can do to alter identities in ways that advance morality and social justice (see Bracher 2006b and 2009). First, literature can enhance identity security by providing various forms of recognition for specific identity contents. Whether the recognition takes the form of the narrator's approbation for a character embodying a particular stigmatized content (e.g., gender, sexuality, ethnicity, social class) or of the mere representation of such characters, it can provide much-needed validation for readers whose embodiment of such identity contents makes them psychologically insecure. The value of such recognition has been attested to by stigmatized individuals who have suffered from self-doubt and low self-esteem. Identity security can also be bolstered by offering enactment opportunities for benign contents (e.g., compassion, intelligence, honesty, creativity, skepticism) and by charting more realizable meanings and/or action scripts for various contents (e.g., strength as restraint rather than dominance; success as peaceful coexistence rather than accumulation of wealth). *Uncle Tom's Cabin*, for example, (re)defines success, strength, dominance, and victory in spiritual (rather than physical or material) terms, which are in principle attainable by virtually anyone, since their pursuit does not involve a zero-sum game. And it is also likely that literary study can enhance students' identity security by providing them with techniques, skills, and narrative prototypes to construct a more robust narrative identity, a coherent story of their life that integrates the multifarious events and sometimes contradictory actions of their past into a more or less unified sense of self across time (see McAdams and McLean 2013; Hammack 2008).

Second, literary study can work in several ways to help readers invest in benign identity contents such as compassion, kindness, and generosity. It can do so by eliciting feelings such as sympathy and thus revealing to readers the prosocial qualities in themselves that they had previously been blind to and/or that had lain largely dormant; by depicting these benign qualities as common traits inherent in human nature; by representing these qualities as implicit in other identity contents that readers are heavily invested in; by modeling such qualities and thus inducing automatic imitation of them (see Chartrand and Bargh 1999); and, finally, by highlighting the benefits that result from enacting such identity contents and thus inclining readers to adopt them (see Bandura 1976). Harriet Beecher Stowe employs each of these methods in *Uncle Tom's Cabin* to bring her readers to embrace sympathy as a core content of their identities.

Third, literature can work in a number of ways to separate readers from toxic identity contents and/or harmful action scripts attached to certain identities (see Bracher 2015). It can do so by producing cognitive dissonance through revealing contradictions between a benign content and a toxic content, between a content and a harmful action script, or between a toxic content and a benign component of the self that has not been owned and integrated into the reader's identity. Stowe, for example, emphasizes the contradiction between her readers' Christian identity and their failure to take action to end slavery, and she admonishes her readers to recognize their own compassionate impulses and realize the contradiction between those impulses and their identity as slaveholders or their inaction in the face of slavery. In addition to employing cognitive dissonance, literature can also move readers to divest themselves of toxic identity contents and harmful action scripts by portraying the negative consequences that accrue to those who embody such contents or enact such scripts and/or the positive consequences that result for characters who embody countervailing contents or action scripts. Shakespeare's *As You Like It*, for instance, systematically works on readers' identities in this way by illustrating how heroic masculinity leads to ruin and how compassion and generosity produce gratification and fulfillment (Bracher 2015).

Fourth, literature can foster greater inclusion of others within one's identity or sense of self. It can do so by modeling such inclusion and also by eliciting sympathy and then inducing the recognition that such feelings indicate that what happens to other people also happens to oneself in some way. *Uncle Tom's Cabin* employs both of these techniques.

4. Social Cognition Enhancement Pedagogy

Utilizing literature's capability to enhance students' social cognition and identities could thus, if established as a key curricular element in literary studies from elementary school through graduate school, make a substantial contribution to social justice while also enriching the lives of the students themselves. But what would such a literary pedagogy involve? Consider first the development of the more adequate cognitive schemas that enable students to avoid the distortions of perception and judgment and the resulting harm produced by the schemas of self-determination and social atomism. This pedagogy involves four general practices that research in various fields has identified as key to correcting faulty cognitive schemas (see Bracher 2013b). These practices include

- acquiring declarative knowledge of moral luck and solidarity;
- acquiring exemplars (particular examples) — which are also the building blocks of prototypes (general models) — of moral luck and solidarity, which can serve as templates for perceiving and appraising people's character, behavior, and life outcomes;
- practicing more adequate information-processing routines that enable one to apprehend moral luck and solidarity in real life and real time; and
- practicing metacognition: monitoring one's own appraisals of other people in order to prevent or correct judgments of self-determination and social atomism.

The key to developing each of these forms of knowledge or skill is repetition. Just as learning to drive, play a musical instrument, or execute a complex athletic maneuver requires repeated practice or rehearsal, so too does the development of cognitive schemas, especially those elements of the schemas — exemplars/prototypes, information-processing routines, and metacognition — that rely on either episodic or procedural memory rather than semantic memory (see Bracher 2013b).

Literature teachers have multiple resources for repeatedly engaging students in each of these schema-developing activities. It is useful, first of all, to select texts that involve readers in as many of these activities as possible. I have had success with novels such as *Frankenstein, Uncle Tom's Cabin, Hard Times, Silas Marner, Maggie, The Jungle, The Grapes of Wrath,* and *Native Son.* Simply reading such texts, however, does not usually engage students in sufficient cognitive practice to develop the corrective schemas. Thus it is also important to formulate reading directives, discussion topics, research tasks, writing assignments, and exams that enlist students in schema-developing cognitive activities. Students might begin to develop a declarative knowledge of moral luck, for example, by being directed to look for articulations of this idea in the literary texts themselves. Guided toward questions of causality or responsibility for characters' behaviors, life outcomes, and character traits, students reading *Frankenstein* will particularly note passages such as the one in which Victor explains to Walton how a series of chance events beyond his control was responsible for making him the person he has become, and of the monster's account of how the repeated rejection and violence he suffered were responsible for making him a monster ("I was benevolent and good; misery made me a fiend," [Shelley (1831) 2013: 105]). Reading *Uncle Tom's Cabin* with the same prompt will help students pay special attention to passages such as Augustine St. Clare's articulation of the principle of moral luck when he declares that the notion of human virtue is "trash" (Stowe [1852] 2010: 208), and the narrator's claim that it is not the slave trader himself who is primarily to blame for his debased character and execrable actions but rather the powerful, well-educated people who allow the system of slavery, of which the "poor trader" is but "the inevitable result" (121).

In class discussions, I read such passages aloud and then invite students to paraphrase them. Once the basic idea is clear, we examine it critically. "Is this idea of moral luck valid?" I ask. "Is there any evidence from the psychological sciences or other disciplines that would either support or challenge this idea?" Usually several students will recall the classic experiments of Stanley Milgram, Philip Zimbardo, or John Darley and Daniel Batson, which demonstrated that being placed in a certain situation can cause people to do bad things that neither they nor anyone else would have guessed they were capable of. Often one or two students will be familiar with Zimbardo's book *The Lucifer Effect: Understanding How Good People Turn Evil*, in which the author concludes that "any deed that any human being has ever committed, however horrible, is possible for any of us—under the right or wrong situational circumstances" (Zimbardo 2008: 211). After an exposition of this empirical evidence corroborating moral luck has been provided (ideally by students who are familiar with it), I summarize the moral luck schema by diagramming it.

In addition to this abstract declarative knowledge, correcting the faulty self-determination schema also requires that one acquire concrete examples of individuals whose behavior, character, and/or life outcomes were significantly affected by forces beyond their control. The literary texts themselves usually provide such exemplars. In *Frankenstein*, Shelley presents the three protagonist-narrators formed by conditions and experiences beyond their control: Walton, Victor, and the monster. The same is true of numerous characters in the other novels I teach. In each case, I engage students in identifying and inferring the various uncontrollable factors that contributed to the character traits, behaviors, and/or life outcomes of these characters. For example, if Victor had not stumbled upon the alchemy books, his life would have probably taken a very different course, and if any number of chance factors had not been in place—e.g., the family taking an outing to this particular inn, the rain confining him to the inn, his seeking diversion in the inn's library, the presence in the library of the book by Albertus Magnus—he never would have encountered the alchemy books.

During our discussion, I often supplement these examples with instances from my own life in which chance events made a profound difference in the course my life took and in the type of person I became, and I ask students to reflect on their lives to see what examples they might find there. Sometimes I also ask them to write about such instances and imagine how their lives and their very characters might be different if certain events had not occurred or certain conditions had not prevailed in their past. And I also frequently assign them the task of choosing a real-life "monster," gathering some biographical information on the internet, and then writing a short paper explaining how circumstances or experiences beyond the monster's control played a powerful role in determining the monster's character and behavior. The backgrounds of these "monsters"—who include Hitler, Stalin, Charles Manson, Ted Bundy, John Wayne Gacy, Jeffrey Dahmer, Aileen Wuornos, a number of school shooters, and many others—invariably include instances of traumatogenic conditions or experiences that clearly contributed to the "monster's" monstrous character traits and actions.

In addition to stocking their memories with exemplars of moral luck, these assignments also engage students in rehearsing, and thus developing, the corrective information-processing scripts or routines—including those of expectation, attention, information search, memory search, inference, supposition, and categorization—that are key components of the moral luck schema. The novels, by repeatedly directing students' attention to the impact of external conditions, situations, and events on characters' behaviors, character traits, and life outcomes, not only train students to attend to these factors when they encounter them; they also develop students' expectation that they will find such factors and their supposition that such factors exist even when they may not be visible or accessible. The "monster" biography writing assignment, similarly, engages students in supposition, expectation, attention, and information-search for (bad) moral luck, and it also leads them to infer moral luck from various types of biographical information and to categorize these individuals as victims of bad moral luck. For the final exam, I present students with about a dozen study questions (two or three of which will constitute the in-class exam) requiring them to explain moral luck and solidarity and to demonstrate how specific episodes or characters exemplify these abstract principles. The purpose of these questions is to help students consolidate their long-term memory of the declarative knowledge of moral luck and solidarity and of the exemplars that embody this knowledge, and to further their development of moral luck and solidarity prototypes out of the exemplars.

Developing students' metacognition is also often initiated by the texts themselves. *The Grapes of Wrath* presents multiple instances of the fundamental attribution error, in which one character fails to recognize that the behavior of another character is caused not by the person's character traits (e.g., meanness, laziness, or greed) but by the person's circumstances, and at one point the narrator pleads with readers to recognize that the migrants from Oklahoma who are producing social turmoil are "results, not causes. Results, not causes; results, not causes" (Steinbeck [1939] 1997: 151). I use passages such as this to encourage students to recognize their own tendencies to commit the fundamental attribution error, and I often assign a paper requiring them to recall an instance in which they committed the error by becoming angry at someone who committed an offensive act and then to infer or imagine how the offending party's objectionable behavior or character traits might have been caused by forces beyond his or her control.

5. Fostering Compassionate Identities through Literary Study

Many of the literary texts I teach also foster compassionate identities, most fundamentally by inducing students to invest more intensively in compassion itself as a central identity content. This investment is elicited in a number of different ways. One prominent way is by portraying characters who exhibit involuntary empathy, sympathy, or compassion. *Uncle Tom's Cabin* and *The Grapes of Wrath* are replete with characters who embody these qualities, and my students and I discuss relevant episodes at length. This focus on fictional instances of compassion highlights the universality of the compassion impulse, revealing to students that they, too, are compassionate at their core, whether or not they recognize and embrace this powerful feature of their humanity. To further emphasize this point, I discuss recent behavioral, neuroimaging, and evolutionary studies indicating that compassion is not only inherent in human nature but also often powerful enough to override self-interest (see, for example, Brown, Brown, and Penner 2012). And I inform them of other studies revealing that a powerful strain of American (and Western) ideology pinpoints self-interest as the sole motivator of human behavior and thus blinds people to their own and others' inherent compassion and altruistic tendencies (see Miller 1999).

In addition, findings that observing or reading about an action can induce a subtle, subliminal imitation of the action in observers (see Chartrand and Bargh 1999; Bergen 2012) suggest that reading about compassionate characters probably also elicits a subliminal imitation of the observed compassion in the students themselves, with each such experience strengthening the related neural pathways. In some cases, the narrator will provide reinforcement of the compassionate identity by expressing approbation for the act. In other cases, the narrative will further reinforce identity investment in compassion by showing the act to produce positive feelings in the character. Two prominent instances in *The Grapes of Wrath* are Jim Casy taking the blame and going to jail for striking a deputy when Tom Joad is the actual culprit and Rose of Sharon nursing the starving man in the novel's final scene, with both of these characters' smiles exhibiting the gratification that such acts provide for the agent. During discussions of these scenes, I inform students that neuroimaging studies have revealed that helping other people activates the brain's reward networks (Lieberman 2014), and I ask them to reflect on what this fact says about human nature in general and themselves specifically, thus reinforcing their recognition of their own compassionate nature.

Another major means by which texts such as *Uncle Tom's Cabin* and *The Grapes of Wrath* promote compassionate identities is by eliciting readers' sympathy for characters. Each experience of sympathy that readers undergo strengthens the neural substrates of sympathy and thus makes readers' own compassionate impulses both stronger and more easily activated. And when they are prompted either by the text (as *Uncle Tom's Cabin* does on occasion[4]) or by the instructor to recognize and reflect on their own feelings of sympathy, students take another step toward incorporating compassion as a central content of their identity. I like to reinforce this development with writing prompts that ask students to reflect on their own experiences of sympathy and compassion:

- Briefly describe instances in which you experienced each of the three types of empathy that Stowe both represents and induces in her readers (i.e., memory-based, perspective taking, and emotional contagion). These may be in response to other people or in response to characters in movies, TV shows, or books.
- Stowe believes that reducing the suffering of others can be profoundly fulfilling. Is she right? What does your own experience tell you? Recall an instance in which you did something that reduced someone else's

4. On one occasion, for example, Stowe ([1852] 2010: 81) prompts her southern readers to acknowledge their own compassion for suffering slaves.

suffering or distress. How did it make you feel? What does the feeling tell you about yourself? Do you like what it tells you?

In addition to making their own inherent compassionate impulses more available for adoption as identity contents, these prompts provide an opportunity for students to (re)affirm and even (re)enact their compassionate identities. An added benefit is that such self-affirmation reinforces identity security, which in turn makes people less punitive and more altruistic (see Steele 1999; Pyszczynski, Greenberg, and Solomon 1999).

Investment in compassion as a central identity content is also facilitated by helping students replace their social atomism person-schema with a solidarity schema. Stowe facilitates this replacement in *Uncle Tom's Cabin* by invoking the example and words of Jesus — "Inasmuch as ye did it not to one the least of these my brethren, ye did it not to me" (Stowe [1852] 2010: 284) — to model the more inclusive solidarity identity and to elicit the recognition that sometimes when things happen to other people they also, in effect, happen to us, thus demonstrating solidarity to be a component of human nature, in principle available to all as an identity content. I point out that Jesus refers to himself here as the Son of Man, thus indicating that what he is describing is a basic human quality and not some unique capability of the divine or supernatural. I then ask the class if they have ever felt this way or if they can think of any examples of people who are like this. The discussion routinely provides examples in which some people (e.g., parents, people in love, team members) experience what happens to other people (e.g., children, romantic partners, and teammates, respectively) as also happening to them. I often mention the blues song refrain, "When things go wrong, / Go wrong with you, / It hurts me too," and inform the class of neuroimaging studies that have found that our brains process things that happen to other people we are close to in much the same way as they process things that happen to us (see, for example, Iacaboni 2009). These models of compassionate identity are also rehearsed through discussions and final-exam study questions on *The Grapes of Wrath* that promote engaging with these models and internalizing them in long-term memory, where they become available for identification and adoption as key components of the students' identities.

Embracing compassion as a central content of one's identity is also facilitated by promoting divestment from, or redefinition of, identity contents that reject tender feelings of sympathy and prevent compassionate actions. *Uncle Tom's Cabin* presents the most heartless characters (e.g., Haley, Tom Loker, Marie St. Clare, and Simon Legree), whose central identity contents are power, control, or dominance, as not only despised but also miserable and hence pitiable. The novel thus establishes an association in readers' mind-brains between lack of compassion and negative consequences, which leads to the inevitable conclusion, voiced more than once by Uncle Tom, that it must be awful to be such a person. This point is reinforced by Augustine St. Clare's reading of the passage from Matthew in which Jesus says that those who fail to help others in need will experience "everlasting fire." I inform my classes that while some people take this fire to be literal, others interpret it as the emotional or spiritual torment that can result from failing to help someone in need, and I sometimes offer the following writing prompt to engage students in reflecting on such an experience they may have had:

> According to one interpretation of the passage from the Gospel of Matthew quoted in *Uncle Tom's Cabin*, not helping someone in need will cause people spiritual or emotional distress. Describe an instance in which you failed to help someone in need and felt bad about it afterwards. What does your distress tell you about yourself and/or about people in general?

Such discussions and writing assignments help students recognize and value compassion as an inherent quality, the denial of which constitutes a betrayal of their true self, which in turn creates a cognitive dissonance with identity contents that run counter to compassion.

Uncle Tom's Cabin also works to help readers change the meaning or definition of identities that may exclude or even oppose sympathy and compassion. Most notably, Stowe repeatedly aligns Christian identity not with belief (e.g., that Jesus is the Son of God) but with sympathy for anyone in distress. And Stowe redefines masculinity—typically taken to involve a physical toughness and invulnerability (as when Legree boasts of his toughness to his fellow riverboat passengers and invites them to feel how hard his fist is) as well as a mental toughness that is immune to sentiment (as Senator Bird initially takes it to be)—as compassion that reveals itself in sensitivity to suffering and the courage to oppose the forces that cause suffering. This redefined masculinity is modeled in Senator Bird, who weeps over the plight of Eliza and Harry and then incurs considerable risk and expense to help them escape; in Mr. Wilson, who weeps after hearing George Harris's story and then gives him money to facilitate his escape; and in young George Shelby, whose tears over Uncle Tom's suffering and death, we are told, "did honor to his manly heart" (Stowe [1852] 2010: 380). I frequently emphasize the undesirability of such a compassionless identity by recounting research by James Gilligan (1996, 2001) and Terence Real (1997) on the harmful personal and social consequences of a masculine identity that denies one's own vulnerability, tenderness, and sorrow.

These two approaches to literary study—the development of the more adequate cognitive schemas of moral luck and solidarity, which produce more accurate assessments of other people, and of a compassionate identity resulting from greater recognition, ownership, and cultivation of one's own inherent compassion — work synergistically to produce both greater personal fulfillment for students and enhanced well-being for other people in their orbit, an orbit that is today ultimately global. My reseaerch group's empirical assessments of the effectiveness of the schema-development pedagogy (Bracher et al., 2019) mentioned earlier have found that this pedagogy does indeed increase students' compassion. And while our empirical assessments of identity-development pedagogy are just now getting under way, previous studies of the effects of literature on identity, of how identity can be enhanced, and of the impact of identity on people's well-being and behavior provide strong support for the hypothesis that literary study can also foster moral character and promote social justice by developing compassionate identities.

6. The Question of Ethics

But is it ethical to promote character development and advance social justice through literary study? Some contend that such a mission is not the job of literature teachers, and others go so far as to claim that it is actually an abdication of their proper responsibilities. Fish has produced the fullest statement of this position. Rejecting the "Presidents' Declaration on the Civic Responsibility of Higher Education," issued by nine hundred college and university presidents, which states that "higher education has an unprecedented opportunity to influence the democratic knowledge, dispositions, and habits of the heart that graduates carry with them into the public sphere" (Fish 2008: 15), Fish maintains that college and university teachers should do only two things — "teach materials and confer skills" — and that professors "therefore don't or shouldn't do a lot of other things — like produce active citizens, inculcate the virtue of tolerance, redress injustices, and bring about political change" (66).

Although such arguments can be persuasive, the position they defend is ultimately unsustainable. First, even if we were, at present, only teaching materials and conferring skills, that fact should not prevent us from discontinuing this practice if pursuing other learning objectives would be more beneficial to our students and the world at large. Second, not all teachers simply "teach materials and confer skills" with no further aim. Teaching to promote social justice, via character development, is what many of us do. In fact, as Marshall Gregory insists, it is impossible not to affect students' character if one teaches them literature: "exposure to stories is educational and therefore formative" (Gregory 2009: 3, see also 26). Education theorists Chickering and Reisser (1993: 208) go even further, declaring that "in the global society of the twenty-first century, where change is the only certainty, . . . identity formation becomes the central and continuing task of education." Third, forming character and teaching skills are not mutually exclusive. The assumption that they are rests on a misapprehension of human character and/or flawed notions about the potential of literary study.

Other objectors to teaching for moral development and social justice claim that such a practice does a disservice to the literary work, deemphasizes the work's "literariness," and conscripts literature to perform a task for which it was not intended (see Fish 2008: 171). But why should students serve literature, rather than vice versa? Literature, as Kenneth Burke ([1941] 1973) insisted, is basically "equipment for living," and our aim as teachers should be to use texts in whatever ways will best serve the well-being of our students and the world at large — as Craig Womack (2012: 45–46) puts it, "to reduce human and nonhuman suffering" and "make the world a better place."

More importantly, however, on what grounds should developing canonical and technical knowledge and skill rather than social cognition and healthy identities be the objective of literary study? Literature is a multifarious, historically contingent set of artifacts and practices, and its study should serve our individual and collective needs. The only defensible reason for using public resources to teach and study anything is to ultimately produce benefits for students and the world at large. Thus, rather than being derived from some presumed essence of literature or authorial intentions, the pedagogical aims and practices of literature courses and curricula should be determined by answers to these questions: What are the most valuable results that literary study is capable of producing, and what are the best ways of using literature to produce these benefits?[5]

The third, and most serious, ethical objection brought against the pursuit of character development and social justice through literary study is that such an agenda violates the rights of students, indoctrinating them, altering their beliefs, values, character, and/or political (e.g., voting) behavior. This objection simplistically equates transformation with brainwashing, refusing to recognize that such alterations can also be produced by knowledge, reason, and

---

5. The logical and moral bankruptcy of the objection to teaching for social justice is most striking in Fish's answer to the question of why literature should be taught at all. According to Fish (2008: 59), literary study exists for the self-gratification of the faculty. Some commentators (e.g., Edmundson 2009 and Culler 2009) suggest that such statements reveal Fish to be a provocateur who is actually satirizing the positions he puts forth. But whatever Fish's intent, the profession of literary studies often conducts itself in a manner that is quite consistent with this attitude. Indeed, the answers given to the question, "Why Teach Literature?" in the 2017 MLA session mentioned above focused primarily on the self-gratification of the teacher. The profession on the whole thus seems disturbingly indifferent to the question of why other people should pay us to do something simply because we like to do it.

truth—precisely what education should be helping students acquire. We literature teachers, like all teachers, have a responsibility to conscientiously pursue learning objectives that, in our best judgment, and based on evidence and logic and subject to the review and criticism of our peers and the general public, will be of greatest benefit both to our students and to the world at large. Learning very often involves introducing students to facts, knowledge, truths, or skills they don't ask for, don't realize they need, and perhaps don't even know exist.

Teaching for moral development and social justice is, of course, not value neutral, but neither is any other pedagogy. Simply by accepting our salaries and teaching our literature classes, we take the position that the study of literature is worth the time and money that it costs our students, their parents, and the general public, and we presume values with every learning objective we embrace (whether implicitly or explicitly), every text we select, every assignment we construct, and every question we pose in our classes. Further, the values that guide teaching for moral development and social justice — truth, compassion, and social justice—are not nearly as controversial and partisan as some values and agendas informing literary study, since they are embraced by most major religions as well as by secular moral philosophies and by both liberals and conservatives in the United States. In fact, value-neutral teaching is untenable both ethically and logically. It is ethically indefensible in that it would have to maintain that positions of opposition to slavery, rape, murder, child molestation, and so on are no better than the practices being opposed, or that racists and antiracists are morally equivalent. And it implodes logically when one recognizes that value neutrality is itself just another value that teachers are trying to impose—a conclusion that deprives value neutrality of any basis for opposing, or privileging itself over, any other pedagogy.

Most problematically, literature teachers and scholars who purport, like Fish and Graff, to engage in value-neutral teaching by providing students with disciplinary knowledge and analytical and rhetorical skills not only perpetuate their students' original indoctrination but actually equip them to do serious harm. For the analytical and rhetorical skills they teach empower violence and injustice just as effectively as they facilitate the pursuit of peace and justice,[6] serving the ends of cold, calculating, narcissistic, selfish, and violent individuals as readily as those of caring, compassionate, altruistic, peaceful people. Without training students to incorporate certain basic truths

6. For a similar argument, see Edmundson (2004: 43–47). Edmundson notes that the form of critical thinking that is most commonly taught is just as easily appropriated by global corporate interests as by humane interests.

about themselves and others into their perceptions and judgments, Fish's approach, as Paul Street has pointed out, would turn professors into submissive servants of power and the status quo (see Fish 2008: 69).[7] Following Fish and Graff's principles would make teachers into little more than intellectual weapons merchants, just as readily arming a Trump or a Putin as a Roosevelt or a Gandhi. The world desperately needs more than this, and literary study can—and should—help meet that need by developing students' social cognition and moral character in ways that benefit both the students themselves and the rest of the planet they inhabit.

References

Ammons, Elizabeth. 2010. *Brave New Words: How Literature Will Save the Planet.* Iowa City: University of Iowa Press.
Aquino, Karl, and Americus Reed II. 2002. "The Self-Importance of Moral Identity." *Journal of Personality and Social Psychology* 83, no. 6: 1423–40.
Bandura, Albert. 1976. *Social Learning Theory.* New York: Prentice-Hall.
Batson, C. Daniel, Johee Chang, Ryan Orr, and Jennifer Rowland. 2002. "Empathy, Attitudes, and Action: Can Feeling for a Member of a Stigmatized Group Motivate One to Help the Group?" *Personality and Social Psychology Bulletin* 28, no. 12: 1656–66.
Bergen, Benjamin, K. 2012. *Louder than Words: The New Science of How the Mind Makes Meaning.* New York: Basic.
Boyd, Brian. 2009. *On the Origin of Stories: Evolution, Cognition, and Fiction.* Cambridge, MA: Harvard University Press.
Bracher, Mark. 2006a. "Teaching for Social Justice: Reeducating the Emotions through Literary Study." *JAC: A Journal of Rhetoric, Culture and Politics* 26, no. 3/4: 463–511.
Bracher, Mark. 2006b. *Radical Pedagogy: Identity, Generativity, and Social Transformation.* New York: Palgrave Macmillan.
Bracher, Mark. 2009. *Social Symptoms of Identity Needs: Why We Have Failed to Solve Our Social Problems and What to Do about It.* London: Karnac.
Bracher, Mark. 2013a. *Educating for Cosmopolitanism: Lessons from Cognitive Science and Literature.* New York: Palgrave.
Bracher, Mark. 2013b. *Literature and Social Justice: Protest Novels, Cognitive Politics, and Schema Criticism.* Austin: University of Texas Press.
Bracher, Mark. 2015. "From Antisocial to Prosocial Manhood: Shakespeare's Rescripting of Masculinity in *As You Like It*." In *Configuring Masculinity in Theory and Literary Practice*, edited by Stefan Horlacher, 95–125. Amsterdam: Rodopi.
Bracher, Mark, Deborah Barnbaum, Michael Byron, Tammy Clewell, Nancy Docherty, Françoise Massardier-Kenney, David Pereplyotchik, Susan Roxburgh, and Elizabeth Smith-Pryor. 2019. "Advancing Social Justice by Improving Social Cognition through Literary Study." Under review.

7. Indeed, Fish (2008: 29) unapologetically admits that, following his principle, "a faculty member in the South in the 1950's could not embrace and urge the idea that segregation is wrong and that students should act to remedy the situation," even though the best social science of the time provided solid evidence, some of it informing the Supreme Court's ruling in *Brown v. Board of Education*, that segregation was based on faulty beliefs about certain populations and social arrangements.

Brown, Stephanie L., R. Michael Brown, and Louis A. Penner, eds. 2012. *Moving Beyond Self-Interest: Perspectives from Evolutionary Biology, Neuroscience, and the Social Sciences.* New York: Oxford University Press.

Burke, Kenneth. (1941) 1973. "Literature as Equipment for Living." In *The Philosophy of Literary Form: Studies in Symbolic Action*, 293–304. Berkeley: University of California Press.

Burke, Peter J., and Jan E. Stets. 2009. *Identity Theory.* New York: Oxford University Press.

Chartrand, Tanya L., and John A. Bargh. 1999. "The Chameleon Effect: The Perception-Behavior Link and Social Interaction." *Journal of Personality and Social Psychology* 76, no. 6: 893–910.

Chickering, Arthur W., and Linda Reisser. 1993. *Education and Identity*, 2nd ed. San Francisco, CA: Jossey-Bass.

Choi, Incheol, Richard E. Nisbett, and Ara Norenzayan. 1999. "Causal Attribution across Cultures: Variation and Universality." *Psychological Bulletin* 125, no. 1: 47–63.

Cialdini, Robert B., Stephanie L. Brown, Brian P. Lewis, Carol Luce, and Steven L. Neuberg. 1997. "Reinterpreting the Empathy-Altruism Relationship: When One into One Equals Oneness." *Journal of Personality and Social Psychology* 73, no. 3: 481–94.

Cook, Guy. 1994. *Discourse and Literature.* New York: Oxford University Press.

Culler, Jonathan. 2009. "Writing to Provoke." *Profession* 1: 84–88.

Djikic, Maja, Keith Oatley, S. Zoeterman, and J. B. Peterson. 2009. "On Being Moved by Art: How Reading Fiction Transforms the Self." *Creativity Research Journal* 21, no. 1: 24–29.

Dodge, Kenneth. 1980. "Social Cognition and Children's Aggressive Behavior." *Child Development* 51, no. 1: 162–70.

Eagleton, Terry. 1983. *Literary Theory.* Minneapolis: University of Minnesota Press.

Edmundson, Mark. 2004. *Why Read?* New York: Bloomsbury.

Edmundson, Mark. 2009. "Against Readings." *Profession* 2009, no. 1: 56–65.

Edmundson, Mark. 2013. *Why Teach?* New York: Bloomsbury.

Epps, James, and Philip C. Kendall. 1995. "Hostile Attribution Bias in Adults." *Cognitive Therapy and Research* 19, no. 2: 159–78.

Felski, Rita. 2008. *Uses of Literature.* Malden, MA: Blackwell.

Fetterley, Judith. 1978. *The Resisting Reader.* Bloomington: Indiana University Press.

Fish, Stanley. 2008. *Save the World on Your Own Time.* New York: Oxford University Press.

Gaunt, Ruth. 2009. "Superordinate Categorization as a Moderator of Mutual Infrahumanization." *Group Processes and Intergroup Relations* 12, no. 6: 731–46.

Gerrig, Richard J., and David N. Rapp. 2004. "Psychological Processes Underlying Literary Impact." *Poetics Today* 25, no. 2: 265–81.

Gill, Michael J., and Stephanie C. Cerce. 2017. "He Never Willed to Have the Will He Has: Narratives, 'Civilized' Blame, and the Need to Distinguish Two Notions of Free Will." *Journal of Personality and Social Psychology* 112, no. 3: 361–82.

Gilligan, James. 1996. *Violence: Reflections on a National Epidemic.* New York: Random House.

Gilligan, James. 2001. *Preventing Violence.* New York: Thames and Hudson.

Goleman, Daniel. 2006. *Social Intelligence.* New York: Bantam.

Graff, Gerald. 2012. "Credo of a Teacher." In Williams and Steffen 2012: 137–39.

Gregory, Marshall. 2009. *Shaped by Stories: The Ethical Power of Narrative.* Notre Dame, IN: University of Notre Dame Press.

Hammack, Phillip L. 2008. "Narrative and the Cultural Psychology of Identity." *Personality and Social Psychology Review* 12, no. 3: 222–47.

Henry, P. J., Christine Reyna, and Bernard Weiner. 2004. "Hate Welfare but Help the Poor: How the Attributional Content of Stereotypes Explains the Paradox of Reactions to the Destitute of America." *Journal of Applied Social Psychology* 34, no. 1: 34–58.

Herman, David. 2013. *Storytelling and the Sciences of the Mind.* Cambridge, MA: MIT Press.

Hitlin, Steven. 2003. "Values as the Core of Personal Identity: Drawing Links between Two Theories of Self." *Social Psychological Quarterly* 66, no. 2: 118–37.

Hudley, Cynthia, and Sandra Graham. 1993. "An Attributional Intervention to Reduce Peer-Directed Aggression among African-American Boys." *Child Development* 64, no. 1: 124–38.

Huesmann, L. Rowell. 1998. "The Role of Social Information Processing and Cognitive Schema in the Acquisition and Maintenance of Habitual Aggressive Behavior." In *Human Aggression: Theories, Research, and Implications for Social Policy*, edited by Russell G. Geen and Edward Donnerstein, 73–109. San Diego, CA: Academic Press.

Hutto, Daniel. 2008. *Folk Psychological Narratives*. Cambridge, MA: MIT Press.

Iacoboni, Marco. 2009. *Mirroring People: The Science of Empathy and How We Connect with Others*. New York: St. Martin's.

Jameson, Fredric. 1982. *The Political Unconscious: Narrative as a Socially Symbolic Act*. Ithaca, NY: Cornell University Press.

Lentricchia, Frank. 1983. *Criticism and Social Change*. Chicago: University of Chicago Press.

Levy, Sheri R., Antonio Freitas, and Peter Salovey. 2002. "Construing Action Abstractly and Blurring Social Distinctions: Implications for Perceiving Homogeneity among, but Also Empathizing with and Helping, Others." *Journal of Personality and Social Psychology* 83, no. 5: 1224–38.

Lieberman, Matthew. 2014. *Social: Why Our Brains Are Wired to Connect*. New York: Broadway.

Mar, Raymond A., and Keith Oatley. 2008. "The Function of Fiction Is the Abstraction and Simulation of Social Experience." *Perspectives on Psychological Science* 3, no. 3: 173–92.

McAdams, Dan P., and Kate C. McLean. 2013. "Narrative Identity." *Current Directions in Psychological Science* 22, no. 3: 233–38.

McDonnell, Elizabeth C., and Richard M. McFall. 1991. "Construct Validity of Two Heterosocial Perception Skill Measures for Assessing Rape Proclivity." *Violence and Victims* 6, no. 1: 17–30.

Miall, David S. 2006. *Literary Reading: Empirical and Theoretical Studies*. New York: Peter Lang.

Miall, David S., and Don Kuiken. 2002. "A Feeling for Fiction: Becoming What We Behold." *Poetics* 30, no. 4: 221–41.

Miller, Dale T. 1999. "The Norm of Self-Interest." *American Psychologist* 54, no. 12: 1053–60.

Nussbaum, Martha C. 1995. *Poetic Justice*. Boston: Beacon Press.

Oatley, Keith. 2011. *Such Stuff as Dreams: The Psychology of Fiction*. Malden, MA: Wiley-Blackwell.

Phillips, Stephen T., and Robert C. Ziller. 1997. "Toward a Theory and a Measure of the Nature of Nonprejudice." *Journal of Personality and Social Psychology* 72: 420–34.

Pyszczynski, Thomas, Jeff Greenberg, and Sheldon Solomon. 1999. "A Dual-Process Model of Defense against Conscious and Unconscious Death-Related Thoughts: An Extension of Terror Management Theory." *Psychological Review* 106, no. 4: 835–45.

Real, Terence. 1997. *I Don't Want to Talk About It: Overcoming the Secret Legacy of Male Depression*. New York: Simon and Schuster.

Reyna, Christine, P. J. Henry, William Korfmacher, and Amanda Tucker. 2005. "Examining the Principles in Principled Conservatism: The Role of Responsibility Stereotypes as Cues for Deservingness in Racial Policy Decisions." *Journal of Personality and Social Psychology* 90: 109–28.

Rorty, Amélie. 1993. "What It Takes to Be Good." In *The Moral Self*, edited by Gil G. Noam and Thomas E. Wren, 30–51. Cambridge, MA: MIT Press.

Ryan, William. 1976. *Blaming the Victim*. New York: Vintage.

Schweickart, Patrocinio P. 1986. "Reading Ourselves: Toward a Feminist Theory of Reading." In *Gender and Reading*, edited by Elizabeth A. Flynn and Patrocinio P. Schweickart, 31–62. Baltimore: Johns Hopkins University Press.

Scully, Diana. 1990. *Understanding Sexual Violence*. London: HarperCollinsAcademic.

Shelley, Mary. (1831) 2013. *Frankenstein*. New York: Penguin.

Sherman, Jeffrey W., Frederica R. Conrey, Steven U. Stroessner, and Omar A. Azam. 2005. "Prejudice and Stereotype Maintenance Processes: Attention, Attribution, and Individuation." *Journal of Personality and Social Psychology* 89, no. 4: 607–22.

Steele, Claude M. 1999. "The Psychology of Self-Affirmation: Sustaining the Integrity of the Self." In *The Self in Social Psychology*, edited by Roy F. Baumeister, 372–90. Philadelphia: Psychology Press.

Steinbeck, John. (1939) 1997. *The Grapes of Wrath*, edited by Peter Lisca and Kevin Hearle. New York: Penguin.

Stets, Jan E., and Michael J. Carter. 2011. "The Moral Self: Applying Identity Theory." *Social Psychological Quarterly* 74, no. 2: 192–215.

Stowe, Harriet Beecher. (1852) 2010. *Uncle Tom's Cabin*, edited by Elizabeth Ammons. New York: Norton.

van Peer, Willie. 2008. "The Inhumanity of the Humanities." In *New Beginnings in Literary Studies*, edited by J. Auracher and Willie van Peer, 1–22. Newcastle, UK: Cambridge Scholars.

Weiner, Bernard. 1995. *Judgments of Responsibility*. New York: Guilford.

Weiner, Bernard. 2006. *Social Motivation, Justice, and the Moral Emotions*. Mahwah, NJ: Lawrence Erlbaum.

Weiner, Bernard. 2014. "The Attributional Approach to Emotion and Motivation: History, Hypotheses, Home Runs, Headaches/Heartaches." *Emotion Review* 6, no. 4: 353–61.

Weiner, Bernard, Danny Osborne, and Udo Rudolph. 2011. "An Attributional Analysis of Reactions to Poverty: The Political Ideology of the Giver and the Perceived Morality of the Receiver." *Personality and Social Psychology Review* 15, no. 2: 199–213.

Williams, Jeffrey J. 2012. "Long Island Intellectual." In Williams and Steffen 2012: 50–56.

Williams, Jeffrey J., and Heather Steffen, eds. 2012. *The Critical Pulse: Thirty-Six Credos by Contemporary Critics*. New York: Columbia University Press.

Wittenbrink, Bernd, Pamela L. Gist, and James L. Hilton. 1997. "Structural Properties of Stereotypic Knowledge and Their Influences on the Construal of Social Situations." *Journal of Personality and Social Psychology* 72, no. 3: 526–43.

Womack, Craig. 2012. "Hearing Losses and Gains." In Williams and Steffen 2012: 42–49.

Zimbardo, Philip. 2008. *The Lucifer Effect: Understanding How Good People Turn Evil*. New York: Random House.

On Punishment and Why We Enjoy It in Fiction: Lisbeth Salander of the Millennium Trilogy and Eli in *Let the Right One In* as Scandinavian Avengers

Margrethe Bruun Vaage
University of Kent

Abstract The article proposes an explanation for why spectators may enjoy excessive punishment when watching fiction, even in Scandinavia where harsh punishment is roundly condemned. Excessive punishment is typically carried out by a vigilante avenger, and in fiction this character is often a fantastic character (e.g., not realistic, taking on superhuman and/or supernatural characteristics). We allow ourselves to enjoy punishment more readily when the character who punishes is clearly fictional. In *The Girl with the Dragon Tattoo* and *Let the Right One In*, fantastic elements seep into an otherwise realistic setting and allow the spectator to fully enjoy the main characters' vigilante revenge. The theory of fictional reliefs posited here holds that this mixture of modes facilitates one of two paths to moral judgment.

Keywords moral psychology of fiction, revenge

Scandinavian countries are renowned for their humane penal systems. Punishment is downplayed in legal reasoning in favor of rehabilitation: the aim of Scandinavian prisons is to rehabilitate the offenders and successfully reintegrate them into society.[1] In commercial Scandinavian fiction, however, punishment can be quite harsh. For example, at the end of *Let the Right One In* (*Låt*

Many thanks to Nancy Easterlin for numerous helpful comments and suggestions.
1. "Prison is not for punishment in Sweden: we get people into better shape," says the director-general of the Swedish prison and probation service in one interview (James 2014).

Poetics Today 40:3 (September 2019) DOI 10.1215/03335372-7558136
© 2019 by Porter Institute for Poetics and Semiotics

den rätte komma in) (dir. Tomas Alfredson, 2008) the vampire Eli tears apart the twelve-year-old Oskar's bullies, who are themselves adolescents. Who would support killing children who bully? As two legal theorists ask, "Why do Eli's actions feel just?" (Crofts and van Rijswijk 2015: 250). Likewise, in the first film adaptation of Stieg Larsson's Millennium Trilogy, Lisbeth Salander takes revenge on her rapist by raping him back: this is an eye-for-an-eye morality far removed from the official consensus of Scandinavian society. The aim of this paper is not to argue that Scandinavians secretly root for harder punishment. Rather, my starting point is an observation made by Arthur A. Raney (2005: 151): when we engage with fiction, we as spectators expect overpunishment.

I propose that the spectator enjoys excessive punishment when watching fiction. In the films considered here, the protagonists who punish wrongdoers excessively are often vigilantes, and vigilante avengers are often fantastic characters: though partially realistic, they take on superhuman and/or supernatural characteristics. Making the vigilante avenger a fantastic character facilitates enjoyment of punishment, because the spectator arguably enjoys overpunishment more readily when the character carrying it out is clearly fictional. I explore how moral psychology sheds light on our moral intuitions and emotions in relation to punishment and then discuss two Scandinavian case studies, *Let the Right One In* and the Swedish film adaptation of Stieg Larsson's trilogy *The Girl with the Dragon Tattoo* (*Män som hatar kvinnor*) (dir. Niels Arden Oplev, 2009), *The Girl Who Played with Fire* [*Flickan som lekte med elden*] (dir. Daniel Alfredson, 2009), and *The Girl Who Kicked the Hornet's Nest* [*Luftslottet som sprängdes*] (dir. Daniel Alfredson 2009). As wholly or partly fantastic characters, Eli and Lisbeth constitute what I elsewhere label *fictional reliefs*: fictional elements that relieve spectators of the obligation to evaluate rationally, allowing them instead to rely on moral intuitions and emotions (Vaage 2013, 2016). These films tease out moral feelings many spectators, especially Scandinavians, might not willingly acknowledge, such as the sheer pleasure of witnessing punishment and revenge.

1. Punishment in Fiction

Perhaps surprisingly, considering that punishment in some form or another features prominently in most commercial fiction, there is not a lot of research on the topic. However, William Flesch (2007) offers a relevant explanation for the human interest in narrative, arguing that the punishment of wrongdoers is critical. In evolutionary psychology, the dominant view is that human morality evolved in order to facilitate collaboration. Our species developed moral emotions and intuitions to ensure the value of cooperation. One of these moral emotions is righteous anger in response to wrongdoing, which is accompanied by the desire to see the wrongdoer punished and by a feeling of pleasure when witnessing the punishment. Indeed, humans are *altruistic* or *prosocial punishers* who desire to see wrongdoers punished even if no harm has been done to them personally (see, e.g., Greene 2013: 57–59, 61, 74).

According to Flesch (2007: 127–28), the tendency to monitor the behavior of others to track their display—or lack—of cooperation is essentially what draws us to fiction:

> Human sociality, or the cooperative or altruistic dispositions of most humans, combines these features: we monitor others, tallying the history of their cooperative behavior; we monitor how others respond or fail to respond to what *they* discover about the history of the cooperative behavior of their fellows; we are moved to punish defectors, even if they do not harm us, and to reward altruists, even if their altruism doesn't benefit us; and we are moved to approve of others who do punish defectors and reward altruism. Much human emotional life consists in and commits us to these responses to the behavior of others, and to these emotions, which impel and guarantee that behavior. Here we have in place all the features needed to explain an interest in narrative.

Thus, our interest in narratives stems from our tendency to want to monitor others, because it is intrinsically interesting to keep track of altruism or its absence. The gratification of seeing wrongdoers punished is given a central role in this theory, and a critic might reasonably object that this explanation for our interest in all kinds of narratives is flawed, since surely there are stories without punishment. Nevertheless, Flesch's observations may explain our enjoyment of stories with wrongdoing. Indeed, in commercial entertainment, there is typically a villain who is punished at the end.

Additionally, much empirical research on a model known as Affective Disposition Theory (ADT) supports the idea that people enjoy stories where wrongdoers are punished and dislike stories where wrongdoers get away with perceived injustices (cf. Raney 2002, 2011; Raney and Bryant 2002; Zillmann 2000; Zillmann and Bryant 1975; Zillmann and Cantor 1977). Yet Raney found one puzzling effect when investigating enjoyment of the so-called justice sequence, defined as "a series of events that portray the committing of a crime and the ultimate consequences experienced by the offender" (Raney and Bryant 2002: 404). In line with ADT, viewers are expected to enjoy stories where offenders are punished proportionately to the crime they committed, but Raney (2005: 151) actually found that

> respondents in the study who enjoyed the drama the most were those who thought that the crime portrayed actually warranted less punishment. Conversely, those who enjoyed the drama the least reported that the villain deserved a greater

punishment. . . . In other words, viewers of crime dramas might tend to expect and demand (for the sake of enjoyment) a punishment that is greater than what is morally acceptable in reality; only such overpunishment will lead to enjoyment.

So viewers' enjoyment of justice sequences is not representative of what we would endorse in real life. We want punishment in fiction to be more severe, and we enjoy the story less if it is not.

Why is that so? In his study of violence in film, Henry Bacon points out that punishment used to be a public ritual where the crowd played a central role. Although he warns that "it is difficult to establish a causal relationship between the decreasing of opportunities to observe real violence in public and the increase of representations of violence in fiction," he suggests that *"representations of executions seem to have the same double function as public executions*: to moralistically impress the people of the mighty arm of law and to give the spectators an experience to be remembered" (Bacon 2015: 19, my emphasis). He ties this to what he labels *the revenge instinct*: we "might not approve of revenge in real life, but we may nevertheless find it profoundly satisfying when in a story those who have been wronged and humiliated succeed in beating their tormentors — or if someone altruistically punishes them" (19). He suggests that punishment in fiction serves as an emotional substitute for public executions of wrongdoers, since modern social systems led to more humane punishment: whereas criminals are punished behind closed doors — or, in Scandinavia, reformed instead — commercial fiction caters to moral emotions, such as righteous anger, and thus offers violent punishment for consumers to enjoy.

However, in spite of Bacon's conclusion that witnessing punishment is intended to impress the onlooker of the power of the law, vigilante avengers are one of the most clear-cut examples of activation of the revenge instinct in fiction, as he also observes. Bacon (2015: 42) argues that this is "one of the most typical narrative patterns in American action films of the past few decades: the ability of the regular law enforcement is seriously flawed and a lonely hero, a vigilante, is needed to punish the baddies." He ties this to the characteristically American resentment of government control and points out that "for one reason or another, law enforcement is not available or is exasperatingly inefficient" (42). One thing to keep in mind is the excessive violence of the vigilante's retribution compared to the punishment that would be meted out by law enforcement, even in the United States. One explanation for the absence of the law in the vigilante narrative may be that it offers the spectator the pleasures of an especially violent revenge.

Bacon sees this narrative pattern as typically American because "it is difficult to think of another film culture which would have produced even in proportional terms so many films on this theme," yet he also recognizes that "the appeal is universal" (43). I think he is right to point to the vigilante's cross-cultural appeal. Although it might be that it is in American film culture that the vigilante has proliferated most prominently, in the transnational exchange of tropes, cycles, genres, and narrative patterns among film cultures, the vigilante has crossed the Atlantic Ocean to Scandinavia.

2. Blending Realism and the Fantastic: The Millennium Trilogy and *Let the Right One In*

Scandinavian crime fiction and film culture are traditionally realistic. Paula Arvas and Andrew Nestingen point out that Scandinavian crime fiction often criticizes social behavior, national institutions, and gender politics and is gloomy, pensive, and pessimistic. They argue that "combined in the Scandinavian crime novel [these factors] form a unique constellation" (Arvas and Nestingen 2011: 2). In a similar vein, Steven Peacock ties Swedish crime fiction to the "fractured dream of the welfare state" and maintains that the "Swedishness" of Swedish crime fiction is to be found in its verisimilitude and realism (Peacock 2014: 3, 16). Quoting Peter Cowie, he links this to the national film culture, which from the 1960s was dominated by realist aesthetics: "Fantasy took second place to a jarring grainy realism that sought to use film if not quite as agit-prop then certainly as an essay form, a vehicle for comment on injustice and corruption" (Cowie quoted in Peacock 2014: 42). Thus, one central topic in Swedish crime fiction is the character who suffers injustice and inequality at the hands of corrupt representatives of the welfare state.

In contrast to this tradition, Lisbeth and Eli, both violent vigilante avengers, stand out from the social realism of the stories in which they appear, resembling characters in American commercial genre films. Careful analysis teases out their defining features as Scandinavian avengers. Let us concentrate on the Millennium Trilogy first. Whereas the trilogy is characterized by realism in many ways, it also goes beyond realism in its portrayal of Lisbeth in particular. Lisbeth embodies the failings of the Swedish welfare state in that she has been subjected to years of abuse by its officials (e.g., she is subject to false imprisonment both in a psychiatric ward as a child and in prison as an adult, declared incapable of managing her own affairs, and raped by her legally appointed guardian). Lisbeth is a victim: disempowered, humiliated, and insignificant in the view of the corrupt powers that be.

However, she is also so much more than this. Lisbeth's story intriguingly borrows from international film culture, American film most prominently. Rikke Schubart maps the female action hero in popular cinema and singles out five female archetypes. One of these is the rape-avenger of the rape-revenge cycle dating back to the 1970s, a subtype of exploitation film which was integrated into mainstream American film culture in the 1980s and into blockbuster films in the 1990s (Schubart 2007: 83–84; see also Clover 1992; Heller-Nicholas 2011; Henry 2014; and Read 2000). The rape-revenge story follows a vigilante narrative pattern, wherein the rape of the female protagonist, typically depicted in gruesome detail, is followed by very violent revenge as she tracks down her rapists and brutally kills them. The rape transforms the main female character and makes her active, transgressive, and violent. One of the best-known examples is *I Spit on Your Grave* (dir. Meir Zarchi, 1978).[2]

The first installment of the Millennium Trilogy is effectively a rape-revenge story. Lisbeth is raped twice by her legal guardian Nils Bjurman and takes revenge on him not by killing him but by brutally raping him back and then tattooing "I'm a sadist pig and a rapist" on his stomach. The spectator later learns that this is not the first time Lisbeth has taken the law into her own hands; as a twelve-year-old child she threw gasoline on her violent father and set him ablaze to prevent him from physically and sexually abusing her mother. Lisbeth is avenging both her own rape and that of her mother. Although Bjurman is not killed (by Lisbeth), she does kill another serial rapist and murderer, Martin Vanger. Lisbeth could save him but instead watches him burn to death. She is scolded for this by her partner, the journalist Michael Blomkvist, who tries to argue that Vanger was a victim of horrible circumstances—most especially, a father who was himself a serial rapist and killer, and who taught Vanger to participate in his crimes from the age of sixteen. Lisbeth, however, brushes this aside and hisses back at Blomkvist to stop talking about victims: Vanger had a choice, as does everyone, and the reason for his behavior was simply that he was a pig who hated women. In this discussion, Blomkvist voices the official Scandinavian view, calling attention to the effects of Vanger's upbringing and thus suggesting that he too should be helped. Lisbeth's response is one of righteous anger and vindictiveness, typical of a vigilante avenger. Their discussion is an explicit articulation of the clash between the vengeful Lisbeth and a reasoned, normative view articulated by Blomkvist.

The Millennium Trilogy is a changing mix of genres that includes aspects of detective, thriller, fantasy, and espionage novels and films (see, e.g., Fister 2013; Leffler 2013; and O'Donoghue 2013). Notably, Lisbeth adds the most markedly unrealistic element to the story; a composite character borrowing

---

2. There are rape-revenge exploitation films to be found in a Scandinavian context in the 1970s too, such as *Thriller—en grym film* (*Thriller: A Cruel Picture*) (dir. Bo Arne Vibenius, 1973).

from all these genres, she evokes clearly fictional associations. In the second installment, moreover, Lisbeth breaks free of the constraints of realism. When she tracks down her father, Zalachenko, who is at the root of all of her problems, the story about her transforms into an action film. The portrayal of Lisbeth in the Swedish adaptation of the trilogy (e.g., her black clothes and her hard, muscular body) arguably derives from Hollywood female action heroines. Philippa Gates (2013: 210–11) maintains that whereas the Swedish film began an "'internationalisation process' of the character of Salander by enacting many mainstream (that is, Hollywood) tropes," the "American [remake of the first instalment by David Fincher] pushed Salander firmly into the role of superhero and action babe." However, Gates overlooks the many action heroine elements present already in the original Swedish novels, which refer abundantly to fiction film whenever Lisbeth takes center stage. For instance, when she decides to find her father: "She was talking to herself. And in a voice she had heard once in a film, she said: *Daaaaddyyyy, I'm coming to get yoooou*" (Larsson 2015a: 498).

Indeed, Lisbeth strongly recalls the Daughter, one of the female archetypes identified by Schubart in popular cinema, whose prototype is found in *La Femme Nikita* (dir. Luc Besson, 1990) and its American remake *Point of No Return* (dir. John Badham 1993). Although transgressive and violent, the main character learns to use her feminine attributes as assets, thus transforming from a girl with a "wrong" masculinity to an acceptable, conventionally feminine woman. Lisbeth's debt to the Daughter archetype, as well as her deviation from it, is apparent in her transformation at the end of the first installment. Here Lisbeth masquerades as Irene Nesser, taking on a traditionally feminine persona to travel internationally and put her hacker skills to use in a massive con operation that leaves her a billionaire. But contrary to forerunners such as Nikita, Lisbeth only transforms externally. She knowingly masquerades as Nesser.[3] When she returns to Sweden with a fat savings account, her blonde wig, high heels, and designer miniskirt are gone, and the old Lisbeth in her black hoodie and skinny jeans is back; she has not really changed in the way that Nikita changes.

In many ways, Lisbeth epitomizes the action heroine, playfully taking up a number of conventions in the wave of action films with strong, violent female characters in the 1980s and 1990s. As Jeffrey A. Brown (2011: 76) points out, one of the distinguishing conventions of the action heroine in film is her relationship to her father. Schubart also explores how the Daughter's strength

3. Similar to Schubart's claim that the Daughter stereotype does not subvert traditional gender roles is the often ambivalent reception of Lisbeth among feminists. See, for example, the essays collected in King and Smith (2012). For a discussion of masquerading female characters as subversive, see Brown (2011: 20).

stems either from her relationship to her father, on whom she has had to rely excessively, or from masculine qualities that are the result of fending for herself in a distorted upbringing (Schubart 2007: 210). Lisbeth's strength can indeed be tied to her troubled childhood and to her father, who takes on the monstrous features of the supervillain in this story. He even shoots his own daughter several times and buries her (alive, as it turns out). It is when Lisbeth faces her father and his ally, Lisbeth's half-brother Niedermann, that the trilogy is most similar to American action film.

Niedermann brings to mind 1980s action heroes, especially those of Arnold Schwarzenegger, most prominently in the *Terminator* films. Niedermann is a giant, presented as an almost robot-like fighting machine; he has a neurological disorder rendering him incapable of feeling pain. Lisbeth's strength is presented as biologically related to these two villains. Perhaps it is this kinship that enables her to rise from the grave in which her father has dumped her and, as the last survivor, or Final Girl, of the horror film, seek out the monsters for a final confrontation (cf. Clover 1992). Half-dead from numerous injuries, she attacks her father with an axe in a sequence that is far removed from sober, politically minded social critique: this is the Millennium Trilogy turned slasher film. Even in the novel, she is described as looking "like something from a horror film" (Larsson 2015a: 560). Indeed, in the novel (but not the film), the fictional elements are carried one step further in Niedermann's distorted vision of the seething Lisbeth, covered in her own blood and dirt, as a vicious mythological creature:

> The creature on the floor was no girl, but a being that had come back from the other side of the grave who could not be conquered with human strength or weapons known to man.
>   The transformation from human being to corpse had already begun. Her skin had changed into a lizard-like armour. Her bared teeth were piercing spikes for ripping chunks of meat from her prey. Her reptilian tongue shot out and flicked around her mouth. Her bloody hands had razor-sharp claws ten centimetres long. He could see her eyes glowing. He could hear her growling low and saw her tense her muscles to pounce at his throat.
>   *He saw clearly that she had a tail that curled and ominously began to whip the floor* (2015a: 561).

In addition to action and slasher film motifs, the story also draws on other genres and conventions. Lisbeth alludes to Pippi Longstocking, a child superhero with supernatural powers — she can even lift a horse! There are direct references to the Longstocking stories in the trilogy. For example, when Lisbeth buys a luxury flat under a false name, the doorbell says V. Kulla; Pippi's house is Villa Kulla. Additionally, the characterization of Lisbeth borrows from the countercultural hacker chick of science fiction film as well as the first feminist private investigators, models of "independence and resistance," as Barbara Fister (2013: 42) argues (see also Povlsen and Waade 2009). In sum, Lisbeth's characterization, even in the novels and the Swedish adaptations, draws on myriad conventions from a range of fictional genres, such as action, slasher, and exploitation film as well as science fiction and crime stories.

These fictional conventions are fantastical, in contrast to the realism typical of Swedish crime fiction. The trilogy as a whole is socially realistic and makes claims to truth, as social realism typically does (Vaage 2017). For example, the Millennium Trilogy can be seen as a critique of the welfare state, revealing its corruption and, in particular, doing so in its focus on violence toward women in contemporary Swedish society. Yet in spite of the critical edge of this trilogy, its fictionality is flaunted through the character Lisbeth Salander. The range of allusions to clearly fictional genres constitutes a self-reflexive element through which this work advertises its status as fiction. Thus, the spectator is encouraged to enjoy the extreme retribution for which Lisbeth is responsible: fictionality is what supplies a license to do so. This is the fictional relief at work.

A similar mix of social realism and the fantastic is found in *Let the Right One In*, a film scholars identify as a critique of the failings of the welfare state reminiscent of the Millennium Trilogy. Whereas Lisbeth took on various action-heroine conventions, in *Let the Right One In*, a vigilante vampire is needed to set things straight. The twelve-year-old Oskar is severely bullied at school in a social realist coming-of-age drama with firm roots in Scandinavian film culture; however, an eerie supernatural element is introduced into this tale of social realism. Things change when the vampire Eli moves in next-door. Eli befriends Oskar, urges him to fend for himself, and assures him that if things turn really bad, she can help him. Empowered by this friendship, Oskar turns violent and hits one of his bullies. When the bullies retaliate, it is Eli who acts as the story's final avenger in the film's splatter-film-style justice sequence. Rochelle Wright (2010: 56) points out that the film "simultaneously draws on and departs from common themes and motifs of indigenous Swedish film as well as vampire film tradition, combining elements of the horror film, the coming-of-age story and the realistic socio-psychological drama."

Moreover, J. M. Tyree argues that, within the broad horror tradition, such films comment allegorically on historical trauma; he quotes Nina Auerbach, who asserts that each age "gets the vampire it deserves" (Auberbach quoted in Tyree 2009: 32). The 1980s was a time of economic decline in Sweden, and in *Let the Right One In*, "set in 1982, the failures of the welfare state are apparent in [the fictional low-income council estate] Blackeberg's collection of lonely figures, including Oskar and his mother" (Crofts and van Rijswick 2015: 253;

see also Hakola 2015). Oskar is bullied and isolated—the Swedish "Nanny State as empty nest," as Tyree (2009: 35) puts it, unable to take proper care of its inhabitants. Crofts and van Rijswik (2015: 269) argue that Eli is an impossible figure in this social realist setting, without whom Oskar's hope of justice is slim.

In the Millennium Trilogy and *Let the Right One In*, then, the social realism typical of both Scandinavian crime and the coming-of-age story is combined with clearly fictional, fantastic elements. This is how the vigilante avenger is integrated into Scandinavian film culture. I have explored the Millennium Trilogy in greater detail, because Eli is obviously a fantastic character—she is, after all, a vampire. In both cases, it is the introduction of elements borrowed from international film culture and American commercial film in particular—though the vampire did, of course, originate in Europe—that seems to open up and allow for enjoyment of vigilante revenge. The avenger is a clearly fictional character with a combination of supernatural and/or superhuman characteristics.[4]

3. Vigilantism and Fictionality

However, we are still in need of an explanation: Why is it important to make the vigilante undeniably fictional in this context? Perhaps it is because when viewers engage with a story that they know is fiction, they rely heavily on moral intuitions and emotions and bracket the principled moral reasoning they feel obliged to make use of in real life (Vaage 2013, 2016). According to the so-called dual-process model of morality, there are two routes a moral evaluation can take: quick-and-dirty intuitive route and a slower and more cognitively demanding route forged through rational deliberation (see, e.g., Greene 2013). I want to suggest that when engaging with works neatly categorized as fiction, people rely heavily on the intuitive route. Indeed, the difference between moral evaluation in real life and in relation to fictional stories is emphasized by vigilante narratives such as the Millennium Trilogy and *Let the Right One In*. Whereas the majority of Scandinavians support the humane penal system in principle, in fiction, perhaps, they allow themselves to be stirred to righteous anger against the wrongdoer and to enjoy punishment in the subsequent justice sequences. Making the vigilante avenger a clearly fictional character—indeed, a fictional relief who draws on conven-

---

4. In her discussion of female action heroes, Lisa Purse (2011: 81) points out that powerful female characters appear most frequently in films with either a comical and/or fantastical setting, thus setting "the potentially culturally disturbing possibility of female agency and physical power at a distance from our everyday contemporary reality." It is beyond the scope of the present paper to discuss the gendered aspect of these Scandinavian avengers.

tions from action and vampire genres—facilitates enjoyment of severe punishment.

These might not be moral emotions of which we are particularly proud. The relative lack of literature on antipathy toward the villain in stories and the enjoyment of punishment of such characters is one indication that this is an aspect of our emotional engagement with fiction that we are not keen to acknowledge. Carol Clover (1992: 151) makes a related point in her discussion of rape-revenge films such as *I Spit on Your Grave*, reminding us "that lots and lots of the movies and television dramas that we prefer to think of in higher terms are in fact funded by impulses we would rather deny." *I Spit on Your Grave*, she notes, "closes all the intellectual doors and windows and leaves us staring at the lex talionis [law of retaliation] unadorned." Stripped down to its grim two-part structure, this classic rape-revenge film viscerally exposes the horror of rape and the protagonist's undiluted rage as she seeks retaliation. Another way to put this is that it is difficult to escape from extreme emotions and intuitions, such as the pleasure of witnessing violent punishment, when watching rape-revenge films.[5] Thus rape-revenge films likely confront the spectator with intuitions and impulses ordinarily unacknowledged or denied.

Anecdotally, in discussions with students, both in Norway and the United Kingdom, my inquiries about enjoyment of revenge sequences usually elicit a nervous giggle, suggesting to me that the students do perhaps enjoy them but are not sure whether it is acceptable to admit this. We have been taught not to revel in antipathy, righteous anger, and vindictive retribution. The nervous laughter may point to the presence of emotional responses about which we do not really know how to talk. The dual-process model of morality can explain the response: by granting oneself a fictional relief through film, we may enjoy severe punishment intuitively, although rationally we do not endorse it. Asked about this, students feel conflicted and giggle nervously because they cannot justify or defend their response rationally.

Jonathan Haidt, a proponent of the dual-process model for real-life morality, would perhaps say that the students are morally dumbfounded. Haidt and colleagues explain how one can sometimes condemn acts intuitively perceived as wrong when, rationally speaking, there is nothing morally wrong with the act in question. The respondents are morally dumbfounded when they try to find rational-sounding reasons to justify a response that simply is not rational (Wheatley and Haidt 2005; see also Haidt 2012). In a similar manner, my students probably perceive the punishment as morally right

5. For a critical discussion of *The Girl with the Dragon Tattoo* as a rape-revenge film and of enjoyment of Lisbeth's revenge, see Henry (2013).

intuitively, but on closer inspection, they cannot justify their response, and the puzzled giggling ensues.

The important role played by fictional elements in vigilante narratives could also explain the difference between the endings of the two stories discussed here. *Let the Right One In* exhibits clear-cut vigilante revenge in its final justice sequence, in which Oskar's bullies are killed by Eli. This ending fully adheres to the vigilante narrative pattern: as pointed out by several critics, Eli's revenge is indeed perceived as just. I propose that it is the clearly fantastic nature of the avenger that makes us perceive it as such. I doubt the spectator would have enjoyed watching a realistically portrayed human being tearing Oskar's bullies to shreds or seeing Oskar himself killing them single-handedly. Perhaps a film with such an ending would have left its spectators bewildered and shocked from having witnessed a human being's descent from victim to aggressor. In their interesting discussion of this story, Crofts and van Rijswick (2015: 260) argue that Oskar transforms as his innocence is corrupted; the revenge goes beyond self-defense. Although Oskar apparently condones Eli's actions — in the film's final sequence we see him happily leaving Blackeberg with her — it is also essential that it is not Oskar himself who kills.

Interestingly, in the last installation of the Millennium Trilogy, Lisbeth leaves it to the legal system to punish her aggressors. Admittedly, she does not do this by choice, since she is imprisoned and must prove that she did not murder three people. Nevertheless, in Lisbeth's story, justice is ultimately restored by the law. For the trial, Lisbeth again masquerades. Indeed, in the Swedish adaptation, she puts on her most fantastic cyberpunk costume: her black hair in a defiant mohawk, she sports dark makeup (blackened eyes and black lipstick) and wears numerous long metal chains and spiked collars around her neck, spiked belts around her hips, tight, shiny, metallic pants, and platform boots. In the novel, Blomkvist is reminded "of a vampire in some pop-art movie from the '60s" (Larsson 2015b: 588). Lisbeth is thus perhaps at her most fantastic when her case is tried before a judge in a court of law. Donning this outfit might be a strategy to bedazzle her opponents and to make them believe that the case will be easily won, since she is clearly crazy and her claims outrageous (Bergman 2012). Alternatively, it might be an expression of the strength required of Lisbeth to trust the law. Having repeatedly suffered injustice in the law's name, facing her tormentors in a courtroom and relying on a judge to make the right call must be the hardest thing Lisbeth has ever had to do. Her greatest victory is perhaps to make the judge listen, and she wins.

As a little emotional treat for the spectators, after the trial, Lisbeth the violent avenger is back when she stumbles upon her villainous brother Niedermann and a final fight between them takes place. Despite this one last act of violence, Lisbeth's character arc leaves her in a state of relative normalization: in the first novel/film, she transforms from realistic victim to fantastic vigilante avenger, but the story ends with some degree of hope that she might settle down as a regular citizen. Although one can imagine more fantastic adventures in wait for Lisbeth the action hero, one can also hope that, as a regular human being, she will find peace and be able to live her life rather than having to fight for it. In contrast to Eli, who is an entirely fantastic character, Lisbeth is a composite character, partly human and realistic and partly derived from action-hero conventions. Thus, whereas the ending of *Let the Right One In* is in line with the vigilante pattern, the ending of the Millennium Trilogy is more complicated, pointing to the ability of the law to ultimately get things right.

One might speculate that the degree to which a vigilante must be portrayed as clearly fictional, or even fantastic, depends on cultural context. In some cultural contexts, enjoyment of punishment might be less taboo than in Scandinavia. Bacon's historical overview explores the vigilante in Western films, such as *Shane* (dir. George Stevens, 1953), and *The Man Who Shot Liberty Valance* (dir. John Ford, 1962), and the later Dirty Harry films. In particular, the geographically expansive setting and the ideology encouraged in the American Western film could hardly be more different from that of contemporary Sweden. Additional research on the function of the vigilante avenger, the rewards he or she offers the spectator, and the variants of this narrative pattern across cultural contexts would enhance cognitive and moral analyses of these phenomena. Similar studies of vigilante avengers in other cultural contexts that compare fictional depictions to the dominant views on punishment in that culture as well as empirical studies of the audience's view on punishment and enjoyment of justice sequences in fiction would either support or invalidate the suggestion I have made in this paper: that clearly fictional conventions facilitate enjoyment of the excessive punishment in *Let the Right One In* and the Millennium Trilogy.

References

Arvas, Paula, and Andrew Nestingen. 2011. "Introduction: Contemporary Scandinavian Crime Fiction." In *Scandinavian Crime Fiction*, edited by Andrew Nestingen and Paula Arvas, 1–17. Cardiff, UK: University of Wales Press.

Åström, Berit, Katarina Gregersdotter, and Tanya Horeck, eds. 2013. *Rape in Steig Larsson's Millennium Trilogy and Beyond: Contemporary Scandinavian and Anglophone Crime Fiction*. Basingstoke, UK: Palgrave Macmillan.

Bacon, Henry. 2015. *The Fascination of Film Violence*. Basingstoke, UK: Palgrave Macmillan.

Bergman, Kerstin. 2012. "Lisbeth Salander and Her Swedish Crime Fiction 'Sisters': Stieg Larsson's Hero in a Genre Context." In King and Smith 2012: 135–44.

Brown, Jeffrey A. 2011. *Dangerous Curves: Action Heroines, Gender, Fetishism, and Popular Culture.* Jackson: University Press of Mississippi.

Clover, Carol. 1992. *Men, Women and Chain Saws: Gender in the Modern Horror Film.* Princeton, NJ: Princeton University Press.

Crofts, Penny, and Honni van Rijswijk. 2015. "'What Kept You So Long?': Bullying's Gray Zone and the Vampire's Transgressive Justice in *Let the Right One In*." *Law, Culture, and the Humanities* 11, no. 2: 248–69. hdl.handle.net/10453/19014.

Flesch, William. 2007. *Comeuppance: Costly Signaling, Altruistic Punishment, and Other Biological Components of Fiction.* Cambridge, MA: Harvard University Press.

Fister, Barbara. 2013. "The Millennium Trilogy and the American Serial Killer Narrative: Investigating Protagonists of Men Who Write Women." In Åström, Gregersdotter, and Horeck 2013: 34–50.

Gates, Philippa. 2013. "'Hidden in the Snow': Female Violence against the Men Who Hate Women in the Millennium Adaptations." In Åström, Gregersdotter, and Horeck 2013: 193–213.

Greene, Joshua. 2013. *Moral Tribes: Emotion, Reason, and the Gap between Us and Them.* New York: Penguin.

Haidt, Jonathan. 2012. *The Righteous Mind: Why Good People Are Divided by Politics and Religion.* London: Allen Lane.

Hakola, Outi. 2015. "Nordic Vampires: Stories of Social Exclusion in Nordic Welfare States." In *Nordic Genre Film: Small Nation Film Cultures in the Global Marketplace*, edited by Tommy Gustafsson and Pietari Kääpä, 203–14. Edinburgh: Edinburgh University Press.

Heller-Nicholas, Alexandra. 2011. *Rape-Revenge Films: A Critical Study.* Jefferson, NC: McFarland.

Henry, Claire. 2013. "*The Girl with the Dragon Tattoo*: Rape, Revenge, and Victimhood in Cinematic Translation." In Åström, Gregersdotter, and Horeck 2013: 175–92.

Henry, Claire. 2014. *Revisionist Rape-Revenge: Redefining a Film Genre.* New York: Palgrave Macmillan.

James, Erwin. 2014. "Prison Is Not for Punishment in Sweden: We Get People into Better Shape." *Guardian* November 26. www.theguardian.com/society/2014/nov/26/prison-sweden-not-punishment-nils-oberg.

King, Donna, and Carrie Lee Smith, eds. 2012. *Men Who Hate Women and Women Who Kick Their Asses: Stieg Larsson's Millennium Trilogy in Feminist Perspective.* Nashville, TN: Vanderbilt University Press.

Larsson, Stieg. 2015a. *The Girl Who Played with Fire*, translated by Reg Keeland. London: MacLehose.

Larsson, Stieg. 2015b. *The Girl Who Kicked the Hornets' Nest*, translated by Reg Keeland. London: MacLehose.

Leffler, Yvonne. 2013. "Lisbeth Salander as Melodramatic Heroine: Emotional Conflicts, Split Focalization, and Changing Roles in Scandinavian Crime Fiction." In Åström, Gregersdotter and Horeck 2013: 51–64.

O'Donoghue, Heather. 2013. "Old Wine in New Bottles: Tradition and Innovation in Stieg Larsson's *Millennium* Trilogy." In *Stieg Larsson's* Millennium *Trilogy: Interdisciplinary Approaches to Nordic Noir on Page and Screen*, edited by Steven Peacock, 35–57. Basingstoke, UK: Palgrave Macmillan.

Peacock, Steven. 2014. *Swedish Crime Fiction: Novel, Film, Television.* Manchester, UK: Manchester University Press.

Povlsen, Karen Klitgaard, and Anne Marit Waade. 2009. "*The Girl With the Dragon Tattoo*: Adapting Embodied Gender from Novel to Movie in Stieg Larsson's Crime Fiction." *P.O.V.: A Danish Journal of Film Studies*, no. 28: 64–74. pov.imv.au.dk/Issue_28/section_2/artc7A.html.

Purse, Lisa. 2011. *Contemporary Action Cinema.* Edinburgh: Edinburgh University Press.

Raney, Arthur A. 2002. "Moral Judgment as a Predictor of Enjoyment of Crime Drama." *Media Psychology* 4, no. 4: 307–24. doi.org/10.1207/S1532785XMEP0404_01.

Raney, Arthur A. 2005. "Punishing Media Criminals and Moral Judgment: The Impact on Enjoyment." *Media Psychology* 7, no. 2: 145–63. doi.org/10.1207/S1532785XMEP 0702_2.

Raney, Arthur A. 2011. "The Role of Morality in Emotional Reactions to and Enjoyment of Media Entertainment." *Journal of Media Psychology* 23, no. 1: 18–23. doi.org/10.1027 /1864–1105/a000027.

Raney, Arthur A., and Jennings Bryant. 2002. "Moral Judgment and Crime Drama: An Integrated Theory of Enjoyment." *Journal of Communication* 52, no. 2: 402–15. doi.org /10.1111/j.1460–2466.2002.tb02552.x.

Read, Jacinda. 2000. *The New Avengers: Feminism, Femininity, and the Rape-Revenge Cycle.* Manchester, UK: Manchester University Press.

Schubart, Rikke. 2007. *Super Bitches and Action Babes: The Female Hero in Popular Cinema, 1970– 2006.* Jefferson, NC: McFarland.

Tyree, J. M. 2009. "Warm-Blooded: *True Blood* and *Let The Right One In.*" *Film Quarterly* 63, no. 2: 31–37. doi.org/10.1525/FQ.2009.63.2.31.

Vaage, Margre Bruun. 2013. "Fictional Reliefs and Reality Checks." *Screen* 54, no. 2: 218–37. doi.org/10.1093/screen/hjt004.

Vaage, Margrethe Bruun. 2016. *The Antihero in American Television.* New York: Routledge.

Vaage, Margrethe, Bruun. 2017. "From *The Corner* to *The Wire*: On Nonfiction, Fiction, and Truth." *Journal of Literary Theory* 11, no. 2: 255–70. doi.org/10.1515/jlt-2017–0023.

Wheatley, Thalia, and Jonathan Haidt. 2005. "Hypnotic Disgust Makes Moral Judgments More Severe." *Psychological Science* 16, no. 10: 780–84. doi.org/10.1111/j.1467–9280 .2005.01614.x.

Wright, Rochelle. 2010. "Vampire in the Stockholm Suburbs: *Let the Right One In* and Genre Hybridity." *Journal of Scandinavian Cinema* 1, no. 1: 55–70. doi.org/10.1386/jsca.1.1.55_1.

Zillmann, Dolf. 2000. "Basal Morality in Drama Appreciation." In *Moving Images, Culture, and the Mind*, edited by Ib Bondebjerg, 53–63. Luton, UK: University of Luton Press.

Zillmann, Dolf, and Jennings Bryant. 1975. "Viewer's Moral Sanction of Retribution in the Appreciation of Dramatic Presentations." *Journal of Experimental Social Psychology* 11, no. 6: 572–82. doi.org/10.1016/0022–1031(75)90008–6.

Zillmann, Dolf, and Joanne Cantor. 1977. "Affective Responses to the Emotions of a Protagonist." *Journal of Experimental Social Psychology* 13, no. 2: 155–65. doi.org/10.1016 /S0022–1031(77)80008–5.

III. HEALING PLANET, SPECIES, AND SELF

Why We Care about (Non)fictional Places: Empathy, Character, and Narrative Environment

Alexa Weik von Mossner
University of Klagenfurt

Abstract Cognitive ecocriticism draws on research in neuroscience and cognitive narratology to explore how literary reading can lead us to care about natural environments. Ann Pancake's novel *Strange as This Weather Has Been* (2007) serves as an example of a novel that cues both direct and empathetic emotions for an actual environment—the Appalachian Mountains—that is wounded and scarred. I argue that the novel's protagonists allow readers to imaginatively experience what it is like to love an environment and then witness its destruction by mountaintop removal mining. Pancake's decision to relate large parts of the story through the consciousness of teenagers allows for highly emotional perspectives that have the potential to engage readers in the social and moral issues around resource extraction.

Keywords cognitive ecocriticism, empathy, emotion, embodied simulation, character

When fifteen-year-old Bant Turrell follows her father beyond a "No Trespassing" sign in the Appalachian Mountains, she catches her breath. Confronted with the sight of "Yellowroot Mountain blasted to bits," the teenage protagonist of Ann Pancake's novel *Strange as This Weather Has Been* (2007) is shaken by bouts of horror and disgust as she stares at the "pure mountain guts" that have been exposed by mountaintop removal mining (Pancake 2007: 20). The "strange rocks" seem to push Bant physically away, and she

Poetics Today 40:3 (September 2019) DOI 10.1215/03335372-7558150

is horrified when she must touch the "gooey liquid stuff" between them with her hands to avoid "slip[ping] and skin[ing] an ankle, let it get in [her] blood" (21). That the girl reacts so violently to the destruction of a beloved mountain is not surprising. It is in our evolutionary makeup to engage emotionally with the environment that surrounds us, especially when it's threatened or threatening to us.[1] What is more remarkable, though, is that readers can share Bant's feelings and perceptions in this moment even though she is a fictional character. Her vivid first-person account invites them to simulate both her feelings and the environment as she perceives it, and her use of the word "guts" cues them to envision that environment as a living thing that has been violated, ripped open, its intestines spilling out of a gaping wound.[2] The narrative thereby enables readers to understand not just cognitively but also viscerally and emotionally the effects of a mountaintop removal mine on the natural environment and on the people living in it.

In this essay, I use a cognitive ecocritical approach to explore how readers come to care about a literary environment and to consider whether such caring can have any impact on their beliefs, attitudes, and actions in the actual world. Pancake's novel lends itself particularly well to such an exploration, because it fictionalizes highly contested sites of environmental and social exploitation in West Virginia with a stated political purpose. Recent research in cognitive science has given new credence to the claim that reading literature can develop cognitive and affective capabilities that are essential for responsible citizenship and social justice. Such claims have been made by literary scholars (Booth 1988; Koopman 2010), philosophers (Nussbaum 1997), social scientists (Dromi and Illouz 2010; Lewis, Rodgers, and Woolcock 2008) and developmental psychologists (Hoffman 2000), and they are increasingly supported by empirical studies in the psychology of fiction (Green and Brock 2000; Mar, Oatley, and Peterson 2009; Johnson 2013; Kidd and Castano 2013). Cognitive literary scholars with an interest in character (Hogan 2011; Keen 2007; Vermeule 2010), emotional persuasion (Sklar 2013), and the relationship between literature and social justice (Bracher 2014) have taken up such claims and contributed greatly to our understanding of how cultural texts cultivate moral feelings for fictional humans. In recent years, scholars with a more ecocritical bent have also turned our

---

1. Emotions, social anthropologist Kay Milton (2002: 4) reminds us, "operate in the relationship between an individual organism and its environment; they are induced when an organism interacts with objects in that environment" and motivate the organism to action.

2. Psychologists Rozin, Haidt, and McCauley (2010: 757) note that "violations of the exterior envelope of the body (including gore and deformity)" are a strong elicitor of disgust. Imagining the unearthed pieces of rock as a bodily violation, therefore, cues the corresponding disgust response in readers.

attention to the complex relationship between readers, characters, and the environments that surround them, demonstrating that we need to go far beyond the traditional idea of the "setting" that simply provides the background to the foregrounded action.

Regardless of whether they work with the notion of place (Easterlin 2012), the concept of the storyworld (James 2015) or that of a narrative environment (Weik von Mossner 2017), these ecocritically minded scholars all explore literary representations of "the mind's [variously] positive and troubled relationships with nonhuman nature" (Easterlin 2012: 93). In doing so, they analyze literary representations of human-nature relationships and insist on the central importance of narrative environments for plot and character development. The present essay draws on this rich interdisciplinary archive to explore how a novel such as *Strange as This Weather Has Been* can lead us to feel and care about its narrative environment — and its real-world counterparts — through vivid sensual imagery and character identification.

1. Narrative Environments, Empathy, and Emotion

Ecocritical investigations into literary texts tend to have clearly defined ethical and political dimensions. In Cheryll Glotfelty's (1996: xix) influential and deliberately open definition, ecocriticism is "the study of the relationship between literature and the physical environment," but scholars in the field have emphasized the approach's ethical "commitment to environmentalist praxis" (Buell 1995: 430) and described it as an "avowedly political mode of analysis" (Garrard 2011: 3). These ethical and political commitments, acknowledges Easterlin in her contribution to Lisa Zunshine's *Introduction to Cognitive Cultural Studies*, may seem to make "the prospect of a cognitive ecocriticism an unwarranted conjunction" (Easterlin 2010: 257), since cognitive literary studies "takes as its starting point human mental processes" rather than the ethical implications of human-nature interactions. However, as Easterlin also points out, this apparent incompatibility is a misconception, because "knowledge of the mind is relevant to any literary account of the environment" (257). If we are interested in how narrative renderings of imaginary places affect readers during and beyond the reading experience, we can find valuable analytical tools in theoretical approaches that draw on the latest insights of cognitive science for textual analysis. Combining cognitive and ecocritical modes of analyses both gives us a better understanding of the multifaceted ways in which literary characters interact with their environments and sheds light on how such interactions engage readers.

Cognitive literary scholars such as Marco Caracciolo and Elaine Scarry have likened literary narratives to "instruction manuals" (Caracciolo 2013:

83) that contain "a set of instructions for mental composition" (Scarry 2001: 244) and invite readers to follow those instructions. The metaphor of the instruction manual is an interesting one: it stresses the active role of the reader as someone who *performs* the narrative, as psychologist Richard Gerrig (1998: 12) puts it. Just like actors on a stage, Gerrig proposes, readers engage in acts of simulation during which "they must use their own experiences of the world to bridge the gaps in texts" and must invest their own emotions to "give substance to the psychological lives of characters" (17).[3] This suggests that the mental performances of readers will be idiosyncratic to some degree, but we can also expect similarities across readers. Like instruction manuals, literary narratives "'invite' their readers to entertain certain imaginings" in a certain way (Caracciolo 2013: 83). The physiological processes that allow us to entertain such imaginings are similar in all humans.

These physiological processes can be explained through the concept of *liberated embodied simulation*, which, in the words of Hannah Wojciehowski and Vittorio Gallese (2011: n.p.), is "a process enabling a more direct and less cognitively mediated access to the world of narrated others and mediating our capacity to share the meaning of their actions, basic motor intentions, feelings, and emotions." Gallese was one of the neuroscientists at the University of Parma who, in the early 1990s, discovered a group of specialized neurons in macaque monkeys that they called the mirror neuron system and that was later also found in humans and other mammals.[4] Mirror neurons are cells in our brains that fire both when we carry out an action and when we watch another person carrying out the same action, allowing us to understand the other person's action on a visceral level. Importantly, the mirror system helps humans recognize the actions of others, and, moreover, allows them to attribute mental states such as sensations, attitudes, and emotions (Rizzolatti and Sinigaglia 2008: xii). That is why researchers have linked mirror neurons to social cognition and communication. Just as important for cognitive narratology is the finding that these neurons are also activated when we read about a fictional character in a novel (Iacoboni 2009: 5). As Gallese (2011: 443) explains, "The MNS [mirror neuron system] is involved not only in understanding *visually presented* actions, but also in mapping acoustically or visually presented action-related *linguistic expressions*." The same is true for linguistically presented perceptions and emotions, which

3. Psychologists such as Richard Gerrig (1999) and Keith Oatley (2011) have developed simulation accounts of reading that are based on appraisal theories of emotion (for a critique of such accounts, see Mumper and Gerrig, this issue). The accounts of liberated embodied simulation that I employ here are based on different theories of emotion that have been developed in the interdisciplinary field of embodied cognition.

4. For more detailed information on the mirror neuron system, see Iacoboni (2009).

is why mirror neurons offer a plausible neurophysiological explanation for Gerrig's (1999: 17) observation that we use our own emotions to "give substance to the psychological lives of characters" and for the notion that narrative texts are imaginative "instruction manuals."

How, then, can these insights about our neural engagement with literary characters be transferred to our imaginary experience of narrative environments and characters' interaction with those environments? To answer this question, we must consider literary perspective and the kind of information we receive about a given environment from a narrator and any number of characters. In other words, how we imagine and feel about the virtual environment we encounter during literary reading is to a large degree a question of focalization.[5] "Determining focalization," writes narratologist James Phelan (2001: 58), "is just a matter of answering the question *who perceives?*," and since as readers we cannot directly perceive a narrative environment, our imaginative experience of it is dependent on—and to some degree determined by—our simulations of a focalizer's perceptions, thoughts, and feelings in relation to that environment. In the case of a single first-person narrator, we literally receive no information about the environment that is external to the narrator's mind. Even if the narrator provides us with such information—for example, in the form of another character's dialogue, a text he or she reads, or a news show he or she watches—we cannot access that information directly but receive it filtered through the consciousness of the narrator, who may or may not be reliable. If several first-person narrators are used, or an omniscient third-person narrator who conveys the subjective experiences of several characters in the text, we are provided with a variety of perspectives on the narrative environment, perspectives that may complement or contradict one another. Whether the presence of a variety of perspectives facilitates our understanding of the narrative environment or instead complicates it depends not least on literary style.

Ecocritics have frequently made the argument that realistic storytelling, with its predilection for detail and conscious striving for representational mimesis, is best suited to evoke in readers a vivid image of a given environment. And indeed, attention to descriptive detail can help us create vivid mental simulations of narrative environments. Scarry (2001: 9) has argued that imaginary vivacity "comes about by reproducing the deep structures of perception." What is simulated in literary reading, she maintains, "is not only the sensory outcome (the way something looks or sounds or feels beneath the hands) but the actual structure that gave rise to the perception; that is,

---

5. The notion of focalization was first developed by Gérard Genette in his seminal *Narrative Discourse* (Genette 1980).

the material conditions that made it look, sound, or feel the way it did" (9). Research on embodied simulation suggests that we not only see such material conditions before some inner eye but literally feel them. Neuroscientist Arthur Jacobs and literary scholar Raoul Schrott (2014: 130) explain that "reading the sequence of letters that makes up the word 'radish' causes various sensory-response areas of the brain to become active, while 'ball' also causes movement centers to be active, and 'kiss' serves those that deal with emotions. The brain actually experiences events it is actually only reading about, and this power of simulation (mimesis, reliving) is an important basis of immersion." How much mimetic detail we need to be able to simulate the bodily-perceptual feel of a narrative environment depends in part on our own previous experience and related emotional memories. But there is no question that we need some kind of mental "instruction manual" to experience it vividly.

There are at least two features of narratives, then, that enable readers to experience what Scarry (2001: 9) calls the "non-actual, mimetic perception" of a narrative environment: one is a vivid account of sensory outcomes — experienced through the conscious bodily experience of a focalizer — and the other one the evocation of the material conditions that give rise to those outcomes. It is in this evocation of material conditions where the detailed, mimetic storytelling of realism may be an advantage, because it helps readers imagine concrete objects, spatial relations, and other material aspects of the narrative environment. However, what matters most is the vivacity of a description as well as its affective charge, not necessarily the amount of descriptive detail. As Anežka Kuzmičová (2012: 23) has noted, "there is no straightforward relation between the degree of detail in spatial description on one hand, and the vividness of spatial imagery and presence on the other." Rather, the illusion of presence arises from complex processes of sensorimotor simulation and resonance.[6] As I have argued elsewhere (Weik von Mossner 2017: 56), it may therefore be a fallacy to assume that detail-oriented realistic storytelling is necessarily the most effective in engaging readers imaginatively and emotionally in a narrative environment. Ann Pancake's *Strange as This Weather Has Been* demonstrates this well, since it offers an intriguing mix of realism and more postmodern elements, such as the use of multiple perspectives and narrative styles.

6. G. Gabriele Starr (2013: 80) notes that when visual imagery is processed during reading, it activates the sensorimotor cortex in the reader's brain in much the same way as if he or she had perceived that environment directly.

2. Perspective, Experience, and Ethics in *Strange as This Weather Has Been*

Pancake's novel about the environmental and social costs of mountaintop removal mining in the Appalachian Mountains allows readers to experience its narrative environment through no less than six focalizing characters. Most of them are teenagers and belong to the Turrell family, which for generations has struggled to make its home in a small coal-mining community in West Virginia. In addition to the fifteen-year-old Bant, there are her three younger brothers Dane, Corey, and Tommy, who grow up in the same toxic wasteland but do not feel intense anger and mourning about the loss of the mountains. Those feelings Bant shares only with her mother Lace, who is old enough to remember the environment still untouched by surface mining and who learned from her own mother "how to live off these hills" (Pancake 2007: 94). Like Bant, Lace tells her story in the first person, whereas the perspectives of Dane and Corey are conveyed by third-person narrators that slip into their young minds and present their perceptions, thoughts, and feelings in immediate, breathless prose.[7] Through these different perspectives and modes of narration, the novel creates a multifaceted prism that allows readers to vividly imagine an environment that is both dying and deadly. As Jack Pendarvis (2007) puts it in his review for the *New York Times*, "Ann Pancake's fine, ambitious first novel is about something simple: what it's like to live below a mountaintop-removal strip mine."

Mountaintop removal mining is an environmental extraction practice that is vastly more detrimental than underground mining. Historian Duane A. Smith (1994: 3) reminds us that any form of mining leaves behind "gutted mountains, dredged-out streams, despoiled vegetation, open pits, polluted creeks, barren hillsides and meadows, a littered landscape, abandoned camps, and burned out miners." What distinguishes mountaintop removal mining is that it is a particularly striking example of what Timothy LeCain (2009: 210) calls a profit-driven "system of mass destruction" that uses explosives to remove up to four hundred vertical feet of mountain and leaves behind a wasteland of toxic coal slurries and "valley fills." The experience of what it is like to live below such a mine is one that Pancake underwent herself, albeit only indirectly through empathetic engagement with people who are affected. She has stated in interviews that she had the initial idea for her novel when, in 2000, she accompanied her sister Catherine to their home state West Virginia to make a documentary film about surface mining.

Up to that point, Pancake had taken pains to never mix her political activism with her fiction writing. In a 2013 article, she explains that she

---

7. Readers learn about the youngest boy, Tommy, only indirectly, through the accounts of his siblings.

"simply didn't believe fiction could put a scratch in contemporary social and political problems" (Pancake 2013: 404). That belief radically changed after she and Catherine visited the Reeds, a poor miner family with four young children who lived right below a mountaintop removal mine and had been repeatedly hit by the severe flash floods caused by it. "The tough little barefoot kids told me how ... scared they were of the floods," Pancake recalls, "how they lay in their beds terrified of what might come down off that mine" (404). Witnessing the ecological devastation wrought by mountaintop removal mining with her own eyes had an impact on the author, but what left an even deeper impression were the personal experiences of those who had to grow up within that devastation. "About two weeks after I went up Seng Creek," she explains in the interview, "I heard in my head the voice of a fictional fourteen-year-old who lived under that mountaintop mine.... I figured it was a short story, but a few days later, the voice of another kid in that family came, and a little while after that, a third voice. About this time, I realized that what I was writing wasn't a short story, but a novel" (404). And not only was it a novel, but it became what Pancake herself calls "a political novel" (404), and thus the kind of text she thought she would never write.

That Pancake's empathetic identification with actual people played a central role in her creation of the novel is nothing unusual. Suzanne Keen (2007: vii) explains in *Empathy and the Novel* that authors inevitably rely on their empathetic capacities when creating fictional characters.[8] Keen has also argued that politically minded authors often deliberately and strategically use their authorial empathy to guide readers' sympathies and emotional responses. Evoking Gayatri Chakravorty Spivak's ([1985] 1996: 214) notion of strategic essentialism, Keen explains that such *authorial strategic empathizing* "occurs when an author employs empathy in the crafting of fictional texts, in the service of 'a scrupulously visible political interest'" (2010: 83). When writing *Strange as This Weather Has Been*, Pancake did have such an overt political interest, and she has openly stated her belief in the "unique abilities literature, including fiction, has to educate, move, and transform audiences" (Pancake 2013: 408). Literature, the author believes, "is one of the most powerful antidotes we have to "psychic numbing," because it "immerse[s] the reader in the personal stories of individual people," compelling him or her to "actually 'live the life' of a person who is a subject of injustice" (408). These stated beliefs about the potential real-world effects of processes of liberated embod-

8. Given this centrality of authors' empathy to the creative process, it is unsurprising that novelists tend to be above-average empathizers. A study conducted by Marjorie Taylor, Sarah D. Hodges, and Adèle Kohányi (2003: 377) found that writers of both genders were "particularly off the charts" for fantasy and perspective taking, two traits that are central to the creation of narrative environments and the characters that populate them.

ied simulation during novel reading echo those voiced by Nussbaum and others. So it is not surprising that the novel's use of focalization and narrative style invites readers to feel with and for characters who—like the Reed family—suffer greatly from the ruthless exploitation of people and places in the Appalachian Mountains. I want to briefly consider all those characters and their relationships to their environment, starting with the mother of the Turrell family, Lace.

It is Lace's first-person narration that opens the novel, and from the very beginning her voice foregrounds the complex dynamics between people and their environments. When she was young, Lace remembers, she did not yet fully understand how deeply interconnected she was with the mountain landscape around her. "You could take one look at them," she writes of her parents, "and see how they fit" (Pancake 2007: 3), but as a teenager Lace cannot share the older generation's feelings of rootedness and place attachment. Instead, she begins to separate herself from the mountains and the community alike, because "nothing on TV, nothing in books, nothing in magazines looked much like our place or much like us, and it's interesting, how you can believe what's on TV is realer than what you feel right under your feet" (3). Those who grow up in this place, she explains, learn early on through the media "that [their] place is more backward than anywhere in America and anybody worth much will get out as soon as they can" (3). At the age of eighteen, Lace does not want to be associated with backwardness, nor does she want to be considered worthless. And so she dissociates herself emotionally from her home and decides that she is "newer than all this here" (3).

It is only when she moves away for college and winds up lonely and miserable that Lace begins to understand that something important is missing in her life. "It was like I was all the time feeling like I wasn't touching nothing," she explains, "and wasn't nothing touching me back, and yeah, they had hills in Morgantown, but no backhome hills, and not the same feel backhome hills wrap you in" (4). Her homesickness and felt lack of connection to Morgantown lead Lace to hitchhike back to her parents' house, and it is only when she is physically present in it that she can see it "again how [she'd] seen it before [she] left. Grubby, grim, gritty, covered with that asphalt shingle stuff with fake brick shapes pressed in it" (10). Confused, she tries to understand what it is "about this place" that casts such a spell upon her and realizes that her very being is connected to it: "I'd learned the smallness of me in the away. I understood that when I left, I lost part of myself, but when I stayed, I couldn't stretch myself full" (10). This insoluble tension between a place attachment that is also expressed in her vernacular writing style (mimicking local dialect) and her vague longing for expansion marks Lace's relationship to Yellowroot and Cherryboy Mountains throughout the novel.

Lace's conflicted feelings about both her home and new locations echo research in the social sciences, revealing that human understandings of place are hardly objective reflections of a given space. Instead, they emerge from a range of cognitive and affective processes that are carried out in relation to the environment. Drawing on research in the interdisciplinary field of place studies, Easterlin (2017: 828) suggests that place is a process that emerges from "an array of components, including emotion, intellection, memory, self-definition, sociality, culture, and physical location." Much of this dynamic construction of place is unconscious and the result of an embodied experience that involves seeing, hearing, smelling, and touching a material environment as well as moving around in it, measuring its extension and physical properties through climbs, walks, leaps, and other physical activities. The central tenet of place studies is that all such understandings are affectively mediated and ever-changing, and Easterlin (2017: 828) claims that they are consistent with evolutionary exigencies: "Humans, like other animals, have a species-typical, self-interested orientation toward the environment." The embodied experience of place (and the memory of such experience), then, has a downright existential dimension, in that it functions to ensure well-being and survival.

How important embodied experience is for Lace's understanding of the mountains around her becomes clear after she has made the fateful decision to have sex with a fifteen-year-old "beautiful boy" (Pancake 2007: 6) they call Jimmy Make and becomes pregnant. Jimmy is too young and overwhelmed to provide for Lace and their daughter Bant, and so Lace asks her mother to show her how to forage in the mountains to make some badly needed money. However, the foraging has some unexpected effects:

> When I first got started, it was just plants I'd expected Mom to reteach me, things I could sell, but she knew she couldn't teach one without the other, and when I look back now, I see how much else I relearned. The names of all the little streams off Cherryboy. How the game paths went. Where you could find a safe drink of water, where you could duck under overhangs to shelter out of storms. It was shortcuts across ridges from hollow to hollow, it was how easiest — footholds, handholds — to scale a particular draw.... All those quiet hours in the woods, I couldn't help paying attention, I started listening in other ways. (139)

It is the embodied experience of the mountain environment — the conscious and attentive exploration of streams, game paths, shortcuts, footholds, and shelters — that deepens Lace's knowledge as well as her emotional attachment to it, and this attachment is further intensified by the presence of her daughter. "We kept following the seasons," she writes, "first Bant on my back, and then Bant waddling, stumbling, picking herself up, and finally Bant working with us" (140). The loving memories of seeing her child grow up becomes an integral part of Lace's remembered experience, and her feelings for the mountains are continuous with her feelings for the people who are important in her life, above all her family. Here Pancake's fictional depiction of the continuity between familial affection, learning, and place attachment is consistent with research in developmental psychology and place studies.

The chapters that are narrated from Lace's perspective thus give readers insight into the development of her place attachment from something that is mostly unconscious and visceral to something that is consciously understood and lived. They furthermore demonstrate what happens to such attachment when the place itself is transformed into something unrecognizably different. Typically, "the perception of place . . . will inevitably . . . be affected or in fact transformed by changes in both social or family relationships and the physical environment" (Easterlin 2016: 232). It is exactly this combination of transformations that affect Lace later in life, when she is a mother of four and stuck with a sloppy, angry Jimmy Make, who is now her husband. At this point, she has lost both of her beloved parents and most of her dreams for the future. The physical environment, too, is changing in horrifying ways: "Killing the trees," she writes, "I knew that's what they did first, and I knew it didn't necessarily mean an impoundment was going in. But it for certain meant the death of Yellowroot" (Pancake 2007: 300). Looking at the murder site "head-on" is too hard for Lace to bear because she has come to understand that "through all those hard, hard years . . . as I'd lost my self, my dream, my dad, my mom—it was place that crept in and filled the lack" (300). But now she is losing place as well, and her home is in constant danger of being engulfed by a toxic flood. The "death of Yellowroot" therefore also constitutes another and just as personal loss that affects the very core of Lace's existence.

Jimmy Make—who works for the mining companies if he works at all—shares his wife's anger, but he cannot relate to her intense feeling of loss. The only member of her immediate family who can is Bant, who—unlike her younger brothers—used to accompany her mother on her foraging trips across the mountains. Like Lace, Bant relates her experience of the mountain environment in the first person, but her narrative is much less reflective than her mother's. Instead, it offers a vivid and highly immediate account of Yellowroot's destruction. Whereas Lace tells readers about her relationship to the changing environment, Bant shows them what if feels like in a way that cues liberated embodied simulation. "When I was real little," she writes, "moving over this land, I never saw myself, felt myself as separate from it" (100). Now that the land is being "taken" by the mining companies, however, she feels "a distance more in time than in space" and fears that she is losing part of herself as she hears "the machines destructing overhead. . . . noises separated out—revving motors and backup beepers and crashes and bangs. Scrape of that humongous shovel against rock" (101).

Unlike her mother, Bant feels a deep need to witness the mountain murder site with her own eyes, and so she trespasses onto the company territory to face it. At first, she feels mostly empathetic pain as she imagines how her dead grandmother would react to the devastation. But then she is able to "feel the hurt for [her]self. . . . It was like they were knocking down whatever is inside of you that holds you up. Kicking down the blocks that hold your intestines, kicking, until what the blocks kept up falls and leaves you empty inside" (103). Whereas Lace's narration cues readers to perceive the mountain as a living being, Bant's chapters do this and more: through the use of second person as well as direct reference to human organs, she creates an immediate, three-way, physical connection between the bodies of the mountain, character, and reader. Here and elsewhere in the novel, Bant uses her own body—and the fact that our mirror neurons will fire when we read about another human's bodily movements, feelings, and perceptions—to give readers a sense of what it feels like to behold the remnants of a violated mountain. Her mind, Bant remembers, "didn't have any way to hold the dead" mountains, and is unable "to see it as real" until she forces herself to look:

> I stared my eyes into Yellowroot, I opened my eyes so wide they burned, and, *show me*, I thought. Pushing my hardest towards the real. *Show me.*
>
> And sudden, like waking up, my mind did let it in. My mind opened and let it past my eyes. The recognition hit my scalp and collared my throat, and my mouth swelled thick—but I couldn't hold the realness for more than a few seconds. I had to drop my face away from what I saw. But all I had to drop it to were those rocks, those rocks fresh from the center of the earth and what those rocks carried, some warning from the world, and always the end of something. (106)

If Lace's voice gives readers a cognitive understanding of the larger context of mountaintop removal mining and its effects on her family, it is Bant who allows them to understand on the visceral level how it hurts those who are affected by it.

The other focalizers of the novel—Bant's brothers Dane and Corey, their uncle Mogey, and the family friend Avery—all add new dimensions to readers' imagined experience of the devastated environment. Pancake insinuates early on that "something is wrong" with Dane, but the exact nature of his disability is never revealed. What becomes clear from the chapters that are channeled through his mind is that the oddly shaped twelve-year-old is immature for his age. And yet the sensitive and timid boy is anything but cognitively impaired. Unlike his younger brothers, Dane is deeply affected by a recent flash flood that almost washed away his family home, and so the predominant emotion in the chapters that are channeled through his mind is fear. Pancake does not use a first-person narrator to relate Dane's subjective experience, but the choppy, present-tense narration in the chapters that are focalized through him suggests that he may be referring to himself in the third person:

> When Dane thinks back now, what scares him most is not the water wall, although the wall scares him bad. It's how he didn't move. He just seized up halfway between back door and outhouse, prickled sharp in his scalp . . . his eyes swelling and bulging out this head. Like if only those eyes could get closer to the water, they might understand, Dane trying to make sense — creek on the wrong side of the road, water on its end — while Mrs. Taylor screamed at him from the back door, 'Move, boy! Move!' But he did not. (47)

Despite, or perhaps because of its use of cognitive estrangement, the narration of Dane's perspective adds an important dimension to Lace's and Bant's more easily decipherable accounts, cueing readers to simulate the immediate sensual impression of environmental disaster.

Unlike the older family members, Dane is not able to fully understand what is happening around him, but his naive account of his perceptions and feelings offers a kind of immediacy that even Bant's narration lacks. "I'm only twelve years old," he thinks to himself, "And I'm going to see the End of the World" (74). While this may be an overstatement, Pancake's use of strategic empathy throughout Dane's chapters allows readers to slip into his shoes and feel sympathy for the terrified boy. This sympathy is bound to increase when Dane's pervasive fear is echoed in the harrowing experience of Avery "Bucky" Taylor, Mrs. Taylor's son and the only focalizing character in the novel who does not belong to the Turrell family. The novel inhabits Avery's mind for just one chapter, but one that is bound to leave a lasting impression, since it conveys what it meant for another twelve-year-old boy to live through the (historical) Buffalo Creek flood that killed more than one hundred people on February 26, 1972.

Pancake uses authorial empathy strategically throughout the chapter to align readers with Avery's gruesome memories of a near-death experience. He is a grown man now, but back in 1972, he was no older than Dane is now when he almost drowned in the toxic flood that submerged his world after the burst of a coal slurry impoundment dam of the Pittston Coal Company. Before he knows what is happening to him, "Bucky," as Avery is called as a boy, finds himself without his pajama bottoms somewhere far down "on the hollowside with a dog curved against his body" (222). His shivering, half-naked body is covered with "coal-dirt all over. His hair is crunchy with it, coal-dirt is greasy in his ears, and he digs in to clear them only to discover that his fingertips are greasy, too" (222). Once again, Pancake limits the narrative perspective to a child's immediate sensual experience of a situation that defies comprehension, using present tense and a range of verbs and adjectives that cue readers to simulate that experience in their minds and bodies. In his conversations with others, Avery pretends he does not remember what happened to him on the long way down to the bottom of the valley, but the chapter reveals that he is in fact haunted by extremely vivid dreams of the horrifying moment when he lost his best friend Tad in the gushing water, the moment when he screams "grab hold of my arm!" and Tad "is no longer there" (243). Avery's horrifying and highly subjective account of the Buffalo Creek flood from the perspective of a child cues sympathy in readers by conveying the trauma that haunts not only him and Dane, but all the characters in the novel and, by extension, the people who lived through the actual events in 1972.

By contrast, readers are bound to feel differently about the chapters that are told from Corey's perspective. Unlike his siblings Bant and Dane, the ten-year-old boy strives to emulate his father and, just like Jimmy Make, he has no affective connection worth mentioning to his environment. When Bant takes Corey up to Yellowroot Mountain to make him aware of the devastation, she cannot know what effect it will have on him. Where she sees a "monster shovel claw[ing] the dirt" (165) and feels that clawing in her own intestines, Corey only sees a "vast mountain-handling piece of gorgeous machinery" (164). Throughout the novel, Corey displays unkind and cruel behavior toward the people in his life as well as an unhealthy fascination with technology, which he conceptualizes as a mighty instrument of power. "Corey is full of metal," observes Dane, "a little steel-made man" (108). Dane admires his younger brother, who seems so much tougher than he is, but Corey's perspective nevertheless serves as a counterpoint to those who are more attuned to their environment and who can perceive its beauties as well as its dangers. "Corey's world," writes Pendarvis (2007), "is full of toxic but irresistible junk that is washed down from deluged dumping grounds." Pendarvis is right to assert that, like the other children in the novel, Corey lives in a kind of hell on earth; yet Corey's deep fascination with the very machinery that produces this hell makes him different from anybody else. His utter lack of empathy and kindness also make him a difficult character to connect to, although several chapters are channeled through his consciousness. Not even when he dies a terrible death in an accident with a stolen four-wheeler are readers likely to feel much compassion for the boy.

This, too, is a result of Pancake's strategic use of empathy, since she chooses to narrate the tragic moment of Corey's death from Dane's cognitively estranged perspective, which makes it difficult to imagine the events in a way that would trigger strong emotions. Howard Sklar (2013: 28) has argued that readers' sympathy results from at least two basic components: "the heightened awareness of the suffering of another" and "a judgment of the explicit or implicit unfairness of that suffering." Both conditions are not entirely met in the case of Corey who, until his untimely death, seems not to suffer as much as the other characters from the destruction of his environment and who arguably brought his final suffering upon himself through his amoral and ruthless behavior and lack of concern for others. However, it can be argued that this behavior and lack of concern is a coping mechanism—a form of psychic numbing—and thus in itself a result of the violent environment the boy has grown up in.[9] Once it is recognized as such, readers might more easily feel compassion with the boy, but they have to make the additional cognitive effort in order to arrive at that realization.

Pancake's use of strategic empathy combined with variable focalization thus guides readers' understanding of both the unfathomable destruction of the Appalachian environment for the sake of profit and their sympathy for the people who live and die in it. In the end, the novel wants readers to grasp the moral wrongness of that destruction. People who care about the place they have grown up in cannot just pack up their things and leave, even if they could afford it. Watching that place turn into something unrecognizably different and toxic fuels feelings of anger, grief, and despair, and the complex blending of those feelings that Glenn Albrecht (2005: 45) has called "solastalgia." Albrecht defines solastalgia as a "homesickness one gets when one is still at 'home'" and identifies it as feeling of distress that results from the "recognition that the place where one resides and that one loves is under immediate assault" (45).[10] Arguably, all the adult characters in the novel suffer from this kind of distress, but Lace has learned over the years that "anger is easier [to bear] than grief" (Pancake 2007: 300), and so she decides to channel her anger into the fight against the mining companies. It is a

9. A study by Michael A. Godkin (1980) suggests that place alienation sometimes corresponds to a troubled primary place attachment or home.

10. Albrecht (2005: 55) explains that the term "solastalgia has its origins in the concepts of 'solace' and 'desolation'" and that it "literally . . . is the pain or sickness caused by the loss or lack of solace and the sense of isolation connected to the present state of one's home and territory." Unlike nostalgia, which takes as its object a place that is lost, people feel solastalgia in relation to a place that is still here but in the process of being destroyed or altered in other negative ways.

fight that mirrors that of actual environmentalist groups in the Appalachian Mountains, and while it may be in vain, both Lace and Bant have learned "in times like these, you have to grow big enough inside to hold both the loss and the hope" (357).

3. Conclusion

Ann Pancake has come a long way from the writer who did not believe that fiction could have any impact on social and political reality to the one who self-consciously writes an environmental justice novel that, in its acknowledgments, directs readers to several websites where they can "find out more about mountaintop-removal mining" (Pancake 2007: n.p.). Ironically, some critics have condemned *Strange as This Weather Has Been* for exactly the feature that Pancake for so long tried to avoid: its openly political stance. In his review of the novel, Danny Miller (2007: 259) complains that he felt "beat over the head" by Pancake's intense focus on the environmental havoc wreaked by mountaintop removal mining, maintaining that "most of the time ... the breathtaking beauty of her writing is smothered by didacticism." Miller's criticism makes clear that his main criterion for the quality of a novel is its aesthetic qualities and its ability to immerse him in its narrative world with a minimal degree of what Keen (2010: 83) calls "a scrupulously visible political interest.'" This returns us to the age-old questions of whether successful fiction can have a political agenda and whether narrative immersion in an imaginative world and aesthetic pleasure is all that we should look for in a novel.

There is bound to be disagreement among literary critics and scholars on both of these questions, and to this we must add the question, explored by Keen and others, whether politically motivated fiction can actually have an impact on real-world attitudes and behaviors. As far as this last question is concerned, the empirical evidence so far is inconclusive, but the studies that exist suggest that reading fiction does enhance theory of mind and empathetic capacities while reducing outgroup prejudice.[11] What a cognitive ecocritical approach can add to the scholarly debate is a teasing out of the narrative means by which a novel like *Strange as This Weather Has Been* invites us to care about an endangered environment and raises our awareness of the situation of actual mining families in the Appalachian Mountains—families like the Reeds.

11. See, for example, Kidd and Castano (2013); Mar, Oatley, and Peterson (2009); and Johnson (2013).

References

Albrecht, Glenn. 2005. "'Solastalgia': A New Concept in Health and Identity." *PAN*, no. 3: 41–55.

Booth, Wayne C. 1988. *The Company We Keep: An Ethics of Fiction*. Berkeley: University of California Press.

Bracher, Mark. 2014. *Literature and Social Justice: Protest Novels, Cognitive Politics, and Schema Criticism*. Austin: University of Texas Press.

Buell, Lawrence. 1995. *The Environmental Imagination: Thoreau, Nature Writing, and the Formation of American Culture*. Cambridge, MA: Harvard University Press.

Caracciolo, Marco. 2013. "Blind Reading: Toward an Enactivist Theory of the Reader's Imagination." In *Stories and Minds: Cognitive Approaches to Literary Narrative*, edited by Lars Bernaerts, Dirkde Geest, Luc Herman, and Bart Vervaeck, 81–106. Lincoln: University of Nebraska Press.

Dromi, Shai M., and Eva Illouz. 2010. "Recovering Morality: Pragmatic Sociology and Literary Studies." *New Literary History* 41, no. 2: 351–69.

Easterlin, Nancy. 2010. "Cognitive Ecocriticism: Human Wayfinding, Sociality, and Literary Interpretation." In *Introduction to Cognitive Cultural Studies*, edited by Lisa Zunshine, 257–75. Baltimore: Johns Hopkins University Press.

Easterlin, Nancy. 2012. *A Biocultural Approach to Literary Theory and Interpretation*. Baltimore: Johns Hopkins University Press.

Easterlin, Nancy. 2016. "Ecocriticism, Place Studies, and Colm Tóibín's 'A Long Winter': A Biocultural Perspective." In *Handbook of Ecocriticism and Cultural Ecology*, edited by Hubert Zapf, 226–48. Berlin: DeGruyter.

Easterlin, Nancy. 2017. "Place-in-Process in Colm Tóibín's *The Blackwater Lightship*: Emotion, Self-Identity, and the Environment." In *The Palgrave Handbook of Affect Studies and Textual Criticism*, edited by Thomas Blake and Donald Wehrs, 827–54. Basingstoke, UK: Palgrave Macmillan.

Gallese, Vittorio. 2011. "Mirror Neurons and Art." In *Art and the Senses*, edited by Francesca Bacci and David Melcher, 441–49. New York: Oxford University Press.

Garrard, Greg. 2011. *Ecocriticism: The New Critical Idiom*, 2nd ed. New York: Routledge.

Genette, Gérard. 1980. *Narrative Discourse: An Essay in Method*. Oxford, UK: Blackwell.

Gerrig, Richard J. 1999. *Experiencing Narrative Worlds: On the Psychological Activities of Reading*. Boulder, CO: Westview Press.

Glotfelty, Cheryll. 1996. "Introduction: Literary Studies in an Age of Environmental Crisis." In *The Ecocriticism Reader: Landmarks in Literary Ecology*, edited by Cheryll Glotfelty and Harold Fromm, xv–xxxvii. Athens: University of Georgia Press.

Godkin, Michael A. 1980. "Identity and Place: Clinical Applications Based on Notions of Rootedness and Uprootedness." In *The Human Experience of Space and Place*, edited by Anne Buttimer and David Seamon, 73–85. New York: St. Martin's.

Green, Melanie C., and Timothy C. Brock. 2000. "The Role of Transportation in the Persuasiveness of Public Narratives." *Journal of Personality and Social Psychology* 79, no. 5: 701–21.

Hoffman, Martin. 2000. *Empathy and Moral Development: Implications for Caring and Justice*. Cambridge: Cambridge University Press.

Hogan, Patrick C. 2011. *Affective Narratology: The Emotional Structure of Stories*. Lincoln: University of Nebraska Press.

Iacoboni, Marco. 2009. *Mirroring People: The Science of Empathy and How We Connect with Others*. New York: Picador.

Jacobs, Arthur, and Raoul Schrott. 2014. "Captivated by the Cinema of Mind: On Toggle Switches, Madeleine Effects and Don Quixote Syndrome during Immersion in Textual Worlds." In *Concentration*, edited by Ingo Niermann, 118–49. Berlin: Fiktion, fiktion.cc/books/concentration.

James, Erin. 2015. *The Storyworld Accord: Econarratology and Postcolonial Narratives*. Lincoln: University of Nebraska Press.

Johnson, Dan R. 2013. "Transportation into Literary Fiction Reduces Prejudice against and Increases Empathy for Arab-Muslims." *Scientific Study of Literature* 3, no. 1: 77–92.

Keen, Suzanne. 2007. *Empathy and the Novel*. New York: Oxford University Press.

Keen, Suzanne. 2010. "Narrative Empathy." In *Toward a Cognitive Theory of Narrative Acts*, edited by Frederick Louis Aldama, 61–94. Austin: University of Texas Press.

Kidd, David Comer, and Emanuele Castano. 2013. "Reading Literary Fiction Improves Theory of Mind." *Science* 342, no. 6156: 377–80.

Koopman, Emy. 2010. "Reading the Suffering of Others. The Ethical Possibilities of 'Empathic Unsettlement'." *Journal of Literary Theory* 4, no. 2: 235–51.

Kuzmičová, Anežka. 2012. "Presence in the Reading of Literary Narrative: A Case for Motor Enactment." *Semiotica* 189, no. 1/4: 23–48.

LeCain, Timothy. 2009. *Mass Destruction: The Men and Giant Mines That Wired America and Scarred the Planet*. New Brunswick, NJ: Rutgers University Press.

Lewis, David, Dennis Rodgers, and Michael Woolcock. 2008. "The Fiction of Development: Literary Representation as a Source of Authoritative Knowledge." *Journal of Development Studies* 44, no. 2: 198–216.

Mar, Raymond A., Keith Oatley, and Jordan B. Peterson. 2009. "Exploring the Link between Reading Fiction and Empathy: Ruling Out Individual Differences and Examining Outcomes." *Communications: The European Journal of Communication* 34, no. 4: 407–28.

Miller, Danny. 2007. "Review of *Strange as This Weather Has Been* by Anne Pancake." *Journal of Appalachian Studies* 13, no. 1–2: 257–59.

Milton, Kay. 2002. *Loving Nature: Towards an Ecology of Emotion*. New York: Routledge.

Nussbaum, Martha C.. 1997. *Cultivating Humanity: A Classical Defense of Reform in Liberal Education*. Cambridge, MA: Harvard University Press.

Oatley, Keith. 2011. *Such Stuff as Dreams: The Psychology of Fiction*. Malden, MA: Wiley-Blackwell.

Pancake, Ann. 2007. *Strange as This Weather Has Been*. Berkeley, CA: Counterpoint.

Pancake, Ann. 2013. "Creative Responses to Worlds Unraveling: The Artist in the Twenty-First Century." *Georgia Review* 67, no. 3: 404–14.

Pendarvis, Jack. 2007. "Buried Alive." *New York Times Sunday Book Review*, October 14. www.nytimes.com/2007/10/14/books/review/Pendarvis-t.html.

Phelan, James. 2001. "Why Narrators Can Be Focalizers—and Why It Matters." In *New Perspectives on Narrative Perspective*, edited by Willie van Peer and Seymour Chatman, 51–65. Albany: State University of New York Press.

Rizzolatti, Giacomo, and Corrado Sinigaglia. 2008. *Mirrors in the Brain: How Our Minds Share Actions and Emotions*. Oxford: Oxford University Press.

Rozin, Paul, Jonathan Haidt, and Clark R. McCauley. 2010. "Disgust." In *Handbook of Emotions*, 3rd ed., edited by Michael Lewis, Jeanette M. Haviland-Jones, and Lisa Feldman Barrett, 757–75. New York: Guilford.

Scarry, Elaine. 2001. *Dreaming by the Book*. Princeton, NJ: Princeton University Press.

Sklar, Howard. 2013. *The Art of Sympathy in Fiction: Forms of Ethical and Emotional Persuasion*. Amsterdam: John Benjamins.

Smith, Duane A. 1994. *Mining in America: The Industry and Environment, 1800–1980*. Boulder: University Press of Colorado.

Spivak, Gayatri Chakravorty. (1985) 1996. "Subaltern Studies: Deconstructing Historiography." In *The Spivak Reader*, edited by Donna Landry and Gerald MacLean, 203–35. London: Routledge.

Starr, G., Gabrielle. 2013. *Feeling Beauty: The Neuroscience of Aesthetic Experience*. Cambridge, MA: MIT Press.

Taylor, Marjorie, Sarah D. Hodges, and Adèle Koháiyi. 2003. "The Illusion of Independent Agency: Do Adult Fiction Writers Experience Their Characters as Having Minds of Their Own?" *Imagination* 22, no. 4: 361–80.

Vermeule, Blakey. 2010. *Why Do We Care about Literary Characters?* Baltimore: Johns Hopkins University Press.

Weik von Mossner, Alexa. 2014. *Cosmopolitan Minds: Literature, Emotion, and the Transnational Imagination.* Austin: University of Texas Press.

Weik von Mossner, Alexa. 2017. *Affective Ecologies: Empathy, Emotion, and Environmental Narrative.* Columbus: Ohio State University Press.

Wojciehowski, Hannah, and Vittorio Gallese. 2011. "How Stories Make Us Feel: Toward an Embodied Narratology." *California Italian Studies* 2, no. 1. escholarship.org/uc/item /3jg726c2.

Nonhuman Fictional Characters and the Empathy-Altruism Hypothesis

Erin James
University of Idaho

Abstract Highlighting a trend in current models of narrative empathy that suggests that readers' ability to empathize with nonhuman characters is dependent wholly on anthropomorphization, this essay explores two narratives that feature chimp characters—Colin McAdam's *A Beautiful Truth* and Karen Joy Fowler's *We Are All Completely Beside Ourselves*—to consider the challenges that nonhuman characters pose to such models and the empathy-altruism hypothesis. It first considers the cognitive differences between humans and chimps to stress just how difficult it is to represent chimp cognition and emotion in narrative and the resulting challenges that this difficulty poses for models of narrative empathy. It then discusses the mechanisms by which written narratives that refuse to anthropomorphize nonhuman characters, such those by McAdam and Fowler, might inspire a real-world ethics of care among readers for nonhuman subjects. Ultimately, this essay proposes an expansion to current models of narrative empathy by which we recognize the potential of human bridge characters to foster real-world care among readers for nonhuman subjects.

Keywords empathy, altruism, anthropomorphization, nonhuman

1. Narrative Empathy and Nonhuman Characters

Colin McAdam's novel *A Beautiful Truth* (2013), about the various types of captivity faced by chimpanzees today, comes with a powerful endorsement on its back cover. Executive Director of Save the Chimps Jo Sullivan celebrates the novel for "telling the stories of chimpanzees in captivity today

Poetics Today 40:3 (September 2019) DOI 10.1215/03335372-7558164
© 2019 by Porter Institute for Poetics and Semiotics

and ... help[ing] people understand why these amazing souls should be loved, respected, and protected in their natural habitat." She declares, "We hope everyone reads this book and comes to see chimpanzees as we do." Her recommendation is buoyed by the fact that a portion of the sale of the book benefits Save the Chimps. A similar suggestion appears in the conclusion of Karen Joy Fowler's novel *We Are All Completely Beside Ourselves* (2013). Narrator-protagonist Rosemary Cook is about to embark on a publicity tour for a book about her and her sister, Fern. But this is a book with a twist: Fern and Rosemary are not actually sisters, but a chimpanzee and a human, respectively, who were raised as siblings until Fern is sold to a research facility when they are five years old. Rosemary calls on her narratee to do something to improve the lives of chimps in captivity: people "must come to see how beautiful she [Fern] is.... They must storm the prison and demand her release.... So rise up already" (Fowler 2013: 300). She notes that all profits stemming from the sale of the book will go directly to the Center for Primate Communication, in which Fern is currently housed.

A key assumption lies in the marketing plans of both books: that each story will resonate so powerfully with readers that it will prompt changes in their real-world attitudes and behaviors toward nonfictional chimpanzees. This assumption will be familiar to scholars of narrative empathy, since it draws heavily on what Suzanne Keen (2006: 224) calls the "empathy-altruism hypothesis," or the idea that novel reading, "by eliciting empathy, encourages prosocial action and good world citizenship." Narrative empathy is the "imaginative process whereby readers temporarily adopt the perceptual, emotional, or axiological perspective of a fictional character," and the processes and mechanisms by which it occurs is a key discussion within cognitive literary studies (Bernaerts et al. 2014: 73). Indeed, Keen (2015: 347) argues that the boom of work on narrative empathy means that it can "now be considered an aspect of literary cognitivism's project. Understanding narrative empathy involves the psychology of intersubjectivity, and sensitivity to context, as well as universals of cognition and emotion: all facets of contemporary cognitivism."

The empathy-altruism hypothesis is controversial. While humanist scholars such as Martha Nussbaum and Steven Pinker have long celebrated the ability of narratives to foster empathic, intersubjective bonds between readers and characters of a different race, class, gender, ethnicity, and/or sexuality,[1] Keen (2007: vii), in the most substantial work on the subject, finds little evidence that a link between novel reading, experiences of narrative empathy, and altruism exists. Nonetheless, she sketches out a model of narrative empa-

1. See Nussbaum (1997: 111) and Pinker and Goldstein (2004).

thy that assumes a direct correlation between any potential real-world ben-
eficiaries of altruistic behavior and the characters with whom readers empathize, and she queries which narrative structures, if any, might facilitate
empathic connections between readers and fictional characters.

The empathy-altruism hypothesis becomes especially controversial in its
application to nonhuman characters. While Keen (2007: 69) posits that *"empathy
for fictional characters may require only minimal elements of identity, situation, and feeling,
not necessarily complex or realistic characterization*," her theory also implies that one
of the essential requirements for character identification is a certain human-
ness. She relies on readers' testimony of their empathic connections with the
horse protagonist of *Black Beauty* to foreground their "ready identification
with nonhuman figures" (68). And she also notes that "character identification routinely overcomes the significant barrier of species difference." Her
implicit suggestion is that basic elements of character identification, such as
"a name, a recognizable situation, and at least implicit feelings," anthropomorphize nonhuman characters, which in turn makes empathy possible (see
also Keen 2011: 137). Luc Bernaerts et al. (2014: 71) similarly argue, in their
recent essay on nonhuman narration, that nonhuman narrators, via their
very ability to narrate, "spring from and require the conceptual integration of
human and non-human traits." Such narrators "exploit non-human experientiality in varying degrees and . . . call upon our ability to attribute consciousness to non-human entities and even to empathize with them" (72).
For these scholars, nonhuman narrators exist within a dialectic of defamil-
iarization and empathy; such narrators both task readers with recognizing
the otherness of nonhuman life and consciousness and induce readers to
engage empathically with impossibly humanized nonhuman minds. Once
again, empathy and anthropomorphization go hand in hand, such that the
former is dependent wholly upon the latter. To empathize with a nonhuman
character or narrator, readers must engage with a humanized version of a
real-world nonhuman subject. Narrative empathy for nonhuman characters
thus always runs the risk of false empathy, or what Keen (2007: 159) defines as
readers' incorrect belief that they have "caught the feeling of suffering others
from a different culture, gender, race, or class."[2]

In what follows, I grapple with these complications of narratives, nonhuman characters, anthropomorphization, empathy, and real-world altruism
by exploring the sometimes surprising ways in which Fowler's and McAdam's
novels inspire care for real-world chimps among readers. My discussion of
the representation of chimps in these texts highlights the special challenges
that nonhuman characters pose for current models of narrative empathy and

---

2. I suggest that we add "species" to this list.

the empathy-altruism hypothesis. These two novels are especially suited for this discussion, given their representations of chimp cognition as distinct from that of humans and thus alien and unknowable. Unlike other recent novels featuring chimp characters, such as James Lever's *Me Cheeta* (2008) and Benjamin Hale's *The Evolution of Bruno Littlemore* (2011), McAdam's and Fowler's novels do not feature speaking or narrating chimp characters and provide readers with little insight by which to connect with characters such as Fern, emotionally or cognitively. Yet both narratives suggest that readers, upon coming to understand fictional chimps as worthy of love and protection, will happily support real chimpanzees. This causes me to ask, Can novels that refuse to anthropomorphize nonhuman characters inspire care for real-world nonhuman subjects while also avoiding the illusion that readers have direct access to the minds and emotions of nonhuman characters?

In this essay, I first consider the cognitive differences between humans and chimps to stress just how difficult it is to represent chimp cognition and emotion in narrative and the resulting challenges that this difficulty poses for models of narrative empathy. Written narratives are especially prone to producing false empathy for nonhuman characters. Second, I explore the mechanisms by which written narratives that refuse to anthropomorphize nonhuman characters might inspire a real-world ethics of care among readers for nonhuman subjects. Keen's theorization of the bridge character as one who ushers readers into the world of the text suggests an affective link, generating real-world cross-species altruism within narrative.[3] Modifying Keen, I conceptualize the bridge as a character who fosters concern for a second character with whom it is impossible for those readers to empathize; the bridge character, as Keen suggests, is a member of an in-group who helps readers to cross a "significant barrier of difference."

In my model of narrative empathy, the bridge character acts as a conduit between readers and the unknowable character with whom those readers cannot empathize. A path to real-world altruism thus might look something like this: readers empathize with a familiar bridge character, the bridge character cares for a second character that readers cannot fully know, and readers — via narrative empathy with the bridge — mimic the bridge's fictional ethics of care in real life to benefit nonfictional counterparts of the unknow-

3. Keen mentions bridge characters at several points in her work, both within discussions of narrative empathy and postcolonial literature; she writes of Michael Ondaatje "rebuff[ing] readers who seek ... an easy bridge character with whom to travel for a voyeuristic thrill" in *Anil's Ghost* and argues that Edwidge Danticat's short stories "provid[e] one avenue for narrative empathy through her use of bridge characters: literate, creative children and teenagers whose very bookishness or eloquence invites a book-reader on the other end of the narrative transaction into the storyworld" (Keen 2007: 152; 2015: 353).

able character. While neither McAdam's nor Fowler's novels provide ample material to understand what it is like to be a real-world chimp, both texts provide readers with an abundance of textual cues by which to temporarily adopt "the perceptual, emotional, or axiological perspective" of human fictional characters that feel deep love and compassion for the chimpanzees in their lives via explicitly human modes of cognition. In so doing, these novels navigate the tricky terrain of representing chimp cognition as separate from and alien to human cognition while simultaneously inspiring an ethics of care for real-world chimps among readers.

2. Chimp and Human Cognition

Because of the similarities between humans and chimps, fictional chimpanzees make a particularly interesting case study for exploring the intertwined complications of nonhuman narrative characters, anthropomorphism, empathy, and real-world altruism. Genetically, humans and chimps are strikingly similar, with comparisons of proteins on the surface of human and chimp cells suggesting that humans are 99.6 percent chimp and vice versa (Bekoff 2000: 31). Chimps and humans also share many points of cognitive overlap, such that chimp minds and chimp modes of meaning-making are not as alien to human minds as those of other nonhuman subjects, such as dogs and bats. Chimps and other higher primates have been the subject of extensive cognitive and behavioral study over the years, most notably in the work of primatologists including Jane Goodall and Frans de Waal. Individual chimps trained by linguists and scientists to communicate in human languages have become famous examples of animal intelligence: husband and wife team Beatrix T. Gardner and R. Allen Gardener trained Washoe (1965–2007) to communicate via approximately 350 sign language words in the 1960s, while Herbert Terrance and his team of graduate students trained Nim Chimpsky (1973–2000) to communicate via 125 signs in the 1970s. While controversial in its findings,[4] this work highlights the social, cultural, and political

4. The exchange titled "Can Chimps Converse?" between Herbert Terrance and Peter Singer in the November 24, 2011, issue of the *New York Review of Books*, prompted by the release of the documentary film *Project Nim* earlier that year, provides insight into the lasting controversies of the "ape language wars" that originated in the 1960s and 1970s with the work of Terrance and the Gardeners. In this exchange, Terrance stands by his claim that the work of the Gardeners "amounted largely to a few fascinating anecdotes, not a collection of rigorously vetted scientific data," while the illusion of Nim Chimpsky's acquisition of grammatical, recursive language in his own study was a "false positive" produced by teachers prompting their charge to make the same or similar signs as them (Terrance and Singer 2011). Singer responds by discussing evidence from further studies, such as those by Sue Savage-Rumbaugh's testing of bonobo language acquisition and David Premack and Guy Woodruff's work on chimp theory of mind

sophistication of chimp societies and draws attention to the evolutionary closeness of human and chimpanzee species.

One point of overlap between human and chimp cognition that is especially important to discussions of narrative empathy is theory of mind (ToM). In 1978, David Premack and Guy Woodruff published a seminal study of chimp ToM and in doing so posed a research question which primatologists still pursue today. Premack and Woodruff's (1978: 515) original study concluded that a chimpanzee demonstrated the ability to attribute mental states to a human actor, or "understood the actor's purpose." In the decades following Premack and Woodruff's study, other scholars pursued their research question with mixed results. Yet consensus today suggests that "there is solid evidence from several different experimental paradigms that chimpanzees understand the goals and intentions of others, as well as the perception and knowledge of others" (Call and Tomasello 2008: 187; see also de Waal 2008: 285).

Evidence of chimp ToM has led primatologists, comparative psychologists, and ethologists to suggest that chimps are also capable of empathy. De Waal makes this case forcefully in his writing on chimp emotions. Describing observations of chimps demonstrating consolation, morality, and sympathetic concern by himself and other ethologists, he argues that the animals "not only reciprocate favors within positive relationships, but also take revenge upon those who have previously acted against them" (de Waal 2008: 291). For de Waal, such behavior is indicative of the type of emotional contagion which makes empathy possible, because it indicates that chimps have empathy for those with whom they have a positive relationship and suppress empathy for strangers and defectors. Other scholars suggest that chimps are capable of empathizing not only with members of their own species but also with human companions. In their foreword to Lori Gruen's *Entangled Empathy* (2014), Amy Fultz and Cathy Willis Spraetz describe their observations of chimp-to-chimp and chimp-to-human empathy. They note that the chimps with whom they work at Chimp Haven, a sanctuary for chimpanzees rescued from biomedical research, show concern for their ill human handlers and display happiness and joy at seeing human friends (Fultz and Spraetz 2014: xiv).

The cognitive similarities between chimps and humans make it especially tempting to anthropomorphize chimps. Ethologists such as de Waal, Gordon Burghardt, and Mark Bekoff argue that thinking of chimps in human terms is

---

(which I discuss below). This work leads Singer to argue that "it is now clear beyond any reasonable doubt that Terrance's 1979 *Science* article presented an unduly negative view of the abilities of apes to communicate spontaneously."

essential to the study of chimp behavior and advocate for "critical anthropomorphism," or an approach to studying animals that both recognizes the inevitable anthropocentric bias of human researchers and attempts to imagine the world from the perspective of the particular species under observation. Critical anthropomorphism views human and animal intelligence as differences in degree rather than kind; it positions human cognition as a variety of animal cognition, and thus suggests that human researchers are well equipped to make reliable, informed predictions about animal behavior. Importantly for discussions of narrative empathy, critical anthropomorphism demands certain imaginative work from researchers, in that it tasks researchers with inhabiting imaginatively the perceptual world, or *umwelt*, of each individual species.

The issues of critical anthropomorphism, animal perspective-taking, and explorations of species *umwelt* are also of interest to literary scholars in their study of representations of nonhuman subjects. Bart Welling (2011: 671) argues that literary critics should engage in critical anthropomorphism when analyzing representations of animals on film, because such an approach would help them distinguish between superficially anthropomorphic representations of nonhuman experiences and more accurate ones. Speaking in explicitly narratological terms, David Herman (2011: 159) posits that graphic novels featuring nonhuman characters can create a bridge between the human and the nonhuman by "figuring the lived, phenomenal worlds [or *umwelten*] of creatures whose organismic structure differs from our own." Alexa Weik von Mossner (2017) also is optimistic about the ability of narrative to capture the experiences of nonhumans. In her writing on trans-species empathy, she notes that, although some aspects of animal experience remain impenetrable to human minds, humans can approximate it, in part because of important continuities between human and nonhuman experiences, such as the human/ chimp similarities that I discuss above.[5]

The work of Welling, Herman, and Weik von Mossner highlights the ability of narratives to engage humans imaginatively and emotionally in the experiences of nonhumans. Ecocritics and new materialists echo this call for critical anthropomorphism, pointing out what scholars across the humanities have to gain from imagining themselves in worlds of nonhuman others.[6] Yet critical anthropomorphic approaches to representations of chimpanzees are

5. Weik von Mossner (2017: 111) argues, "In fact ... such trans-species consciousness attribution is something that we do all of the time, be it in our day-to-day interaction with actual animals or in our imaginative engagement with creatures.... The process is not so different from attributing consciousness to humans."

6. For examples, see Armbruster (2013), Bennett (2010: 99), and Iovino and Oppermann (2012: 82).

troubled by essential differences between chimp and human cognition and communication. Individual chimps such as Washoe and Nim Chimpsky have learned to communicate with their human handlers via visual images, but no documentation exists of even a rudimentary system of signs naturally occurring in wild chimpanzee communities. Cognitive psychologist Merlin Donald (1991: 134) makes the phylogenetic argument that, while captive apes can learn a significant number of signs and string together two or three signs appropriately, "it is evident that apes do not have anything like the human capacity for syntactically complex, high-speed communication." Furthermore, studies indicate that while chimpanzees and other apes possess the ability to perceive events and situations, they lack the cognitive capacity for narrative construction and interpretation. It is this capacity for narrative thinking that leads Donald to make a clear distinction between human and ape cognition: "Our genes may be largely identical to those of a chimp or gorilla, but our cognitive architecture is not. . . . Humans are utterly different. Our minds function on several phylogenetically new representational planes, none of which are available to animals" (382).

Donald (1991: 16) and others argue that the evolution of narrative thinking, which Donald places during the transition from *Homo erectus* to *Homo sapiens*, brought with it a unique set of cognitive skills that even our closest genetic relatives lack. Social psychologist Jerome Bruner (1990: 77) argues that meaning-making via narrative requires humans to prioritize human goal-directed action, sequential order, sensitivity to what is normal and abnormal, and the perspective of a narrator. According to Bruner, humans "enter into meaning" by making narrative sense of the world around them, and this cognitive inclination toward narrative is a defining characteristic of the species (68). Indeed, he sees the innate disposition to narrative organization as so essential to human cognition that he maintains it is a precursor to language acquisition.

It is thus narrative mentation, and not language, which originally set human cognition apart from that of other species. Cognitive narratologist H. Porter Abbott (2000: 250) agrees and develops the work of Bruner and Donald to claim that the development of narrative meaning-making has allowed humans to exist in their own constructed realities:

> Freed from regularity, time could now contract or expand in myriad ways—ways that could even accommodate the regularity of natural rhythms, though without being chained to it. Narrative time is constructed time, organized according to creatural priorities. If hominids found themselves, like all other creatures, thrown into a world governed by the seemingly eternal regularities of days and seasons,

they found in narrative a way to impose shapes of their own devising back upon the universe.

Taken together, this work suggests that narrative thinking directs humans to foreground human activity and engage in perspective-taking (via a narrator) as well as to reorganize time according to their own priorities. The capacity for narrative thought is uniquely human and provides humans with a distinctive relationship to themselves and the world around them.

Given these stark differences between chimp and human cognition, I am interested in exploring the dynamics of empathy not only in narratives that productively anthropomorphize nonhuman characters but also in texts that refuse to anthropomorphize such characters. I am especially concerned with what this second set of texts, committed to highlighting the cognitive differences between humans and other species, might look like, and what they can teach readers about real-life nonhuman subjects. Although he too is optimistic about the benefits of anthropomorphized representations of nonhuman characters, Marco Caracciolo holds that the politics of perspective-taking and empathy are especially complicated in written narratives.[7] He argues that because the ability to handle complex language systems is a uniquely human skill, written figurations of animal consciousness are inevitably anthropomorphizing and thus always reflect human beliefs, values, and experiences.[8] For Caracciolo, as well as for Keen and other scholars of narrative empathy and nonhuman characters, written representations of animal emotion and cognition are never simply about animals alone; they are "character-centered

---

7. I agree that these questions are especially pressing for written narratives. The shared focus on visual narratives by Welling, Herman, and Weik von Mossner implies that visual and auditory evidence in films and graphic novels may play a vital role in animal perspective-taking. Weik von Mossner is most explicit about the importance of such nonlinguistic evidence, especially in her argument that graphic displays of animal suffering such as the dolphin slaughter scene in *The Cove* cue negative emotions in viewers. Weik von Mossner (2017: 105) notes that this scene contains "no commentary, no narration, just long minutes filled with images of relentless, brutal slaughter," and she posits that the sounds and sights of dolphins "as they try to writhe away from the boats or dive out of the water in frenzied motion, blood covering their sleek bodies" are essential to the scene's power. She contends that scenes such as this are painful to watch for human spectators as viewers "empathize with nonhuman animals, feeling their joy, their fear, their terror and their pain" (106). Much of her discussion of tran-species empathy relies upon the ability of readers to read visually the faces and bodies of nonhuman subjects, reaffirming the idea that graphic images and sounds are especially powerful conduits to cognitive and emotional sharing.

8. As Caracciolo (2016: 144) states explicitly, "Literature does not provide tools to validate insights into animal experience — it can only offer imaginary reconstructions whose perceived plausibility reflects the biases (and limitations) of the human imagination." See also Nancy Easterlin's (1999) work on bioepistemology, in which she makes the more global point that all species perspectives are inherently species-centric.

illusion[s]" that give readers the misperception of direct access to the consciousness of nonhuman subjects (Caracciolo 2016: 144).

The empathy for nonhuman characters in written narratives that produces real-world altruistic behavior thus relies on readers adopting the perspective of a figurative, personified version of a subject that does not exist outside of human imagination. This marks an essential difference between the potential real-world results of narrative empathy for nonhuman and human characters; while a written narrative might not, for instance, represent accurately what it is like to be a black, female, and/or queer subject, its representation of a black, female, and/or queer character does not necessitate mapping traits and consciousness onto that character that do not and cannot exist in the real world. The fundamental differences between human and chimp cognition also heighten Caracciolo's warnings about the politics of anthropomorphization in written narratives. The cognitive capabilities that distinguish humans from other species are not based upon complex linguistic systems alone, as he implies. Narrative itself is a cognitive capacity available only to humans. Narratives enable humans not only to produce complex constructions of the self but also to order the world around them to reflect their priorities. Narrative, and especially written narratives free of the direct sights and sounds of other species, cannot exist without foregrounding the perceptual, emotional, or axiological perspective of humans.

3. Connecting to the Nonhuman via Human Bridges

Although very different in their narrative structures and tones, neither *We Are All Completely Beside Ourselves* nor *Beautiful Truth* anthropomorphizes its central nonhuman characters. This assertion may initially surprise readers familiar with Fowler's novel, as one of the hallmarks of the text is Rosemary's trick of narrative timing; she allows her narratee (and thus the text's readers) to assume happily that Fern is a human child for the first seventy-six pages of her story. Speaking of her imaginary childhood friend Mary, Rosemary opens chapter 5 with a bald statement:

> There's something you don't know yet about Mary. The imaginary friend of my childhood was not a little girl. She was a little chimpanzee.
> So, of course, was my sister Fern. (Fowler 2013: 77)

This revelation is shocking, because it immediately calls into question Rosemary's reliability as a narrator and tasks readers with reinterpreting the textual cues with which they have thus far modeled the character of Fern. But Rosemary is willing to risk the vexation of her narratee to make her point about Fern. She explains that if she had told you that Fern is a chimp, you would have been unable to see Fern as she really is: "I tell you Fern is a chimp and, already, you aren't thinking of her as my sister. You're thinking instead that we loved her as if she were some kind of pet. . . . Fern was not the family dog" (77–78). Chapter 5 of Fowler's novel thus opens with a counterintuitive admission. To help her narratee see Fern as a chimp and not a human, Rosemary must first trick the recipients of her narrative into seeing her sister as a person and not a pet.

But this emphasis on Fern's personhood does not mean that Rosemary anthropomorphizes her sister. Much of Rosemary's narration focuses on the utter unknowability of Fern and the mysteriousness of Fern's interior emotional and cognitive life. Throughout the novel, Fowler emphasizes Fern's physicality: "I do remember her. I remember her sharply—her smell and touch, scattered images of her face, her ears, her chin, her eyes. Her arms, her feet, her fingers. But I don't remember her fully" (55). Rosemary almost always represents Fern in terms of exterior appearance or actions. Her description of playing in the snow with her sister is illustrative of this habit: "Fern sits on the ground beside me, rests her chin on my arm. . . . She stuffs another handful of snow into her mouth, smacks her protuberant, acrobatic lips, and turns to look up at me, eyes shining" (97). Readers might feel tempted to ascribe emotion to Fern here—to practice ToM—by assuming that her shining eyes indicate mischievousness or delight. But Rosemary quickly frustrates this temptation, explaining that "Fern's eyes seem larger than human eyes, because the whites are not white but an amber color only slightly lighter than the irises." Even in this scene, in which the symbols of emotion and consciousness seem so apparent, Rosemary warns her narratee that Fern's consciousness is unknowable.

Fowler provides no clearer articulation of Fern's foreignness than in Rosemary's ultimate admission that she cannot know her sister:

> That there was something inside Fern I didn't know.
> That I didn't know her in the way I'd always thought I did.
> That Fern had secrets and not the good kind. (270)

Rosemary finally must admit that she and Fern were never true siblings. Rosemary-the-character realizes that she cannot know the inside of her sister, and this barrier prevents Rosemary-the-narrator from making assumptions about Fern's consciousness and emotional state throughout the narrative. Hence, her persistent focus on Fern's exteriority—Fern's body and her physical actions. Rosemary yet again confirms her sister's strangeness in the final moment of her narration, in which she and Fern connect across a glass window pane at Fern's rehabilitation center. Despite physically mirroring each other when they rest their foreheads on the glass, Rosemary admits that "I didn't know what she was thinking or feeling" (308). Rosemary recognizes Fern's body and sees a reflection of herself in the chimp, such that she describes the scene "as if [she] were looking in a mirror" (308). But Fern's interiority remains elusive.

It is the ultimate intangibility of Fern's emotions and consciousness that makes her such a difficult character with whom to empathize. Readers of Fowler's novel are left with little more than physical descriptions by which to cognitively connect to Fern: readers know what Fern looks like and how she moves and behaves, but the narrative never permits readers the luxury of peering into her mind. Beyond this, Fowler also calls into question any attempts to map emotion onto Fern or to interpret her physical actions as being motivated by inner thoughts and feelings. In refusing to anthropomorphize its chimp, Fowler's novel gives readers little by which to identify with the character. Rosemary cannot render Fern's interiority in narrative because to do so would immediately flout what she refers to as Fern's "essential simianness" (77).

Yet while Fowler refuses to imagine what it is like for Fern to be a chimp, she does depict what it is like for a human to have experiences similar to Fern's. In numerous scenes of symbolic twinning, Rosemary acts as a powerful bridge between human and chimp experience. Rosemary's story is chock-full of such moments, in which she represents herself as going through human versions of Fern's chimp experiences. This twinning is most obvious in Rosemary's childhood. Known throughout her school years as "monkey girl," Rosemary's youth is defined by her struggles to socialize as would a normal human child. She recalls her kindergarten teacher telling her parents that she has boundary issues and must learn to keep her hands to herself. Rosemary, learning social cues from her chimp twin, "truly had no idea that other people weren't to be touched; in fact, I'd thought quite the opposite. But I was always making mistakes like that" (30). Rosemary later notes that the same teacher described her as impulsive, possessive, and demanding on her report card that year — "classic chimp traits" that Rosemary would work hard to eradicate (138).

Her struggle to behave as a proper human continues into her adulthood. As a college student, she speaks of feeling a certain "wildness" and notes that she is "a pretty good climber, for a girl" (12, 13). Rosemary makes this college-aged twinning explicit in a long scene that recalls a drunken night on the town and ends with her in jail. The night remains in her adult, narrating mind as a disconnected montage from the hypothetical film *The Monkey Girl Returns*. The parallels between her experience and Fern's overwhelm her:

> After all those years of keeping her out of my head, suddenly she was everywhere. I couldn't not see how I'd been put, drugged, into a cage just the way she'd once been put, drugged in a cage. I was confident of my release come morning, and I wondered if she'd also been confident. It was far worse than imagining her frightened, to think of her certain that this was all a mistake and we were on our way to rescue her, that she'd soon be home in her own room and in her own bed. (173)

Rosemary conflates her experience with Fern's; both sisters are drugged and held captive. Rosemary, in her jail cell panic, even finds herself trying to communicate unsuccessfully in Fern's sign language. There is a key difference in Rosemary's and Fern's experiences, though: the human sister is released in the morning and returns, sober, to her college dorm, while the ape sister remains in her cage to face additional drugging. And readers never do gain insight into Fern's emotional state as she lives in captivity. But scenes such as these make clear that while Fowler's novel does not provide readers with enough textual cues to temporarily adopt a chimp's perspective, it does offer a rich set of qualia by which to temporarily adopt Rosemary's perceptual, emotional, or axiological perspective as she moves through situations similar to Fern's.

Beyond this symbolic twinning, Fowler's narrative also helps readers make sense of Fern's experience via Rosemary's by emphasizing Rosemary's particularly human mode of cognition. The novel's concern with narration and narrativity implicitly speaks to the crucial role that story plays in human sense-making and, specifically, the way in which Rosemary makes sense of Fern's story by rendering it in her own complex narrative. Rosemary frequently punctuates her story with metanarrative interjections, such that she continually reminds her narratee (and readers) of her ability to narrate. Examples of such statements include "Skip the beginning. Start in the middle"; "The story that I told ... obviously that story isn't really from the middle of this story"; "But you'd probably rather get straight to Fern. I'll condense"; "But I'm getting ahead of myself" (2, 46, 204, 234). As this string of metanarrative interjections implies, Rosemary is hyperaware of her organization of narrative time. She stitches together the relevant memories of the story of her and Fern's lives in a way that reorganizes time according to her priorities. Rosemary manipulates the *syuzhet* of her narrative to impose a certain ethical stance upon its *fabula*: Fern is as worthy of love and compassion as a human sister, and Rosemary's particular ordering of narrative events will help her narratee recognize this idea. Furthermore, Rosemary's story is also a complex autobiography, through which she constructs herself for her narratee by reconstructing the reality of her existence. The novel as a whole thus reflects the cognitive process, unique to the human species, by which humans "enter into meaning" by making narrative sense of themselves and the world around them (Bruner 1990: 68).

Like Fowler's novel, *A Beautiful Truth* is also invested in representing non-anthropomorphized chimpanzee characters. But whereas Fowler's text addresses the differences between chimp and human cognition by refusing to illustrate the former, McAdam's narrative gives readers a glimpse into chimp minds by emphasizing the ability of chimps and humans to empathize with each other via physical and visual cues. These connections are most obvious in the scenes featuring the human couple Walt and Judy Ribke and their adopted chimp son Looee, who is regularly affected by the emotions of his parents: "When he saw her [Judy's] fear or anger he got frightened himself and he would run around screaming, trying to find comfort where he could until he felt he could touch her or get a hug" (McAdam 2013: 36). The domestic scenes in the Ribke house play a crucial role in the novel, in that they represent the close emotional connections that are possible between humans and chimpanzees. Walt, Judy, and Looee share each other's emotional states, such that the parents cannot help but see Looee as "an equal—a child perhaps, but certainly not an animal" (37).

Yet the novel also foregrounds the stark differences between human and chimp modes of meaning-making, thus underscoring the inherent foreignness of chimpanzees. Most striking of these representations is the transcriptions of pictograph conversations between the chimp Mr. Ghoul and human primatologist Dave Kennedy. A typical example of these conversations illustrates Mr. Ghoul's ability to use symbols to express his desires but struggle to arrange those symbols grammatically or string them together to tell a narrative:

> Please machine make vodka sentence.
> ? What does Ghoul want.
> Make vodka. Dave. Make sentence.
> ? Ghoul wants sentence or Ghoul wants vodka.
> Vodka sentence.
> That is not right.
> Please Dave vodka sentence Dave.
> ? (21)

Throughout the novel, the narrator makes clear Dave's belief that the differences between chimps and humans are those of degree, not of kind. But despite Dave's excitement when he teaches a chimp to recognize and use a new symbol, the ultimate result of his conversations with Mr. Ghoul and other chimps is confusion. His conversations with the chimps that he studies never progress beyond basic, nonnarrative statements and often end in question marks that signify a communicative impasse between chimp and human researcher. At other points in the novel, the narrator uses non-English words that readers must translate by deduction to accentuate the strangeness of chimp experience, such as "pokol-people" (lab technicians), "plektar" (a plastic window), and "yekel" (a stranger) (18, 22, 70). The cumulative effect of these narrative tics is to suggest the inherent strangeness of chimps. Their experiences, the narrator insinuates loudly, are not human.

Like Fowler, McAdam works around these emotional and cognitive barriers by using human bridge characters to make sense of chimp experiences. The novel is peppered with passages that challenge readers to make sense of chimp experiences via human emotions. Medical lab techs on the wing that ultimately houses Looee when he grows too violent to live with the Ribkes watch chimps dream and then, in turn, "dream their own dreams at home" (192). The conversation of two researchers who study a sociogram that makes clear Mr. Ghoul's isolation drifts "to family and how much it can mean sometimes just to get a phone call" (206); another researcher speaks of her husband's bad summer cold when she treats the respiratory infections of four apes with antibiotics (210). Veterinarian Dr. Meijer has never spoken to the people across the hall in his new apartment building, and in this way resembles Looee, who is ignored by his new chimp neighbors when he moves into the lab (215). The text works a well-worn groove in these passages: the narrator makes familiar chimp behavior for readers via human emotion and experiences. Human bridge characters act as a conduit between readers and alien chimps.

McAdam uses narrativity just as Fowler does, to reinforce readers' cognitive and empathic connections to human bridge characters who exhibit an altruistic ethics of care for chimpanzees. A key difference between this text and Fowler's is its basic narrative structure: McAdam's text features third-person (heterodiegetic) narration with variable focalization, in which an omniscient perspective flits frequently between humans and chimps in various states of captivity, while Fowler's novel employs first-person (homodiegetic) narration, in which a human narrator summarizes the life of her chimp sister. Yet in the climactic moments of *A Beautiful Truth*, the heterodiegetic narrator's voice is overwhelmed by primatologist Dave in a long passage of free direct discourse. The passage opens with the narrator explaining, in present tense, Dave's desire to persuade colleagues at academic conferences to care for chimps as much as he does: "He struggles to describe them sometimes, to make the larger world feel the way he feels" (265). Dave's voice quickly takes over the narration of the conference, such that readers come to know Dave's experience in his own words, unenclosed by quotation marks. "I was the quietest person on the panel," he states; "I kept looking up and down the table and out to the audience thinking we're apes and we're doomed not to know it" (273). Dave later laments that his human peers at the conference collectively talk "about global consciousness and enlightenment and progress and we have no sense of the fact that we are talking apes" (275).

The free direct discourse passage serves as a powerful illustration of a particularly human form of meaning-making, giving readers a picture of a man trying to make sense of a world that he does not understand via self-narration. While initially Dave struggles to describe the chimps, "to make the larger world feel the way he does," by the end of the passage he achieves this task by overwhelming the narrator's voice (265). He speaks of his fears to his wife in the first person, telling her not only of his concerns for Mr. Ghoul and other chimps, but also of how the cruelty of humans toward others has influenced his feelings about the death of his mother and his relationship to his daughter. Importantly, Dave's free direct discourse rearranges time to underscore the connections between humans and chimps; his narration moves fluidly between recalling experiences in his own life and his deeply personal observations of the chimps in his care. McAdam's narrative only returns to the heterodiegetic narrator's voice when Dave finally is able to express contentment about his connection with another human who understands him, his wife: "I'm so glad you're coming home soon. . . . This place is cleaner than you've ever seen it and I've mowed the lawns he says" (279). Dave must tell his own narrative to make sense of his care for chimpanzees and his frustration that other humans do not share his ethics.

The effect of this climactic passage is twofold. First, it places Dave and his deep compassion for chimpanzees at the emotional center of the text. Second, and perhaps more importantly in light of human cognition, it also draws attention to the necessity of narration and narratives in human sense-making. As with Fowler's narrative, McAdam's novel encourages readers to make a strong cognitive connection to a human bridge character via representations of the cognitive processes by which that character makes sense of their world by narrating it. The emotional power of this passage suggests that human interiority from within the consciousness of a bridge character can be one of the most effective means of producing empathy with nonhuman characters. This argues against the implied supposition that empathy correlates with shared consciousness.

Indeed, contrary to current theories of narrative empathy and critical anthropomorphism, literary narratives such as Fowler's and McAdam's that refuse to anthropomorphize nonhuman characters can also be important tools for fostering the altruistic behavior of readers for real-world nonhuman subjects. They facilitate this altruism not by fostering the illusion of shared perceptual, emotional, or axiological perspectives between readers and non-human characters but through their use of human bridge characters that themselves are exemplars of an altruistic ethics of care in action. To use Suzanne Keen's language, characters such as Rosemary and Dave help readers overcome the significant barrier of species difference by allowing those readers to try on the emotional and cognitive states of fictional humans who themselves practice an ethics of care for nonhuman subjects.

References

Abbott, H. Porter. 2000. "The Evolutionary Origins of the Storied Mind: Modeling the Pre-history of Narrative Consciousness and Its Discontents." *Narrative* 8, no. 3: 247–56.

Armbruster, Karla. 2013. "What Do We Want from Talking Animals?: Reflections on Literary Representations of Animal Voices and Minds." In *Speaking for Animals: Animal Biographical Writing*, edited by Margo DeMello, 17–33. London: Routledge.

Bekoff, Mark. 2000. *Animals Matter: A Biologist Explains Why We Should Treat Animals with Compassion and Respect*. Boston: Shambala.

Bennett, Jane. 2010. *Vibrant Matter: A Political Ecology of Things*. Durham, NC: Duke University Press.

Bernaerts, Lars, Marco Caracciolo, Luc Herman, and Bart Vervaech. 2014. "The Storied Lives of Non-human Narrators." *Narrative* 22, no. 1: 68–93.

Bruner, Jerome. 1990. *Acts of Meaning*. Cambridge, MA: Harvard University Press.

Call, Josep, and Michael Tomasello. 2008. "Does the Chimpanzee Have a Theory of Mind?: 30 Years Later." *Trends in Cognitive Sciences* 12, no. 5: 187–92.

Caracciolo, Marco. 2016. *Strange Narrators in Contemporary Fiction: Exploration in Readers' Engagement with Characters*. Lincoln: University of Nebraska Press.

de Waal, Frans. 2008. "Putting the Altruism Back into Altruism: The Evolution of Empathy." *Annual Review of Psychology*, no. 59: 279–300.

Donald, Merlin. 1991. *Origins of the Modern Mind: Three Stages in the Evolution of Culture and Cognition*. Cambridge, MA: Harvard University Press.

Easterlin, Nancy. 1999. "Making Knowledge: Bioepistemology and the Foundations of Literary Theory." *Mosaic* 32, no. 1: 131–47.

Fowler, Karen Joy. 2013. *We Are All Completely Beside Ourselves*. New York: G. P. Putnam's Sons.

Fultz, Amy, and Cathy Willis Spraetz. 2014. "Foreword." In *Entangled Empathy: An Alternative Ethic for Our Relationship to Animals*, by Lori Gruen, xi–xv. New York: Lantern Books.

Herman, David. 2011. "Storyworld/Umwelt." *SubStance* 40, no. 1: 156–81.

Iovino, Serenella, and Serpil Oppermann. 2012. "Material Ecocriticism: Material, Agency, and Models of Narrativity." *Ecozon@* 3, vol. 1: 75–91.

Keen, Suzanne. 2006. "A Theory of Narrative Empathy," *Narrative* 14: 207–36.

Keen, Suzanne. 2007. *Empathy and the Novel*. Oxford: Oxford University Press.

Keen, Suzanne. 2011. "Fast Tracks to Narrative Empathy: Anthropomorphization and Dehumanization in Graphic Novels." *SubStance* 40, no. 1: 135–55.

Keen, Suzanne. 2015. "Human Rights Discourse and the Universals of Cognition and Emotion: Postcolonial Fiction." In *The Oxford Handbook of Cognitive Literary Studies*, edited by Lisa Zunshine, 347–65. Oxford: Oxford University Press.

McAdam, Colin. 2013. *A Beautiful Truth*. New York: Soho Press.

Nussbaum, Martha. 1997. *Cultivating Humanity: A Classical Defense of Reform in Liberal Education*. Cambridge, MA: Harvard University Press.

Pinker, Steven, and Rebecca Goldstein. 2004. "The Seed Salon," *Seed*: 44–52.

Premack, David, and Guy Woodruff. 1978. "Does the Chimpanzee Have a Theory of Mind?" *Behavioral and Brain Sciences* 4, no. 1: 515–26.

Terrance, Herbert, and Peter Singer. 2011. "Can Chimps Converse? An Exchange." *New York Review of Books*, November 24. www.nybooks.com/articles/2011/11/24/can-chimps-converse-exchange/.

Weik von Mossner, Alexa. 2017. *Affective Ecologies: Empathy, Emotion, and Environmental Narrative.* Columbus: Ohio State University Press.

Welling, Bart. 2011. "Critical Anthropomorphism in the 'Age of Biocybernetic Reproduction': A Response to Nicola Merola's 'Monkeys, Apes, and Bears, Oh My!'" *JAC* 31, no. 3/4: 660–85.

The Poetry and Practice of Meditation

Elizabeth Bradburn
Western Michigan University

Abstract Is reading poetry good for you? Drawing on evidence that reading poetry involves some of the same brain structures as those upon which human psychological well-being depends, this essay argues that George Herbert's devotional lyrics, long understood as Christian meditations, center on recurring images in a manner consistent with the modern practice of mindfulness meditation. There is a significant overlap between the way meditation was understood by seventeenth-century Christians and the way it is understood by modern meditators in a secular and therapeutic context. Neurally, meditation means the reduction of activity in the brain's default mode network; phenomenally, it means repeatedly bringing wandering attention back to a chosen meditation object. Poetry can be isomorphic with meditative practice because the image of meditation has an identifying pattern of movement — spontaneous wandering and controlled return — that can be created in several sensory modalities. Complex enough to characterize Herbert's poetry as meditative, the pattern of wandering from and returning to a focal image potentially defines a meditative literary mode with a distinctive relationship to the imagination. The therapeutic potential of meditative poetry speaks to the value not just of poetry but of humanist education in general.

Keywords meditation, meditative poetry, George Herbert, default mode network

Elizabeth Bishop once suggested that she considered George Herbert's *The Temple* (1633) a kind of self-help manual, better than psychoanalysis.[1]

---

1. Referring to a popular book "on how to psychoanalyze oneself," Bishop (1994: 108) wrote to Marianne Moore, "I had infinitely rather approach such things from the Christian viewpoint myself — but the trouble is I've never been able to find the books, except Herbert."

Poetics Today 40:3 (September 2019) DOI 10.1215/03335372-7558178

Is reading poetry good for you? Herbert's friend and fellow poet-clergyman John Donne believed so, saying from the pulpit that the book of Psalms, the acknowledged model for Donne, Herbert, and many other Renaissance lyricists, was "an Oyntment powred out upon all sorts of sores, A Searcloth that souples all bruises, A Balme that searches all wounds" (Donne [1626] 1954, 7: 51). For Donne, the "Oyntment" is a spiritual one, as is the "advantage" that Herbert reputedly hoped would accrue to "any dejected poor soul" who found in *The Temple* "a picture of the many spiritual conflicts that have passed betwixt God and my soul" (Walton [1670] 1995: 380).[2] Bishop, writing three centuries later, saw the healing influence of poetry in psychoanalytic terms. Now, in the age of neuroscience, there is evidence that reading poetry does involve some of the same brain structures as those upon which human psychological well-being depends. I will argue that Herbert's devotional lyrics, long understood as Christian meditations, center on a recurring image in a manner consistent with the modern practice of mindfulness meditation.[3] The neural mechanisms of meditation can help to define the poetic mode of *The Church* (the middle section of *The Temple* containing the devotional lyrics for which Herbert is best known) and explain how it might offer emotional "help" even to a nonbelieving reader like Bishop.[4]

1. What Is an Image?

I use *image* in the neurobiological sense: "a mental pattern in any of the sensory modalities" (Damasio 1999: 9). While literary critics generally think of imagery as pictures painted in words, in the brain, images may be visual, auditory, olfactory, gustatory, or somatosensory. Images may respond to perceived external objects, or they may be constructed through memory. Reading a poem on the page means having an "embodied pattern of experience" (Johnson 2007: 243) in the visual modality while at the same time being prompted to multisensory "imaginative acts occurring under authorial direction" (Scarry 1999: 31). Thus this stanza from "The Temper (1),"[5] in which

2. These words were reported by Izaak Walton in his biography of Herbert. Walton ([1670] 1995: 380) wrote that on his deathbed Herbert instructed his friend Nicholas Ferrar to "read [*The Temple*]; and then, if he can think it may turn to the advantage of any dejected poor soul, let it be made public; if not, let him burn it."
3. Mindfulness meditation, now a secular and clinical practice in the west, derives from Buddhist teachings.
4. The Herbert scholar Joseph H. Summers corresponded at length with Bishop about Herbert's influence on her. Summers (1994/95: 56) quotes from a letter in which Bishop wrote that Herbert's poems "help a bit" in the aftermath of tragic personal events.
5. In *The Church*, a loosely structured (as opposed to strictly sequential) collection of about 160 lyric poems, Herbert frequently gives the same title to more than one poem, a practice whose

the speaker addresses God, creates both visual and auditory mental patterns as the reader looks at the lines on the page and either voices or hears in the mind's ear the rhyme and meter:

> Yet take thy way; for sure thy way is best:
> >   Stretch or contract me, thy poor debtor:
> >   This is but tuning of my breast,
> > >   To make the music better. (Herbert [1633] 1995: 53)

Besides meeting the eyes and ears, these words direct the reader to imagine the sound of music and the bodily sensation of being stretched and contracted. The stanza creates an image involving three sensory modalities, with one (hearing) involved in two separate ways.

This image also includes movement, most apparently in that stretching and contracting are bodily motions. Less obviously, the "music" mentioned in the fourth line of the stanza is a dynamic image. In *Feeling Beauty: The Neuroscience of Aesthetic Experience*, G. Gabrielle Starr (2014: 88) enumerates the many ways in which music evokes motor imagery in the hearer, arguing that "motion and imagined motion are central to music." Reaching a similar conclusion, Mark Johnson (2007: 256) underscores the centrality of metaphors of bodily movement to our *experience* of music. Seventeenth-century writing generally and *The Church* in particular attest repeatedly to the dynamic nature of musical experience. Herbert's poem to "Church-music" exemplifies this motif:

> Sweetest of sweets, I thank you: when displeasure
> >   Did through my body wound my mind,
> You took me thence, and in your house of pleasure
> >   A dainty lodging me assign'd.
>
> Now I in you without a body move,
> >   Rising and falling with your wings: (Herbert [1633] 1995: 63)

If theorists such as Johnson and Starr are correct, then this healing flight on the wings of music is no mere poetic conceit, but an expression of a common, perhaps universal, phenomenal experience of music. The "tuning of my breast" in "The Temper" uses the same conceptual metaphor to suggest that the "stretching and contracting" are simultaneously auditory and motor experiences. Further, the auditory image created by the poem's meter is dynamic. According to Starr (2014: 89), "In the case of poetry, metrical writing can evoke not only auditory imagery but the imagery of motion; as we

---

significance I analyze in part 4. Modern editors distinguish these identically titled poems by numbering them. Here I discuss the first of two called "The Temper."

time the words that we 'hear,' motor centers of the brain, including the cerebellum, are also active, perhaps in helping us catch the beat, and what enables the timing of action also enables us to understand and produce metrical speech." "The Temper" prompts us to imagine sound as motion in two ways: by referring to musical experience and by employing poetic meter.

Perhaps most subtly of all, the arrangement of the lines on the page forms an image of movement. A visual form may seem frozen, but Starr (2014: 85–86) explains that even abstract paintings create a dynamic experience for the viewer:

> It is ... neither necessary to imagine the hand that made a work nor to enact a neural simulation of a body in a work in order to engage the imagery of motion. In Pollock's 1946 *Shimmering Substance*... the yellow spiral or circle that seems to dominate the painting doesn't actually exist on the surface of the canvas: there is no yellow line, only the illusion of a yellow line, which can be constructed around the interruptions of white, blue, green, and pink pigment. The circular image is produced by the sweep of the eye as it follows an imagined curve and by the standard embroidery of vision ... , and it is strengthened by the suggestive echoes of loops throughout the canvas. The vibrancy of the painting—its "shimmering"—comes through our own visual and imagined engagement, the sense of motion that comes from the eyes and from the filling in of the golden curve as it draws the viewer on and in to the painting's perceptual and formal logic.

In other words, the act of visual perception itself can summon motor imagery—in the case of poetry, by following lines of verse across and down the page. While I am not claiming that a poem should be viewed as a painting, I do insist that the physical layout of a poem contributes to its dynamic imagery. Concrete (or "shape") poems, of which Herbert includes two in *The Church*, make this contribution explicit. I will return to Herbert's shapes (abstract and concrete) later. For now, I wish to emphasize, following Starr, that the visual form of poetry "engage[s] the imagery of motion."

To return to the "tuning" stanza from "The Temper," then: while there is almost nothing in it that constructs an image in the sense usually meant by literary critics (a picture in the mind's eye), the lines do create a complex image in the neurobiological sense. There are sounds heard, lines and white spaces seen; in imagination, the stretching and contracting of the body, the sound of music, the experience of being "tuned" by dramatic emotions; even the humble gesture of submission ("sure thy way is best") in the stanza's first line. And, far from being unique to the sixth stanza of "The Temper," this complex multisensory motor imagery occurs in every poem in *The Church*. This matters because the same type of imagery, imagery in the neurobiological sense, defines the practice of meditation and accounts for its effectiveness. In the next two sections I will explain how this is so and how the link between aesthetic experience and meditative practice can define a meditative poetic mode. Finally, I will return to *The Church* to show how Herbert designed an image of meditation into his book that resonates with modern, non-Christian readers.

2. An Image of Meditation

What do meditators do? Meditation is a mental and emotional process, and there is a significant overlap between the way that process was understood by seventeenth-century Christians and the way it is understood by practitioners of modern mindfulness meditation. This overlap constitutes an image of meditation shared by the two cultures. Again, I use *image* in the neurobiological sense: meditators perceive their practice as one of those "patterns by which the contours of our experience take shape and undergo transformation" (Johnson 2007: 243). Verbal descriptions of and instructions for meditation prompt the imagination, often through metaphor. The imagery evoked by a seventeenth-century meditation manual can tell us something about how Herbert and his contemporaries experienced Christian meditation, with important implications for understanding meditation as both a cross-cultural practice and a literary mode.

To understand seventeenth-century meditation phenomenally, I turn to *The Art of Divine Meditation* (1606), a manual by Bishop Joseph Hall.[6] Like modern meditation teachers, Hall ([1606] 1981: 80) instructs meditators to set up their environments by reducing external stimuli: he recommends "solitariness of place" and "composedness" of the body (82), either by adopting a still position or by walking alone. With this framing established, "our divine meditation is nothing else but a bending of the mind upon some spiritual object" (72). As the word *bending* suggests, Hall's image of meditation follows a rhythm of wandering and then returning to the meditation object. "As the mind," he explains, "if it go loose and without rule, roves to no purpose, so, if it be too much fettered with the gyves of strict regularity, moveth nothing at all" (88).[7] In his theory, the undisciplined mind tends to

6. Two influential studies of seventeenth-century lyric identify Hall's manual as both popular in its time and historically appropriate for the study of seventeenth-century poetry generally and *The Church* specifically (Martz 1954: 62; Lewalski 1979: 150–51). A more recent article by Ben Faber (2016), which I discuss in part 4, examines *The Art of Divine Meditation* in detail to argue for its direct influence on Herbert.

7. The context for Hall's comment is to caution against the strictures of an overly "subtle scale of meditation" (87), a concern not immediately applicable to my argument. I quote the passage only to show that Hallean meditation, along with mindfulness meditation, acknowledges the

"rove." Meditation acknowledges this spontaneous wandering and practices the controlled return of attention to a chosen object.

A similar pattern of experience characterizes modern mindfulness meditation. Neuroscientists who study the effects of meditation try to correlate phenomenal descriptions with neural patterns observed using functional magnetic resonance imaging (fMRI). In Damasio's (1999: 318) terms, they try to establish a connection between an image, which "can be accessed *only in a first-person perspective*," and a neural pattern, which "can be accessed *only in a third-person perspective*." Modern minds, like early modern ones, tend to wander (to the past, to the future, to projections of the self) in the absence of a sufficiently engaging external stimulus. In mindfulness meditation, the meditator minimizes external stimuli (as in Bishop Hall's method) and then uses "focused attention" and "voluntary control of mental content" (Travis and Parim 2017: 86) to repeatedly return the wandering mind to a meditation object (typically the meditator's own breathing). The motor image here, of wandering and returning, is no mere figure of speech, but a mental pattern "built with the tokens" (Damasio 1999: 318) of the somatosensory modality.

What happens in the brain during and as a result of meditation? Using fMRI technology, researchers have found evidence that meditation "targets" a brain system known as the default mode network (Brewer et al. 2011: 20257). The default mode network supports specific forms of internal cognition, including "autobiographical memory retrieval, envisioning the future, and conceiving the perspectives of others" (Buckner, Andrews-Hanna, and Schacter 2008: 1), as well as navigation (Buckner and Carroll 2007). As its name suggests, the default mode network is "preferentially active when individuals are not focused on the external environment" (Buckner, Andrews-Hanna, and Schacter 2008: 1). When meditators minimize external stimuli, they create a situation in which the default mode network would normally be active and then use focused attention and mental control to train the mind away from its default mode of wandering. Meditation both reduces the activity of the default mode network and strengthens the connection between the default mode network and other brain structures that support cognitive control (Brewer et al. 2011; Jang et al. 2011; Garrison et al. 2015), thus giving the brain a "more present-centered" (Brewer et al. 2011: 20255) default mode.

Meditation is a cross-cultural experience. Neurally, it means the reduction of activity in the default mode network; phenomenally, it means repeatedly

mind's tendency to wander and recognizes that it must be gently trained to focus rather than rigidly immobilized.

bringing the wandering attention back to a chosen meditation object. What, then, does meditation mean poetically? In the next section, I explain what meditation has in common with poetry and how these shared qualities could help define a meditative literary mode.

3. Meditation and Imagination

The default mode network is involved not only in meditation, but also in "intense aesthetic experience" (Starr 2014: 8). Using fMRI technology to track the neural patterns of subjects viewing art, Starr and her colleagues concluded that aesthetic experiences increase activity in the default mode network (Vessel, Starr, and Rubin 2012). Developing the implications of these findings, Starr (2014: 98) suggests that complex imagery, which requires high-level creative cognition to process, provides a "gateway" to the default mode network, enhancing its capacity for imaginative self-projection. "Imagery," she writes, "integrates and remakes knowledge, and, enacted in the brain and in the mind, it can take powerful hold of the self" (99).

From this perspective, meditative poetry may seem like a contradiction in terms. It appears that both meditation and art engage with the default mode network, but in different ways:

- In meditation, the meditator creates an environment, the absence of external stimulus, where the default mode network would normally be active, and uses attentional focus to train it to be less active. Imaginative self-projection decreases.
- In aesthetic experience, the viewer enters an environment, the presence of a complex and engaging external stimulus, where the default mode network would normally be inactive; and, if the experience is intense enough, the default mode network is activated. Imaginative self-projection increases.

The opposition I have sketched here corresponds to a distinction made by Alan Richardson in a critique of neuroscientific theories of the imagination that take an unqualified view of that faculty as adaptive and creative. Referring to Randy L. Buckner's work, Richardson acknowledges imagination as the mind's "default" mode, but insists that it is not necessarily or uniformly healthy and adaptive. "In the Buddhist tradition," Richardson (2011: 686) points out, imagination "makes us miserable, drawing us away from the present moment and poisoning our lives." Richardson cites Samuel Johnson as an example of a British writer who drew on the Christian meditative tradition to take a negative view of imagination (687).

There may, however, be more to meditative poetry than direct opposition between an imaginative/default-mode-network-on mode and a meditative/default-mode-network-off mode. The two descriptions above are as analogous as they are opposed. In both situations, the brain's default response is reversed: meditation decreases default mode network activity where it would normally occur, and intense aesthetic experience increases default mode network activity where it would normally be quiet. Perhaps what the meditating and the art-experiencing brains have in common is not the level of activation in the default mode network but the adjustment of neurological connections to the default mode network. Starr (2014: 64) surmises that the activation of the default mode network in profound aesthetic experiences might register insight, the integration of "computational reward into a complex experience of emotions and intense aesthetic feeling." If meditative poetry evokes a particular kind of imagery, as I will argue in the next section, then it too involves the imagination. The meditative mode may not suppress or negate imagination so much as call up a particular kind of image that helps the default mode network define its relationship to itself, as happens purposely in meditation.

The possibility of a meditative mode of poetry defined against an imaginative one was first suggested by William W. Bevis in a study of Wallace Stevens. Bevis (1989: 9) argues that Stevens "somehow became a master of meditative detachment," a detachment visible in Stevens's oeuvre as a direct counter to the poet's imaginative mode. Establishing that Stevens could have had little contact with Buddhism, Bevis takes a phenomenological rather than a historicist approach, drawing on the neuroscience of meditation (as it stood in the 1980s) to argue that Stevens discovered meditative states and Zen philosophical attitudes for himself and sought to represent them in his poetry. Bevis calls meditative poetic form "a true fragmentation, made of an endless series of associations that follow one from another but which fail to progress, to maintain a single principle, or to form a coherent picture of the speaker" (281). Although this consciously modernist description does not fully apply to *The Church*, it does sketch out an image similar to the one that I will define as meditative in Herbert's poetry.[8]

8. Bevis argues that a study of Christian meditative poetry such as Martz's (cited in note 6) cannot be applied to Stevens's poetry, which exhibits an intuitive sense of "Eastern negation." He does acknowledge, however, that even where doctrines differ, the experience of meditation may be universal (Bevis 1989: 235). In drawing on the neuroscience of meditation, as Bevis does, I have argued for a cross-cultural understanding of meditation.

4. Herbert's Poetry of Meditation

In section 1, I offered a neurobiological definition of imagery, explaining how poetry creates images of movement in multiple sensory modalities. According to Starr (2014: 91, 98), it is not just imagery but multisensory motor imagery specifically that underwrites aesthetic experience and provides access to the default mode network. The centrality of movement to poetic imagery makes it possible to define a meditative poetic mode. Poetry can be "isomorphic" (Tsur 1992: 417) with meditative practice because the image of meditation has a distinctive pattern of movement—spontaneous wandering and controlled return—that can be created in several sensory modalities. In this section, I will elaborate on this image of meditative movement as it appears in *The Church*, showing how it shapes the relationships between the poems and their titles, the overall structure of the collection, and Herbert's distinctive use of visual and auditory motor imagery.

In meditation, the mind moves obliquely, progressing in lateral steps, neither driving forward toward a predetermined goal nor going in a circle. The sense is of discovering something that has always been there; there is wandering and returning to an object, but in some ways the path itself is the object. In sketching this image of meditative movement, I modify Ben Faber's analysis of Hallean meditation in Herbert's poetry. Faber (2016: 80) identifies what he calls a "zig-zag path" of movement in *The Church*, one characterized by "controlled spontaneity" (74). He claims, however, that this oblique movement is also goal directed (80)—primarily, it seems, to distinguish it from the circularity of sin (81). I argue that the rhetoric of a typical Herbert poem progresses in zigzagging steps without either returning to its starting point or driving linearly toward a predetermined goal. This explains Herbert's many surprising endings, in which the speaker, rather than reaching a conclusion toward which he has been moving incrementally, seems to turn in place and express a significant change of heart.

The resolution of "The Temper," one stanza of which I discussed in part 1, is one of many examples. Here is the poem in full (Herbert [1633] 1995: 52–53):

> How should I praise thee, Lord! how should my rhymes
> > Gladly engrave thy love in steel,
> > If what my soul doth feel sometimes,
> > > My soul might ever feel!
>
> Although there were some forty heav'ns, or more,
> > Sometimes I peer above them all;
> > Sometimes I hardly reach a score,
> > > Sometimes to hell I fall.

O rack me not to such a vast extent;
    Those distances belong to thee:
    The world's too little for thy tent,
        A grave too big for me.

Wilt thou meet arms with man, that thou dost stretch
    A crumb of dust from heav'n to hell?
    Will great God measure with a wretch?
        Shall he thy stature spell?

O let me, when thy roof my soul hath hid,
    O let me roost and nestle there:
    Then of a sinner thou art rid,
        And I of hope and fear.

Yet take thy way; for sure thy way is best:
    Stretch or contract me, thy poor debtor:
    This is but tuning of my breast,
        To make the music better.

Whether I fly with angels, fall with dust,
    Thy hands made both, and I am there:
    Thy power and love, my love and trust
        Make one place ev'ry where.

The turn in place occurs at "yet" (line 21). The poem does not progress sequentially toward a static goal. Instead, it expresses a series of emotional shifts (marked by "O") that bring about a change of state, a new insight or acceptance on the part of the speaker. There is no lesson learned or aim achieved; rather, the speaker finds something that has always been there, and the trajectory of the poem is the speaker's emotional acceptance of this. The speaker, as Hall ([1606] 1981: 88) recommends, follows the mind "through all ... those 'places' which natural reason doth afford us." This poem presents an image of meditation in the mode of bodily movement; instead of dramatizing a scene or story of personal meditation, it evokes the emotional dynamic described by Hall: "Being lifted up with our estate of joy, it [the mind] is cast down with complaint; lift up with wishes, it is cast down with confession, which order doth best hold it in ure [i.e., in practice] and just temper and make it more feeling of the comfort which followeth in the conclusion" (103). The lifting and falling, stretching and contracting, are emotional as well as physical, "tempering" the mind to be able to accept comfort and stability.

Herbert's highly experimental titles often contribute to the meditative movement in his poems. John Hollander (1985: 223) calls Herbert's titles "radical, in that their expressive character is in each case part of the poem's

fiction" and "modern . . . in their systematic obliqueness" (224). In a detailed
analytical study of titles in *The Church*, Anne Ferry (2008: 66) points out that
most of Herbert's titles are "single noun[s] referring to an abstraction pur-
ported to be the subject of the poem." They serve as meditation objects: not
goals, but foci to which the poems repeatedly and often indirectly return, as
in this sonnet titled "Prayer" (Herbert [1633] 1995: 49):

> Prayer the Church's banquet, Angels' age,
>> God's breath in man returning to his birth,
>> The soul in paraphrase, heart in pilgrimage,
> The Christian plummet sounding heav'n and earth;
> Engine against th' Almighty, sinners' tower,
>> Reversed thunder, Christ-side-piercing spear,
>> The six-days-world transposing in an hour,
> A kind of tune, which all things hear and fear;
> Softness, and peace, and joy, and love, and bliss,
>> Exalted manna, gladness of the best,
>> Heaven in ordinary, man well drest,
> The milky way, the bird of Paradise,
>> Church-bells beyond the stars heard, the soul's blood,
>> The land of spices; something understood.

The paratactic structure places these images in lateral relationship to each
other rather than in a vertical hierarchy; in Chanita Goodblatt's (1990: 51)
terms, the catalog is a succession, not a sequence. Goodblatt's essay, which
is about Walt Whitman, distinguishes between illustrative and meditative
catalogs, arguing that the latter are characterized by "a focus on sensory
perception" (50). While Herbert's catalog doesn't begin to approach Whit-
manesque levels of sensuality, it nevertheless qualifies as meditative. The
catalog includes auditory and tactile as well as visual images; presents "an
ongoing perceptual experience as a succession of images" (49) as opposed to a
narrative sequence; and is written, except for the final phrase, in the present
tense.[9] And even the final shift to past tense does not complete the succession
of images or retroactively hierarchize them. Rather, it indicates that the
paratactic catalog has deepened the speaker's understanding of prayer.
Drawing on the revision history of *The Church*, Ferry (2008: 76) asserts that
Herbert crafts his titles to "[shift] attention away from the poet, and from the
poem as an example of his performance in a literary genre." The title and
structure of "Prayer" illustrate this principle perfectly. "Prayer" is not itself a
prayer but a meditation on prayer.

9. I draw these criteria from Goodblatt's (1990: 50–52) instructive comparison of Whitman's
meditative catalogs with a nonmeditative catalog from Milton's *Paradise Lost*.

Herbert's systematic use of titles throughout *The Church* also evokes an image of meditative movement in the work as a whole. A succession rather than a sequence, *The Church* often returns to the same poem titles. There are, for instance, three poems called "Love" and two called "Jordan." The modern editorial practice of numbering these identically titled poems can misleadingly suggest that they form sequences. Some poems with the same title appear next to each other, but many are pages apart, and, as Ferry points out, "for widely spaced poems with the same title [Herbert] never used the same form. In its association Herbert's title allowed the reader to approach the text [of an individual lyric] as if it were an entry in a commonplace book. . . . In the fiction enacted, the volume is then a compilation of passages collated under commonplaces" (76). To read *The Church*, then, is neither to "rove without purpose" nor to be "too much fettered with the gyves of strict regularity." Rather, the effect is of repeatedly coming back to the same places and meditating on them anew, much as the speaker of "The H. Scriptures" (Herbert [1633] 1995: 56) does:

> This verse marks that, and both do make a motion
>   Unto a third, that ten leaves off doth lie:
>   Then as dispersed herbs do watch a potion,
> These three make up some Christian's destiny: ·
> Such are thy secrets, which my life makes good,
>   And comments on thee: for in ev'ry thing
>   Thy words do find me out, and parallels bring,
> And in another make me understood.

The zigzagging "motion" of reading to discover something that was already there describes the meditative image found in the overall collection as well as in its individual poems.

Besides emerging from the sense of the poems, meditative movement materializes in their visual form. In part 1, I cited Starr's explanation of how visual art can call up motor imagery, and here I will go into detail about how the shapes of Herbert's poems evoke the special kind of oblique movement I am associating with meditation. A look through *The Church* suggests that Herbert aimed to deploy every possible shape of stanza, and in fact the volume includes over one hundred different stanza patterns, most of which are unique not only in Herbert but in all of English poetry (Hayes 1938: 43). Herbert cues the reader to attend to visual form by including two shape (or concrete) poems among the variety of stanzas in *The Church*, one of which, "The Altar," opens the collection.

The more famous shape poem, however, is probably "Easter Wings" (Herbert [1633] 1995: 40–41), which uses its visual form to evoke imagery of movement in two ways. First, the stanzas are in the shape of wings, thus creating a visual image that supports the specific kind of movement (flight) referred to in the poem. But following the margins of the lines with the eye reveals yet another dynamic image:

> Lord, who createdst man in wealth and store,
> Though foolishly he lost the same,
> Decaying more and more,
> Till he became
> Most poor:
> With thee
> O let me rise
> As larks, harmoniously,
> And sing this day thy victories:
> Then shall the fall further the flight in me.
>
> My tender age in sorrow did begin:
> And still with sicknesses and shame
> Thou didst so punish sin
> That I became
> Most thin.
> With thee
> Let me combine,
> And feel this day thy victory:
> For, if I imp my wing on thine,
> Affliction shall advance the flight in me.

Here is a lateral movement between wide and narrow, as though the poem itself is contracting and then expanding again. Herbert verbally cues the reader to notice this: lines 5 and 15, where the poem is most contracted, read "most poor" and "most thin." The edges of the lines move back and forth laterally, forming an oblique margin.

Indeed, any stanza form that combines long and short lines, as most of Herbert's do, would evoke this image of lateral movement. In "The Temper," for instance, the dynamic image of contracting and stretching is both verbally cued and visually presented in the change of line lengths. Each stanza begins with a pentameter line, contracts laterally with two tetrameter lines, contracts further with a trimeter line, and then, at the beginning of the next stanza, stretches out again into a pentameter line. The poem's title and theme make clear that this movement is not goal directed. That is, although the stanza shape determines that the last line of the poem is "contracted," the content does not suggest a state of contraction as a goal or conclusion; rather, the resolution is the speaker's recognition that he is being "tuned" by the back-and-forth movement. The stanza form represents this dynamic tempering: the longest and shortest lines frame two "medium" lines, "tuned" in the sense that they are the same length as each other.

Thus these stanzas do not just produce lateral movement; more precisely, in them the vertical and the horizontal interact in a way that brings forward the image of the oblique. In "The Temper" the notion of tempering or tuning shapes the image. "Grace" (Herbert [1633] 1995: 58) uses the title concept to shape the stanza and line length dynamic. Here is the first stanza of that poem:

> My stock lies dead and no increase
> Doth my dull husbandry improve:
> O let thy graces without cease
> > Drop from above!

Each of the six stanzas uses this form, with the refrain "drop from above" as the fourth line of each. Here the words cue an image of vertical movement: the fourth line looks as though it is being dropped from the line above. This effect depends equally, however, on the horizontal dimension. Moving the fourth line to below the end of the third line creates the image of dropping, which would not be there if the fourth line began at the left margin. This zigzagging evokes meditation in that it suggests the focusing motions of the human mind in meditation as it prepares for—but, in Herbert, never presumes to have achieved—contact with the divine in the vertical dimension.

Finally, the oblique movement of the poems' margins on the page also evokes imagery in the auditory modality. The stanza forms probably evoked auditory imagery for Herbert because their variety originated in music (Low 1978: 30). "Denial" illustrates how the combination of visual with auditory motor imagery creates a meditative mode. Most of Herbert's stanza forms use contrapuntal rhyme; that is, Herbert "construct[s] the pattern of his line lengths independently of the pattern of his rimes" (Hayes 1938: 48). In the quatrains of "The Temper," for instance, traditional lyric harmony would require that the second and third tetrameter lines rhyme. Instead, each rhymes with a line of a different length. These lines are "tuned" visually and rhythmically, but not phonemically. Herbert's use of contrapuntal rhyme may heighten his visual forms' evocation of meditative movement by emphasizing the variation in line length and diminishing slightly the closural effects of end rhyme.[10] But he deploys contrapuntal rhyme in an even more complex (if not especially subtle) way in "Denial" (Herbert [1633] 1995: 77):

---

10. This may be an example of the "sensory competition" that Starr (2014: 114) says accounts for some aesthetic pleasures.

When my devotions could not pierce
        Thy silent ears;
Then was my heart broken, as was my verse:
        My breast was full of fears
            And disorder:

My bent thoughts, like a brittle bow,
        Did fly asunder:
Each took his way; some would to pleasures go,
        Some to the wars and thunder
            Of alarms.

As good go any where, they say,
        As to benumb
Both knees and heart, in crying night and day,
        Come, come, my God, O come,
            But no hearing.

O that thou shouldst give dust a tongue
        To cry to thee,
And then not hear it crying! all day long
        My heart was in my knee,
            But no hearing.

Therefore my soul lay out of sight,
        Untun'd, unstrung:
My feeble spirit, unable to look right
        Like a nipt blossom, hung
            Discontented.

O cheer and tune my heartless breast,
        Defer no time;
That so thy favours granting my request,
        They and my mind may chime,
            And mend my rhyme.

The obvious gimmick here (that the fifth line of each stanza but the last is unrhymed) may be made somewhat oblique by the use of contrapuntal rhyme: it is not clear which line "should" be rhymed. As the poem proceeds, however, the lateral movement of the lines across the page along with the meter return the reader's eye repeatedly to the same place, a place where a rhyme should be but isn't. As a result, the reader can't know ahead of time what will be found there — only what will not be found there. The last stanza "corrects" the pattern, retrospectively indicating the meaning of the un-rhymed places. This concludes the poem in one sense, but it cannot be understood as a goal toward which the poem progresses, because the unrhymed stanzas do not incrementally advance to the rhymed one; they just keep marking the place of meaning. What the reader finds in that place is "Denial," from which the poem rhythmically wanders and to which it repeatedly returns. In multisensory, dynamic imagery, the poem meditates upon, rather than enacts, denial.

The pattern of imagery that I have described occurs repeatedly in *The Church*, both in individual poems and at a higher structural level. Because the image of meditation is dynamic and integrates multiple sensory modalities, it is complex enough to define Herbert's poetry as meditative and potentially to define a meditative literary mode. If practicing mindfulness meditation and reading seventeenth-century meditative lyrics generate similar mental and neural patterns, then meditative literature need not be limited to a particular religious context or a particular literary culture. The meditative mode could be understood in neurobiological terms.

This would explain why Elizabeth Bishop found Herbert's poetry psychologically comforting apart from its theological content. Besides the common image I have described, seventeenth-century meditation and modern mindfulness meditation share a therapeutic purpose. Just as modern mindfulness meditation can help to treat "psychological disorders involving emotional dysregulation" such as depression and anxiety (Taylor et al. 2013: 4; Brewer et al. 2011: 20254), early modern Christian meditation explicitly claims to comfort the meditator and develop emotional stability. In "the art of meditation . . . we make use of all good means, fit ourselves to all good duties; by this we descry our weakness, obtain redress, prevent temptations, cheer up our solitariness, temper our occasions of delight, get more light unto our knowledge" (Hall [1606] 1981: 71). Ferry (2008: 82) concludes her analysis of Herbert's titles by suggesting that he imagined *The Church* as "a devotional commonplace book modeled on the Psalter." That is, Herbert really did believe that his poems could comfort and heal the reader, just as the Psalms were thought to do.

Reading poetry is good for you—and this conclusion speaks to the value not just of poetry but of humanist education in general. The meditative quality of *The Church* is expressed not as a literal verbal message but through a complex interaction of aesthetic images. It requires a reader sensitive and attentive to visual, auditory, and sensorimotor imagery as well as rhetorical patterns. Such attentiveness in turn requires education and training. By making the psychological benefits of meditative poetry available to students, literary humanities make an irreplaceable contribution to their well-being.

References

Bevis, William W. 1989. *Mind of Winter: Wallace Stevens, Meditation, and Literature*. Pittsburgh, PA: University of Pittsburgh Press.

Bishop, Elizabeth. (1928–1979) 1994. *One Art: Letters*, edited by Robert Giroux. New York: Farrar, Straus, Giroux.

Brewer, Judson A., Patrick D. Worhunsky, Jeremy R. Gray, Yi-Yuan Tang, Jochen Weber, and Hedy Kober. 2011. "Meditation Experience Is Associated with Differences in Default Mode Network Activity and Connectivity." *Proceedings of the National Academy of Sciences*, no. 108: 20254–59.

Buckner, Randy L., and Daniel C. Carroll. 2007. "Self-Projection and the Brain." *Trends in Cognitive Sciences* 11, no. 2: 49–58. doi.org/10.1016/j.tics.2006.11.004.

Buckner, Randy L., Jessica R. Andrews-Hanna, and Daniel L. Schacter. 2008. "The Brain's Default Network: Anatomy, Function, and Relevance to Disease." *Annals of the New York Academy of Sciences*, no. 1124: 1–38. onlinelibrary.wiley.com/doi/10.1196/annals .1440.011.

Damasio, Antonio. 1999. *The Feeling of What Happens: Body and Emotion in the Making of Consciousness*. San Diego, CA: Harcourt.

Donne, John. (1626) 1954. *The Sermons of John Donne*, edited by Evelyn M. Simpson and George R. Potter, 10 vols. Berkeley: University of California Press.

Faber, Ben. 2016. "The Art of Divine Meditation in George Herbert's *The Temple*." *Christianity and Literature* 66, no. 1: 73–89. doi.org/10.1177/0148333116679117.

Ferry, Anne. 2008. *By Design: Intention in Poetry*. Stanford, CA: Stanford University Press.

Garrison, Kathleen A., Thomas A. Zeffiro, Dustin Scheinost, R. Todd Constable, and Judson A. Brewer. 2015. "Meditation Leads to Reduced Default Mode Network Activity beyond an Active Task." *Cognitive, Affective and Behavioral Neuroscience* 51, no. 3: 712–20.

Goodblatt, Chanita. 1990. "Whitman's Catalogs as Literary Gestalts: Illustrative and Meditative Functions." *Style* 24, no. 1: 45–58.

Hall, Joseph. (1606) 1981. *The Art of Divine Meditation*. In *Bishop Joseph Hall and Protestant Meditation in Seventeenth-Century England*, edited by Frank Livingstone Huntley, 65–118. Binghamton, NY: Medieval and Renaissance Texts and Studies.

Hayes, Albert McHarg. 1938. "Counterpoint in Herbert." *Studies in Philology* 35, no. 1: 43–60.

Herbert, George. (1633) 1995. *Complete English Works*, edited by Ann Pasternak Slater. New York: Knopf.

Hollander, John. 1985. *Vision and Resonance: Two Senses of Poetic Form*, 2nd ed. New Haven: Yale University Press.

Jang, Joon Hwan, Wi Hoon Jung, Do-Hyung Kang, Min Soo Byun, Soo Jin Kwon, Chi-Hoon Choi, and Jun Soo Kwon. 2011. "Increased Default Mode Network Connectivity Associated with Meditation." *Neuroscience Letters* 487, no. 3: 358–63. doi.org/10.1016/j .neulet.2010.10.056.

Johnson, Mark. 2007. *The Meaning of the Body: Aesthetics of Human Understanding*. Chicago: University of Chicago Press.

Lewalski, Barbara Kiefer. 1979. *Protestant Poetics and the Seventeenth-Century Religious Lyric*. Princeton: Princeton University Press.

Low, Anthony. 1978. *Love's Architecture: Devotional Modes in Seventeenth-Century English Poetry*. New York: New York University Press.

Martz, Louis L. 1954. *The Poetry of Meditation: A Study in English Religious Literature of the Seventeenth Century*. New Haven: Yale University Press.

Richardson, Alan. 2011. "Defaulting to Fiction: Neuroscience Rediscovers the Romantic Imagination." *Poetics Today* 32, no. 4: 663–92. poeticstoday.dukejournals.org/content /32/4/663.

Scarry, Elaine. 1999. *Dreaming by the Book*. New York: Farrar, Straus, Giroux.

Starr, G. Gabrielle. 2014. *Feeling Beauty: The Neuroscience of Aesthetic Experience.* Cambridge, MA: MIT Press. ProQuest e-book.

Summers, Joseph H. 1994/95. "George Herbert and Elizabeth Bishop." *George Herbert Journal* 18, nos. 1 – 2: 48 – 58.

Taylor, Véronique A., Véronique Daneault, Joshua Grant, Geneviève Scavone, Estelle Breton, Sébastien Roffe-Vidal, Jérôme Courtemanche, Anaïs S. Lavarenne, Guillaume Marrelec, Habib Benali, and Mario Beauregard. 2013. "Impact of Meditation Training on the Default Mode Network during a Restful State." *Social Cognitive and Affective Neuroscience* 8, no. 1: 4 – 14. doi.org/10.1093/scan/nsr087.

Travis, Frederick, and Niyazi Parim. 2017. "Default Mode Network Activation and Transcendental Meditation Practice: Focused Attention or Automatic Self-Transcending?" *Brain and Cognition*, no. 111: 86 – 94. doi.org/10.1016/j.bandc.2016.08.009.

Tsur, Reuven. 1992. *Toward a Theory of Cognitive Poetics.* Amsterdam: Elsevier.

Vessel, Edward A., G. Gabrielle Starr, and Nava Rubin. 2012. "The Brain on Art: Intense Aesthetic Experience Activates the Default Mode Network." *Frontiers in Human Neuroscience* 6, no. 66. doi.org/10.3389/fnhum.2012.00066.

Walton, Izaak. (1670) 1995. "The Life of Mr. George Herbert." In Herbert [1633] 1995: 338 – 85.

Notes on Contributors

Marshall Alcorn is professor of English and chair of the English department at George Washington University. He is the author of *Changing the Subject in English Class* (2002) and *Resistance to Learning* (2013). His research interests are neuroscience, affect, and trauma studies.

Paul B. Armstrong is professor of English at Brown University. His most recent books are *How Literature Plays with the Brain: The Neuroscience of Reading and Art* (2013) and a Norton Critical Edition of Joseph Conrad's novella *Heart of Darkness* (5th ed., 2017). His book *Stories and the Brain: The Neuroscience of Narrative* is forthcoming (2020).

Katalin Bálint is assistant professor in media psychology in the Department of Communication Sciences, VU University Amsterdam. She researches the experience of cinematic and literary narratives and the effect of noncontent formal features on viewers' social cognition responses. Her papers have been published in *Frontiers, Projections: The Journal of Movies and Mind, Journal of Media Psychology*, and *Scientific Study of Literature*. She has coedited several journals and handbooks, including *Narrative Absorption* (2017).

Mark Bracher is professor of English and director of the Neurocognitive Research Program for the Advancement of the Humanities at Kent State University. His most recent books include *Literature and Social Justice: Protest Novels, Cognitive Politics, and Schema Criticism* (2013), *Educating for Cosmopolitanism: Lessons from Cognitive Science and Literature* (2013), and *Social Symptoms of Identity Needs: Why We Have Failed to Solve Our Social Problems and What to Do About It* (2009). He is currently completing a book on compassion-cultivating pedagogy.

Elizabeth Bradburn is associate professor of English at Western Michigan University and editor of *Comparative Drama*. She has published several articles on cognitive neuroscience and seventeenth-century British literature.

Poetics Today 40:3 (September 2019)   DOI 10.1215/03335372-7558192

M. Soledad Caballero is professor of English at Allegheny College. Her work in British Romanticism focuses on travel writing, empire, and gender studies; she is also a poet. With psychologist Aimee Knupsky, she has published in *Romantic Praxis*; additional coauthored essays are forthcoming in *Critical Collaboration Communities: Academic Writing Partnerships, Groups, and Retreats*. Caballero and Knupsky have been awarded the Expanding Collaboration Grant *Interdisciplinary Team Teaching across the Arts/Humanities and Sciences*, funded by the Mellon Foundation, as well as a National Endowment for the Humanities Connections planning grant focused on the application of ethical interdisciplinarity to humanities programs and student experiences at Allegheny College.

Nancy Easterlin is a research professor of English and professor of women's and gender studies at the University of New Orleans. She is author *A Biocultural Approach to Literary Theory and Interpretation* (2012) as well as author and editor of numerous essays on and special issues about cognitive-evolutionary theory and interpretation. Her current work applies place studies to the dynamic relationship among locale, identity, sociality, gender, ideology, and other factors in narrative representations.

Richard J. Gerrig is professor of psychology at Stony Brook University. His research focuses on audience design in language use as well as people's experiences of narrative worlds. He is the author of *Experiencing Narrative Worlds* (1993), which draws on several disciplinary traditions to explore the processes by which people are transported to narrative worlds and the consequences of that transportation. With his students, he has developed the participatory perspective on narrative experiences. He has published research demonstrating how participation explains both general and person-specific aspects of readers' experiences.

Erin James is associate professor of English at the University of Idaho. Her monograph *The Storyworld Accord: Econarratology and Postcolonial Narratives* (2015) won the 2017 International Society for the Study of Narrative's Perkins Prize and was a finalist for the Association for the Study of Literature and Environment's Ecocriticism Book Award (2017). Her previous publications include essays in the *Journal of Commonwealth and Postcolonial Literature*, *The Bioregional Imagination* (2012), *Teaching Ecocriticism and Green Cultural Studies* (2012), *The Language of Plants: Science, Philosophy, Literature* (2017), and the *Journal of Narrative Theory*.

Aimee C. Knupsky is associate professor of psychology at Allegheny College. Her work in cognitive psychology focuses on how we learn and communicate in academic settings. With literary scholar M. Soledad Caballero, she explores interdisciplinary connections among emotion, affect, and literature through grant-funded research, teaching, and scholarship, including the Expanding Collaboration Grant *Interdisciplinary Team Teaching across the Arts/Humanities and*

Sciences, funded by the Mellon Foundation. They were awarded a National Endowment for the Humanities Connections planning grant focused on the application of ethical interdisciplinarity to humanities programs and student experiences at Allegheny College. With Caballero, she has published in *Romantic Praxis* and has work forthcoming in *Critical Collaboration Communities: Academic Writing Partnerships, Groups, and Retreats.*

Anežka Kuzmičová is a postdoctoral fellow in the Department of Culture and Aesthetics, Stockholm University, and an adjunct researcher at the Institute of Literature, Czech Academy of Sciences. Working in the area of reading research, she has authored numerous theoretical and empirical studies on literary reading and leisure reading practices, in journals such as *Communication Theory, Convergence, Language and Literature, Semiotica, Style* and others. In 2014–19, she served as working group leader in COST Action IS1404 E-READ (Evolution of Reading in the Age of Digitisation). Her doctoral monograph, *Mental Imagery in the Experience of Literary Narrative: Views from Embodied Cognition* (2013), is freely available online.

Micah L. Mumper researches theoretical issues in psycholinguistics, with an emphasis on the interaction between readers' life experiences and their narrative experiences. His publications include "On the Origins of Readers' Outcome Preferences" with Richard Gerrig and Kelsey Bagelmann (2016), "How Readers' Lives Affect Narrative Experiences" with Richard Gerrig (2016), and "Leisure Reading and Social Cognition: A Meta-Analysis," with Richard Gerrig (2017). A recent graduate of the doctoral program in cognitive science at Stony Brook University, Mumper brings a fresh perspective and new empirical evidence to the role of ordinary memory processes in emotional inferences in his dissertation.

Michael O'Neill is a lawyer specializing in constitutional law and is presently writing a book about the effect of critical American literary texts on the quest for legal equality. His research interests are in neuroscience, evolutionary psychology, and law and literary studies.

Margrethe Bruun Vaage is a lecturer in film at the University of Kent. Specializing in cognitive film theory, she explores the spectator's imaginative, emotional, and moral engagement in fictional films and television series. Her latest book is entitled *The Antihero in American Television* (2016). She has published widely in journals such as the *British Journal of Aesthetics* and *Midwest Studies in Philosophy* and *Screen* as well as in *The Routledge Encyclopedia of Film Theory* and anthologies such as *Cognitive Media Theory* and *The Oxford Handbook of Cognitive Literary Studies.*

Alexa Weik von Mossner is associate professor of American studies at the University of Klagenfurt in Austria. Her research explores contemporary environmental culture from a cognitive ecocritical perspective with a particular focus on affect and emotion. She is the author of *Cosmopolitan Minds: Literature, Emotion, and the Transnational Imagination* (2014) and *Affective Ecologies: Empathy, Emotion, and Environmental Narrative* (2017), the editor of *Moving Environments: Affect, Emotion, Ecology, and Film* (2014), and the coeditor (with Sylvia Mayer) of *The Anticipation of Catastrophe: Environmental Risk in North American Literature and Culture* (2014).